SOCIETIES OF BRAINS

A Study in the Neuroscience of Love and Hate

THE INTERNATIONAL
NEURAL NETWORKS SOCIETY SERIES

Harold Szu, Editor

Alspector/Goodman/Brown • *Proceedings of the International Workshop on Applications of Neural Networks to Telecommunications* (1993)

Pribram • *Rethinking Neural Networks: Quantum Fields and Biological Data* (1993)

Pribram • *Origins: Brain and Self Organization* (1994)

Freeman • *Societies of Brains: A Study in the Neuroscience of Love and Hate*

Alspector/Goodman/Brown • *Proceedings of the International Workshop on Applications of Neural Networks to Telecommunications, Vol. 2* (forthcoming)

SOCIETIES OF BRAINS

A Study in the Neuroscience of Love and Hate

Walter J Freeman

The Spinoza Lectures

Amsterdam, Netherlands

It rarely happens that men live in obedience to reason, for things are so ordered among them, that they are generally envious and troublesome to one another. Nevertheless, they are scarcely able to lead a solitary life, so that the definition of man as a social animal has met with general assent; in fact, men do derive from social life much more convenience than injury.
Benedict De Spinoza (1677)

LEA LAWRENCE ERLBAUM ASSOCIATES, PUBLISHERS
1995 Hillsdale, New Jersey   Hove, UK

Lawrence Erlbaum Associates, Inc., Publishers
365 Broadway
Hillsdale, New Jersey 07642

Library of Congress Cataloging-in-Publication Data

Freeman, Walter J.
   Societies of brains : a study in the neuroscience of love and hate
/ Walter J. Freeman.
      p.   cm.
   "The Spinoza lectures."
   Includes bibliographical references and index.
   ISBN 0-8058-2016-7 (c : alk. paper). -- ISBN 0-8058-2017-5 (p :
alk. paper)
   1. Neuropsychology. 2. Love. 3. Hate. 4. Cognition. 5. Brain-
-Philosophy.   I. Title.
   [DNLM: 1.Brain--physiology. 2. Behavior.   3. Mental Processes.
WL 300 F855s 1995]
QP360.F715 1995
152.4--dc20
DNLM/DLC
for Library of Congress   95-4213

Printed in the United States of America

10 9 8 7 6 5 4 3

SOCIETIES OF BRAINS

A Study in the Neuroscience of Love and Hate

Table of Contents

Acknowledgements

I am grateful for 33 years of support for research on Correlation of EEG and Behavior from the National Institute of Mental Health, and for support for my students from the Office of Naval Research for the past 6 years. I am deeply indebted to my father for inspiring me to undertake a career in research on the biology of mental disorders; and to my teachers: Richard McKeon in philosophy; H. T. Chang (now in Shanghai) in electrophysiology; John Fulton in neurophysiology; Harold Saxton Burr in neuroanatomy; Paul Yakovlev in neuropsychiatry; Otto Smith in control systems theory; Aharon Katchalsky in biophysics, for whom I named "K-sets"; Ilya Prigogine, who introduced me to dissipative structures; and Lillian Greeley for insightful discussions of intentionality. This book was occasioned by an invitation from the University of Amsterdam in the Netherlands to lecture from the Spinoza Chair in 1995. It is dedicated to my hardworking and talented students, whose names appear in the bibliographies that list the many publications of our work together: Soo Myung Ahn, Kurt Ahrens, Brett Andrews, Bill Baird, Heinrich Bantli, Cathleen Barczys, John Barrie, Carl Becker, Maria Biedenbach, James Boudreau, Steve Bressler, Stuart Brown, Brian Burke, Henry Chang, Paul Cook, Wes Davis, Jay Edelman, Frank Eeckman, Joe Eisenberg, Jayana Emery, Robert Eshelman, Gershon Furman, Gyöngy Gaál, Teresa Gonzalez-Estrada, David Graham-Squires, Kamil Grajski, Charlie Gray, Michael Greenspon, Herb Highstone, John Horowitz, Sven Jakubith, Mark Lenhart, Leslie Kay, Larry Lancaster, Harrison Leong, Joanne Leong, Stan Leung, Tim Lowry, Diane Martinez, Vinod Menon, Michael Moutoussis, Theoden Netoff, Hasu Patel, Stirling Pickering, Barry Rhoades, Marty Rosenthal, Brandon Savage, Walter Schneider, Masud Seyal, Koji Shimoide, Christine Skarda, Doug Stuart, Dan Sunday, Richard Tang, Steve Truong, Chiyeko Tsuchitani, Bob van Dijk, Gonzalo Viana Di Prisco, Kerry Walton, Xiao-jing Wang, Tommy Joe Willey, and Yong Yao.

Prologue

> Although the universe may not have come from
> chaos, human experience certainly has begun in a
> private and dreamful chaos of its own, out of which
> it still only partially and momentarily emerges.
> George Santayana [1905 p. 39]

Despite notable successes in recent years, brain science is in crisis. The optimism of researchers in basic neuroscience and clinical neurology working with behaviorists and cognitivists has been clouded by mature awareness of the complexity of scientific and human affairs. Pervasive antiscientific fears in the public of what further "progress" may bring recall Mary Shelley's Dr. Frankenstein, and the horrific vision of Yeats in "The Second Coming" (1921):

> Turning and turning in the widening gyre
> The falcon cannot hear the falconer;
> Things fall apart; the center cannot hold;
> Mere anarchy is loosed upon the world ... .

The problem is not information overload. There is always too much information. It is the misdirected search for meaning. Our models are designed to simulate some logical functions of the individual brain. In this they neglect the most important function of brains, which is to interact with each other to form families and societies (Fischer 1990; Brothers 1990), as shown by the necessity for acculturation and education in bringing young people to maturity. Meaning arises in social relations. It comes from inspired visions of isolated individuals only after they have been communicated. Yet each person is terribly alone. Why is this so? How can this isolation be transcended?

This book had its origin in an experimental finding and an insight. First, the finding. I was tracing the path taken by neural activity that accompanied and followed a sensory stimulus in brains of rabbits. I traced it from the sensory receptors into the cerebral cortex and there found that the activity vanished, just like the rabbit down the rabbit hole in "Alice in Wonderland". What appeared in place of the stimulus-evoked activity was a new pattern of cortical activity that was created by the rabbit brain (Section 3.6). My students and I first noticed this anomaly in the olfactory system (Freeman and Schneider 1982), and in looking elsewhere we found it in the visual, auditory, and somatic cortices, too (Freeman and Barrie 1994; Barrie, Freeman and Lenhart 1994). In all the systems the traces of stimuli seemed to be replaced by constructions of neural activity, which lacked invariance with respect to the stimuli that triggered them. The conclusion seemed compelling. The only knowledge that the rabbit could have of the world outside itself was what it had made in its own brain.

As far as I know, this finding has not been made before. It could not have been obtained by introspection, because the process of observation contains within it some well-known operations that compensate for accidental changes in appearances of objects owing to variations in perspective, context, and so forth (Smythies 1994). We are drenched in perceptual constancies, as a necessary condition for daily living. No one can tell from one's own experience or from the constant response R of someone else to a repeated stimulus S that the constant S-R relation is mediated by inconstant patterns of brain activity. I explain the lack of invariance as based on the unity of intentionality, such that every perception is influenced by all that has gone before. An alternative explanation of my data would be to suppose that the observed activity represents an "error function" between a present stimulus and a fixed memory of the stimulus, which is retrieved from "memory banks", but the anatomy of the olfactory system does not support that alternative, and it leads into a morass of Kantian transcendentalism (Section 1.4).

Phenomenology will take a bath in these data, which suggest that a form of *epistemological solipsism* isolates brains from the world. This is not *metaphysical solipsism* (Maturana and Varela 1992), according to which everything that exists is the projection of a brain. That would lead to the absurd conclusion that all of us are the fantasy of a dreaming rabbit. The less extreme view is that all knowledge originates within brains of individuals. Each mind begins within itself to construct its world view and comes later to the realization that other minds must exist, so that "the initial position of every mind must be solipsistic" (Rollins 1967). "Though my experience is not the whole world, yet that world appears in my experience and, so far as it exists there, it is my state of mind" (Leibniz 1947).

Knowledge is not "instilled" by indoctrination, as held by professors who feed information to their students in the way they put data into their computers. It is encouraged to grow by exhortation and example, as held by educators (Santayana 1905).

Solipsistic views reportedly (Rollins 1967) have been held in some degree by many philosophers since Descartes (1637), but they pose difficulties. It is impossible for minds by logic alone to disprove metaphysical solipsism, so how can a mind really be sure that any other mind exists, or, for that matter, the world? How can knowledge be based on the experience of each individual separately, through the sensory systems that form the windows of minds onto the world? How can knowledge of natural laws and mathematics emerge? If knowledge is expressed in a private language within each mind, how can it be shared and verified as being the same in different minds?

These formidable difficulties are not found in the views that knowledge is universal and is there to be imbibed like water, or that it is built into minds as categorical structures in order for minds to exist at all. The neural mechanisms by which solipsistic knowledge can be created, made public, and then validated between individuals become clear only in the context of intentional action. Repeated attempts to answer these questions by logic and computation have not succeeded. Hence, the biological data emerging from animal brain studies and appearing to indicate a solipsistic view offer new and interesting questions. Why do brains work this way, seeming to throw away the great bulk of their sensory input? What part do they keep? Where and how do they keep it? How do they express what they know in themselves? How do they acquire it? How do they mobilize the past to embed it in the future? Above all, how do they communicate with other brains? This problem is not translating or mapping knowledge from one brain onto another. It is the prior establishment of mutual understanding through shared actions, during which brains create the channels, codes, agreements and protocols that precede that reciprocal mappings of information in dialogues. It takes more than a phone line and a dictionary to make a call to a foreign country.

Therefore, to say that a brain is *solipsistic* is to say that it grows like a tree within itself, and that it has a boundary around itself in much the way that a neuron has a bounding

membrane entirely around itself, preserving its unity and
integrity. The barrier is not merely the skin and bone around
each brain. It is the private language in each brain, in some
respects like the labeling of the self by the immune system. Yet
brains arise and are shaped in evolution, not as isolated
entities, each a "society of mind" (Minsky 1986), but as units in
societies ranging upwards from pairs to empires. Rainer Maria
Rilke (1982) described the way in which individuals resonate
together in his poem "Liebeslied":

> Doch alles, was uns anrührt, dich und mich,
> nimmt uns zusammen wie ein Bogenstrich,
> der aus zwei Saiten eine Stimme zieht.
> Auf welches Instrument sind wir gespannt?
> Und welcher Geiger hat uns in der Hand?
> O süsses Lied. [pp. 239-240]

> Yet all that touches us, you and me,
> takes us together like a violin bow,
> that draws one voice from two strings.
> On what instrument are we strung?
> And which violinist has us in hand?
> O sweet song. [My translation]

For biologists, the instrument is brain chemistry, and the player
is evolution. The growth from within each individual is
necessary in order that each brain cope with the infinite
complexity of the world (Section 4.2), but cooperation with
other brains is also a social imperative, because the gulf must
be bridged. Rilke (1984) saw the isolation as having beneficial
aspects by providing ultimate privacy for everyone:

A good marriage is one in which each partner appoints the
other to be the guardian of his solitude, and thus they show
each other the greatest possible trust. A merging of two
people is an impossibility, and where it seems to exist, it is
a hemming-in, a mutual consent that robs one party or both
parties of their fullest freedom and development. But once
the realization is accepted that even between the closest
people infinite distances exist, a marvelous living side-by-
side can grow up for them, if they succeed in loving the
expanse between them, which gives them the possibility of
always seeing each other as a whole before an immense sky.

The use of language is an evolutionary triumph that has made civilization possible (Section 4.8), but the growth and use of language for communication by representations (Section 5.5) requires the prior preparation and shaping of brains by specific neurochemical mechanisms (Section 6.2).

Next, the insight. I have always liked to dance but had no reason to suppose that dancing might be explanatory in neuroscience. Now I see that dancing with others is a quintessential means to bridge the solipsistic gulf. One part of the story is that the necessary chemical mechanisms have been provided through evolution in support of mammalian reproduction (Section 6.6). Another part is that humans have learned how to use these chemical mechanisms to manipulate their own and each other's behavior, in order to build the channels of communication that are required to overcome the solipsistic gulf in forming societies. Music, dancing and sports provide the archetypal techniques. Another is the manner in which common and exotic drugs are used to enhance the isolation and internal pleasures of solipsistic brains, with the price that they destabilize and disintegrate societies (Section 7.6). Yet another is the search by some solipsistic brains for self-projections of a religious nature, or for paranormal, extrasensory contacts with other minds by extending their mental fingers directly and being touched in turn by mental processes from other minds. These belief systems follow logically in the context of the solipsistic gulfs between brains (Epilogue). I conclude that philosophers and physicists may not comprehend brains until they follow Nietzsche (1887) by learning to dance.

Brains consist of neurons, which in turn are composed of organelles, molecules and atoms. They are designed by biological evolution to work in pairs, families, tribes and, by cultural evolution from this biological base, in cities, nations and empires. The numerical sequence in relation to size forms a hierarchy in which each node or level is infinitely complex. To go from one level to another in understanding, we must simplify and abstract to retain only the information that is necessary and sufficient. An isolated molecule, neuron, or brain - for example, one under anesthesia - gives a one-sided view of its properties. The problem raised in this book is that biologists have largely neglected those biological properties by which brains join together in social cooperation, not from lack of interest or technical capacity, but from failure to see the problem, perhaps owing to an emphasis by science and Western society on the individual, whether it is a particle, neuron, brain, mind, or cultural hero like St. George, Isaac Newton, or John Wayne. I wish to advance new ways to understand the biological bases for cooperation among people.

In Chapter 1 I summarize three millennia of exploration of mind and brain, with the conclusions that observations on brain biology in relation to behavior provide our best source of new understanding, that we have sufficient data to provide new insights into the human condition, that we need new concepts by which to organize the data, and that recent developments in nonlinear dynamics can give us the necessary foundation.

In Chapter 2 I review the nature of *state variables*. Dynamics is the study of change in the state of something. In brains that thing has been identified over the centuries with nerve spirits, energy, information, and quanta. I reformulate the mind-brain relation by defining *Neuroactivity* as the structure of brain operations and "mind" as the structure of behavior.

In Chapter 3 I explain how to model Neuroactivity with dynamics from measurements of electrochemical brain operations. To that end I define the emergent activities of masses of neurons forming populations, for which some but not all of their macroscopic properties can be derived from the microscopic properties of their component neurons.

In Chapter 4 I sketch the relations between observed movements of bodies and minds as the structure of behavior. I propose a central role for the limbic system as the organ of intentionality. It provides for the senses of time, space, and expectancy as the contexts for purposes, goals and predictions.

In Chapter 5 I close the loop by calculating statistical relations of Neuroactivity in brains to thoughts I infer from observations of behavior. To that end I define thought as fleeting actualization of intentional structure, and representation as a product of behavior that is used to cross the solipsistic gulf.

In Chapter 6 I describe learning, by which intentional structures stretch forth and change themselves through self-organizing, chaotic dynamics. I infer that neurohumoral mechanisms exist in mammals for unlearning by a meltdown of intentional beliefs without loss of procedural and declarative memories, which enables understanding between self-organizing brains by cooperative actions. We experience this as falling in love.

In Chapter 7 I place qualia of experience inside the solipsistic barrier, with communication only by making representations. The qualia include awareness and its accompanying triad of self, cause, and free will. They are essential properties of societies, individuals having evolved to function in groups, not in isolation.

Whereas in the view of "the brain" as an end object of analysis, the nature, function, and even existence of consciousness can be questioned, from the viewpoint of brains as the material basis for societies, I hold that consciousness, like causality, is an ethical imperative. It does not necessarily follow that consciousness is suitable for scientific study (Jaynes 1976), any more or less than desire, "redness", or conscience (Breasted 1933). The most suitable object for science I take to be intentional structure, which is found functioning in the neuropil of animals having brains as the bases for their goal-directed behaviors. We owe to the eminent comparative neurobiologist Theodore Bullock (1965) the admonition not to write of "the brain", seeing that there are so many kinds, and to the eminent animal psychologist Donald Griffin (1992) not to write of "the mind", seeing that no two are alike, but I assume that all brains and minds are equally real and cohabit one reality, which I call "the world" or environment in its infinite richness and variety.

The usual approach to socialization speaks of bonding in pairs, which is socially if not politically correct for a scientific book. Pair bonds are for geese and beavers. There comes to humans an experience, perhaps once in a lifetime and with the turbulence of a hurricane, which transfigures the sense of self and the belief structure of the possessed. Its object becomes the main source of meaning and inspiration for the self. It is associated with sex, but it is not limited by gender, personhood or age. Plato (1961) described love as "the best of all forms of divine possession" and "the source of the greatest good" (Note 7.3). It "happens" to people, whereby they "fall" not by choice but often with the foreboding sense of "falling ill", due to impairment of the sense of self-control. Yet the process is embedded in volition, for people seek to arrange conditions so that it might be facilitated or avoided, and, once seized, they must choose what to do about it: run, deny, blindly embrace, or explore.

My aim is to give *love* (May 1969) due place and precedence in intentionality, and also to explore its inescapable connection to *hate*, for there is little that exceeds the consuming ferocity and pain of civil wars and the dissolutions of pair bonds that have soured. Loneliness comes with the unity of brain function, hope with brain growth to wholeness in maturity, love with the most intense form of reaching to connect, and hate with the desire to destroy that which threatens unity from outside. These feelings must have brain chemistries, which need further unbashful exploration. They must play essential roles in construction of arenas for rational discourse by mathematicians and logicians and for fair compromises by politicians. Considering Spinoza's "definition of man as a social animal" they are not to be ignored.

This book necessarily touches on many fields. Philosophers have their taxonomy of -isms and -ologies, mathematicians their axioms and theorems, and zoologists their genera and species. My storehouse for such details was filled in medical school with eponyms of signs, symptoms, and diseases, mostly now overlain. I have omitted graphs and figures, which shift the burden of communication from writer to reader. As Hilary Putnam (1990) remarks, "... thought does not consist of a sequence of pictures". A graph is like a pointed finger: readers tend to look at it instead of at what it indicates. My aim is not to explain neuroscience to nonscientists, but to use it to challenge some widely held scientific concepts deriving from philosophers such as Spinoza and Kant, particularly religious, neuroinformational, environmental, and genetic determinisms, which I believe are not merely wrong. They are deeply corrosive to human welfare, dignity, and opportunity. I feel that this situation is a matter of choice, not historical necessity, that it needs to be changed, and that it can be changed by taking a fresh point of view.

Chapter 1

Brains and Minds

What is man, that Thou art mindful of him? ... for Thou hast
made him a little lower than the angels. Psalms 8:2-5

We and our ancestors for countless generations have followed
two roads in pursuit of understanding our minds in relation to
our bodies. One has been observation of the effects of physical
and chemical damage to our bodies on our thinking and behavior.
The other has been introspective reflection on our experiences,
thoughts and feelings, and their relations to similar processes
in other beings like ourselves and those imagined to exist in
animals, objects, events, or pure abstractions not of this world.

1.1 The origin and growth of introspection

Far from being a solitary preoccupation, introspection as
distinct from mere experiencing is an intensely social
enterprise, as much as eating, defecating, being born, and dying.
Reports that we have heard and read from others tell us what to
look for, how to interpret nuances of feeling, and what to accept
or reject as valid or invalid. The task is incomplete until we
have compared our notes with those of others in conferences and
late-night talk shows. Moreover, the capacity for introspection
requires the prior existence of awareness of the self as distinct
from the world and others like the self. The emergence of this
capacity in the evolution of mankind is lost in the remote past,
but it recurs in each individual at some time in childhood. Then
as now the realization of the self must have had catastrophic
consequences. The self comes quickly to the realization that
the self will inevitably die. Children respond to this insight
with denial and levity. They sing:

> Did you ever think as the hearse rolls by
> that you will be the next to die?
> The worms crawl in, the worms crawl out,
> the worms play pinochle on your snout,

and dissolve into laughter. They play

> Ring around the rosy, pocket full of posy,
> ashes, ashes, all fall down,

without realizing that they inherit this game from children 700 years ago, who exorcised their experience of the bubonic plague by re-enactment: the ring of red swelling around lymph nodes in the groin, the openings that drained pockets of pus, the ashes placed on doors and bodies, and the demise of entire villages.

Adults who were faced with death in battle, childbirth, illness, and old age were less able to laugh at the fatal outcome, but they could still deny it.   Then as now the concept must have emerged of the spiritual "I" that could survive the dissolution of its body.   Otto Rank (1932) described this concisely: "... originally, man became soul at his death, while later, living man had a soul which only parted from his body at death."   Egyptian rulers tried to have it both ways by mummifying their bodies and building giant tombs to protect their remains, so that their spirits might live on.   The cost was prohibitively high, and the results unsatisfactory (Breasted 1933).   The conception of the existence of spirits whether or not embodied took deep root and was extended to family and friends, animals, trees, and all manner of identified objects in the world.   It must have been a short step then to attribute causes and effects to thereby inspirited objects of the world, seeing that this is an integral aspect of the way humans understand things (Section 7.3).

Art historians have proposed that the emergence of representations in the forms of statuettes, pictographs, paintings, and abstract designs reflected an effort to concretize and objectify the spirits, as a way of affirming their existence, working out their desires and tactics, and attempting to control them.   "The kind of satisfaction which [artists in primitive cultures] looked to obtain from art was not, as in Western art, that of sinking themselves in the external world, and finding enjoyment in it, but that of depriving the individual thing in the external world of its arbitrary and apparently haphazard character; that is, to immortalize the object in giving it an abstract form and so finding it a resting place in the flight of phenomena" (Worringer 1953).   "Compared with the idea of the soul or its primitive predecessors even the most abstract art is concrete, just as on the other hand the most definite naturalism in art is abstract when compared with nature" (Rank 1932).

With the help of Egyptian social organization and mathematics the Greek philosophers developed complex systems of abstract thought, which culminated in the dialogues of Socrates and Plato. These and their antitheses in co-existing schools still largely define the terms of contemporary introspection. In the past three centuries great advances took place in the works of European and American novelists, who discovered in the process of creating fictional characters a means for examining inner space in richer detail than was possible on the stage. Sigmund Freud and Carl Jung provided systems that mechanized the thermodynamics of inner space, in many ways analogous to the machinations of gods in the Greek and Roman pantheons, giving an aura of scientific respectability to their approaches, though it infuriated James Joyce, among others, to hear attribution to Freud of the discovery of the unconscious. Recent advances have brought introspection new power (Smythies 1994), especially in the visual experience of space (Ramachandran 1992) and in the neuropharmacology of hallucinogens (Fischer 1971).

1.2   Artificial Intelligence (AI) and cognition

The 20th-century mechanization of the laws of thought in Boolean algebra and symbolic logic has given introspection a new twist, in which the artificial intelligentsia propose to simulate or emulate the operations of their minds, as they perceive them, with algorithms implemented in silicon. The intent of the predecessors of AI, Immanuel Kant, Alfred North Whitehead and Bertrand Russell, was to surmount the vagaries of biological minds by distilling the essence of thinking and expressing it in fixed mathematical forms. The movement has undergone transformations in each generation through logical positivism to contemporary cognitive science - not to be confused with cognitive psychology, the study of "Brains [and Minds] in Rats and Men" (Herrick 1926). *Cognition* is the process of learning or constructing knowledge. Within this domain, *conventional cognitivism* holds that knowledge is expressed in symbols, and that *knowing* is the manipulation of the symbols according to logical rules. The symbols are said to exist in minds where the knowing takes place. The problem for strict cognitivists is how to connect symbols in their logical systems with meaningful objects and events. Attempts to get computers to perform simple tasks, like ordering a hamburger in a real-

time unstructured environment like MacDonald's, have foundered
in the infinite complexities of everyday life.   There are solid
reasons for this failure (Dreyfus 1979, 1991; Dreyfus and
Dreyfus 1986; Sections 3.11, 5.6, 6.3).

Biological brains are not logically necessary for minds.   It is
hydrocarbon chauvinism to suppose that minds cannot or should
not exist in silicon, selenium, iron, or interstellar dust clouds,
as Fred Hoyle (1957) speculated.   Grey Walter (1963) built
electronic turtles on wheels with a few relays, two motors, and
two sensors, one for light and the other for touch.   His turtles
learned to prowl his living room and avoid objects while
searching for both an agreeable intensity of illumination and
electric power to replenish their batteries, though sometimes
he found one stuck behind a couch, starved to death.   The point is
that AI as distinct from neuroengineering deliberately avoids
consideration of the properties of brains and deals only with the
perceived properties of minds. Its logical position is that since
one need not know the physics of solid state devices in order to
implement software or use feathers in order to fly, one need not
know the properties of brains in order to do what brains do.   If
AI and other variants of cognitivism (Section 5.7) have failed to
live up to their promise, what essential properties of brains did
they omit in simulations of what they think brains do?

Strict *behaviorists* share this exclusionary thinking with
cognitivists.   In the same decade that Whitehead and Russell
undertook their monumental but failed task of describing human
thought in terms of logic and mathematics, John Watson (1924)
discarded introspection and disavowed the need to know what is
happening between the ears in order to model and control
behavior.   Behaviorists refuse to accept introspection as a
legitimate form of behavior, and suppose that knowledge about
brains is either irrelevant or unattainable.

Philosophers and physicists have recently focused attention on
consciousness, with various responses: delight in discovery;
denial of its existence or suitability for scientific discourse;
attempts to incorporate it as an operational component of
silicon minds (Lucky 1989; Penrose 1994; Dennett 1991; Herbert
1993); or adoption as the *sine qua non* of mind-brain function
(Searle 1992).   For centuries the concept of consciousness has
been regularly re-introduced into biology at intervals of fifty

years or so, suggesting that alternating generations have felt compelled to expel it after those preceding had re-discovered it. Darwin (1872) accepted it, as did the early anesthetists, but Jackson (1884) did not. James (1890) contemplated it, but Watson (1924) excluded it. The last preceding reentry was in 1954 with publication by the senior neurobiologists of their day (Adrian, Bremer and Jasper) of a symposium modestly entitled "Brain Mechanisms and Consciousness" (*and*, not *of*). The book was based on the discovery by Magoun (1958) of the midbrain reticular activating system, where bleeding from head injury as in boxers causes coma. But consciousness was soon discarded or ignored by most neurobiologists, such as Hubel and Wiesel (1962), though not by Sperry (1969). Among current enthusiasts there is little agreement on how to explain it (Section 7.1), and an overview of the turmoil of 20th century philosophy gives a sense of how little has changed in the 2,500 years since the ancient Greeks formulated the terms of debate (Pirsig 1974).

1.3 Brain studies in the material world

Concepts concerning brains as the source of mental life do not grow in isolation. They arise in a framework of ideas about the material world, in which the body is understood as being made of the same substance and conforming to the same laws as the rest of the world. The first written record of such knowledge came from ancient Egyptian glyphs and medical treatises, such as the Ebers papyrus. Illness was described as the result of an escape from the large bowel into other parts of the body of a noxious substance transliterated as "wchdw". Treatment consisted of removal of the poison by cupping, bleeding, sweating, and use of purgatives and emetics. This system has been described as "the dawn of rational medicine", in that the mechanisms of diseases and their treatments were conceived as material processes and not as inhabitations or possessions by spirits and malign powers to be conjured by incantation and magic ritual. These medical procedures persisted unchanged as the backbone of Western medical practice for 3,000 years, into the 19th century, even though, or perhaps because, through the years medicine suffered considerably less favorable regard than its sister science, astrology, which, like AI, had a stronger base in physics and mathematics than in biology.

Observations relating more specifically to brains are manifested by the residual effects of a surgical procedure. Skulls in large numbers from ancient burial grounds all over the world show scars of trephination, which was the opening of the skull by scraping the bone with a sharp stone or by two pairs of crosscuts like a tictactoe. The practice may have been grounded in a materialistic belief that a hole would relieve hydrostatic pressure inducing headache. More likely the ancient surgeons believed that evil spirits were trapped inside, leading to unacceptable behavior in their patients thus possessed. The Inca priests were thought to have chewed coca leaves with lime for alkaline extraction of cocaine and to have spit into the wound, perhaps (as we would say) for local anesthesia, but more likely for the infusion of benign, priestly powers. Many skulls show evidence of healing; some have multiple trephinings in different stages of knitting together, showing that their owners survived the procedure and that, as today, the treatment did not always succeed on the first try.

The next documented step toward a rational basis for explanation of behavior appeared in the writings of the Hippocratic school (probably derived in large part from the Egyptians), in which the material world was conceived as composed of four essences: water, earth, air and fire, each with its associated quality: moist, dry, cold or hot. Human bodies consisted of these elements in combinations forming *humors*, such as blood (fire + water), phlegm (water + air), black bile (water + earth), and yellow bile (earth + fire), whence come our Hippocratic temperaments: sanguine, phlegmatic, melancholic, and choleric. Disease was from an excess or deficiency of one or more humor. It was treated by the Egyptian methods and was prevented by regimens of good diet, clean water, and exercise.

One ought to know that on the one hand pleasure, joy, laughter, and games, and on the other, grief, sorrow, discontent, and dissatisfaction arise only from [the brain]. It is especially by it that we think, comprehend, see, and hear, that we distinguish the ugly from the beautiful, the bad from the good, the agreeable from the disagreeable ... . Furthermore, it is by [the brain] that we are mad, that we rave, that fears and terrors assail us - be it by night or by day - dreams, untimely errors, groundless anxiety, blunders, awkwardness, want of experience. We are affected by all these things when the brain is not healthy, that is, when it is too hot or too cold, too moist or too dry, or when it has experienced some other unnatural injury to which it is not accustomed. (Clarke and O'Malley 1968, pp. 4-5)

These conclusions were solidly based on clinical observations. The authors knew, for example, that damage to one side of a brain was accompanied by convulsions and paralysis on the opposite side of its body, and that the level of severance of the spinal cord was related to the extent of dysfunction below.

Tedious debates occupied physicians for the next 2,500 years concerning the ratios of combination of the four humors. Pythagoras and Aristotle added a fifth essence, whence *quintessential,* which was the *ether* of the heavenly spheres. Some alchemists confused their *ether* with our alcohol, which may have rationalized the actions of many a Bacchanale who drank the nectar of the gods and indulged in orgiastic fertility rites. The entire system was scrapped after the development of the periodic table of the chemical elements by Mendeleev, the slow emergence of organic chemistry from alchemy, and the transforming of fermentations of alcoholic beverages into the bacteriological hypothesis of disease by Pasteur. By these advances surgeons developed the techniques of anesthesia in 1847 and asepsis after Pasteur, which led to improvements in experimental surgery on animals and the more common recovery of individuals with penetrating head wounds particularly in wartime. Some dramatic insights into brain and behavior accrued from the American Civil War (Mitchell, Morehouse & Keen 1864), World War I (Goldstein and Gelb 1939), and World War II (Luria 1966).

1.4 Medicine, philosophy, and intentionality

These reports have not been absorbed as integral components of cognitivism, reflecting the persistence of the classical division between medical science and philosophy. In Greece the primacy of brains as the organ of behavior was a medical view. Philosophers held with Aristotle that the seat of mental faculties was the heart, since brains in dead animals were cool to touch and were thought to act as radiators to cool the blood. This was good physics, since heads are indeed a prime site of heat loss from bodies and should be covered in freezing weather and shaded from hot sun, but it was bad biology. Contrariwise, Aristotle did share with the physicians the medical view that bodies including brains were the material substance of thought, and that the mind was its form, that is, process. The majority of philosophers held the spirit-centered view of Plato, that bodies were mere shadows of the eternal forms of ideas. As a good experimentalist Aristotle said one should not confuse wax with the form taken by the wax, a particularly apt metaphor considering the choice of word by Roman soldiers for brains: *cerebrum* meaning *head-wax*, owing to the consistency of the material on their swords after battle.

Aristotle's views were adopted by the Arabs in the Medieval centuries and were transmitted with few modifications to pre-Renaissance Europe principally by Ibn Senna (Avicenna), an influential translator and commentator on Aristotle and compiler of medical and philosophical lore, with the addition of new fields such as algebra and alchemy. Two fields benefited enormously from this infusion of Egyptian, Greek and Arabic thought. One field was philosophy, wherein the concept of body as substance and mind as process was elaborated by Thomas Aquinas in the 13th century into an intricate theory of Being as derived from Creation. Again, the natures of mind and body were conceived in the larger context of the prevailing theory of the universe, in this case a mathematical structure. Two key concepts were the *unity* of mind by its assertion of a boundary against the outside, and an *intentional relation* betweer. intellect and material objects, in which a mind shaped itself by changes in scale to conform to an object in coming to know it (Basti and Perrone 1993). Thus *intentionality* served to denote the epistemological process (May 1969) by which mind came to enfold the world and understand its unity with God.

The other field was medicine, reportedly through a manuscript published in 1306 by Lafranchi of Milan, which dealt with the process of healing of wounds and described it in two forms. Healing by first intention was the closing of the gap cleanly to leave a narrow scar. Healing by second intention was by suppuration with the "flow of laudable pus" followed by granulation and recovery. To watch closely bodies healing themselves was a profoundly moving experience, for it gave concrete evidence of self-organization in bodies, acting to make them whole, and sharing some of the goal-seeking properties of brains. Physicians and surgeons had little understanding or control of the process. The 16th century surgeon Ambroise Paré, when congratulated on his success in surgical treatments, laconically said, "I bound his wounds. God healed him."

This use of *intention* (from Latin, *stretching forth*) clearly conveyed the sense of tendencies in both brains and bodies toward wholeness and integrity in themselves in achieving their God-given *essence* of being. The intentional relation was unidirectional, in that minds stretched toward external objects but did not invest them, meaning to enter them or to be entered by them in spiritual interpenetration. Following Ibn Senna, who distinguished directing attention toward objects from thinking about objects, logicians adapted the meaning of the words to their own purposes, by which first intention meant perceiving things, and second intention meant thinking about classes of things (comparable to German: kennen *versus* wissen, or French: connaitre *versus* savoir). These mental processes constituted an epistemological growth of mind into the wholeness of intent (action) and perception, expressing the unity of each being. The word *intention* was not synonymous with purpose, though it evolved by metonymy to mean that currently, what Heidegger (1982) called "an erroneous subjectivizing of intentionality" in not accepting the inner/outer distinction (Dreyfus 1991).

This example of two communities, one of practicing surgeons and the other of scholars using the same words having similar roots but context-dependent meanings, also poignantly presaged the present division between neurobiologists and the artificial intelligentsia, who appear to signify the same things with the words "information", "memory", "sign", "symbol", "computation", "representation", "code", and so forth, but in fact are doing so with confusingly different meanings. Among philosophers there is persisting disagreement about the nature of "intentionality" as it has come from Kant (1781) imbued with the concept of representation. Putnam (1990), a contemporary admirer of Kant, identified the two concepts ("... representation - that is to say, intentionality - ..." p.107). He wrote:

Kant's purpose, unlike Berkeley's, was not to deny the reality of matter, but rather to deny that things in themselves are possible objects of knowledge. What we can know - and this is the idea that Kant himself regarded as a kind of Copernican

Revolution in philosophy - is never the thing in itself, but always the thing as represented. And the representation is never a mere copy; it always is a joint product of our interaction with the external world and the active powers of the mind. The world as we know it bears the stamp of our own conceptual activity. [p. 261]

Kant's revolution replaced *intension* (old spelling) with *schema,* and reversed intentionality, so that instead of minds shaping themselves to their sensory inputs from the world, minds shaped sense impressions according to their innate categories, foreshadowing Chomsky's (1975) "deep structure". Kant used his word "Vorstellung" more to mean reproductive than creative imagination. He disdained "experimental sciences" (1781 p. 107) except Newtonian physics as incomplete and provisional, not proving anything.   He sought to construct a self-consistent, self-contained transcendental logic to give a totality of *a priori* cognition.   From the rigidity of his innate architecture of reason the "thing-in-itself" was unknowable.   Kant was the forefather of cognitive science, and his "Kritik" was prototypic software.

Intentionality survived underground through Brentano's idea that consciousness is directed toward objects outside itself, and it resurfaced in the work of his followers Husserl and Heidegger, but with conflicting views on the nature of meanings and beliefs "about" the world.   Putnam wrote that the word has become "a chapter-heading" in philosophy books, and that "intentionality won't be reduced and won't go away", but that he would "try to show that there is no scientifically describable property that all cases of any particular intentional phenomenon have in common" (1988 p. 2).   He succeeded by identifying intensions with Kantian schemata and the contents of belief systems, as did Dennett (1991) in identifying consciousness with content and Crick (1994) in identifying it with the firing of neurons.

Since analytic philosophers have currently bled the concept of intentionality to an anemic *aboutness*, and have failed to reach consensus on what that means, biologists are empowered to reclaim the debilitated corpus and infuse it with fresh blood.   In my usage *intentionality* means the process of a brain in action having the properties of unity, wholeness, and intent (the tension of *taking in* by stretching forth) defined as follows:

An *intentional structure* is a living brain having the capacity to actualize these properties by purposive behavior. *Unity* refers to a state of integration by which a self distinguishes itself from nonself. This property attaches to bacteria, neurons, brains, and the immune systems of multicellular animals. *Wholeness* refers to a bounded process by which through stages a self actualizes its mature form, ultimately to die, holding for plants, animals, brains, and healing bodies. *Intent* refers to a relation in which a self modifies itself into conformance with aspects of nonself.

I propose that, when properly understood, brains alone embody all three properties, but only certain kinds and parts of brains (Section 4.2) and at certain times, and that these *are* proper objects for the study of intentionality.

1.5 The growth of modern neuroscience

Brain science came to maturity by the end of the 19th century from three developments. Studies by German pathologists such as Rudolf Virchow on the diseased organs of dead bodies led to the cellular theory of disease, by which the four humors were supplanted with the concept of the cell as the basic component of all living systems. The new science of chemistry, emerging from alchemy, supported the chemical dye industry that provided the means to stain thin sections of brain tissue, in order to visualize the microscopic structure of nerve cells in brains and the changes that occurred in them with illness and advancing years. Psychiatrists and neurologists prepared detailed clinical descriptions of patterns of function of body, brain and spinal cord over the life spans of normal individuals. They correlated their findings with normal anatomy and with pathological changes in brain structure, and interpreted these dynamic processes in terms of the "evolution and devolution of the nervous system" (Jackson 1958). These three systems of thought became the tripod on which modern neuroscience stands: the cell hypothesis, which is called the Neuron Doctrine when applied to brains; the connections of neurons in brains; and the orderly sequences of changes in structure and function over time of normal brains from conception through birth to maturity and old age, including the ravages of injury and disease.

The century now passing has brought advances in knowledge of magnitudes far exceeding the expectations of even the most imaginative science fiction writers. The energy that has driven researchers to achieve these successes has been the thrill of the sense of closure in constructing codes, maps, lattices, and alphabets by which to organize their new data. These reductionist schemata were implicitly modeled on the major unifying and simplifying constructs of the hard sciences, which are the periodic table in chemistry; the electromagnetic spectrum in classical physics; the set of elementary particles in physics; the genetic code of DNA in molecular biology; and the geochronological continuum in evolutionary biology. Each of these constructs provides a linear scale or a small number of elements to combine in many ways, in order to represent the richness of the material world.

Neurobiologists have focused on the search for elementary components in brains, such as the reflex, the neuron, the chemical transmitter molecule, the action potential that releases the transmitter, the membrane channel that the transmitter opens, and the genes that direct the construction of the gates and the transmitters. Physiologists have measured great varieties of unconditioned reflexes in animal and man as functional components with which to construct hierarchies with which to model the homeostatic regulation of body functions. Behaviorist psychologists have trained animals and humans to perform conditioned reflexes and attempted to extend their studies to explain *higher functions* by decomposing them into chains of reflexes, or more recently to settle for the pragmatic biofeedback regulation in treatment of psychosomatic diseases.

Neuroanatomists have explored the intricate anatomical connections of neurons throughout brains in every animal they could lay their hands on, including jellyfish, squid, octopuses, worms, leeches, lobsters, ants, bees, spiders, fish, frogs, turtles, pigeons, rats, cats, rabbits, elephants, dolphins, monkeys, apes, and humans, aiming to describe the circuitry of each species as one would the network of a telephone exchange, cataloguing the *identifiable neurons* that recur in the same locations and with the same shapes in individuals of the same species, and noting the unique features of each animal with respect to the manner in which it makes its living with specialized sense and motor organs. Electrophysiologists have made detailed maps of functional connections of each array of receptors in the skin, ear, eye, nose, tongue, bones, muscles, and soft tissues of bodies onto their target areas of the cerebral and cerebellar cortices, and of the motor cortices and nuclei onto the muscles, showing the topographies of sensation and motion in pictures like the pages of an atlas of road maps. Developmental biologists have searched for the attractant and repellent chemicals and their diffusion gradients that guide the growth of axons to form maps. Immunologists have identified *cell adhesion molecules* (CAMs) by which neurons find and specifically adhere to each other (Edelman 1987). Mapping of neuronal connections has been the crowning achievement of the present half-century.

Using these wiring diagrams neurochemists have extracted and identified an ever increasing number of chemicals by which neurons transmit pulses to each other across their specialized junctions, the synapses. Neuropsychologists are using the circuits and the array of transmitter substances to identify mechanisms of change in synapses as they condition animals. They are attempting to construct an alphabet of neural changes that mediate various types of learning, such as habituation, sensitization, association, and delayed recall (Alkon 1992).

Neuroradiologists are using computer driven instruments to make noninvasive images of brain functions in humans by techniques called functional MRI and PET (Roland 1993). They show which areas of human brains have elevated metabolic activity or increased blood flow during speaking, writing, reading, silent recall, mental arithmetic, and other cognitive tasks. Because neurons slowly recharge their membrane batteries by burning glucose after they have become active, brain images from these methods are indirect, like measuring the distribution and density of smoke to mark flames of a forest fire. Sharper images are obtained by measuring magnetic and electric fields of brain potentials (Gevins et al. 1989; Barlow 1993), with remarkable results relating brain activity to cognition. The data from the several approaches seem to agree that a functional unit of cerebral cortex may have a diameter of about 2 centimeters (Section 3.6), but mosaics of such units have not been identified in patterns suitable for an atlas of thoughts (Section 5.5). Some researchers propose that brains can be mapped into minds by means of brain images from PET scans, so scientists can make "truth tables" and detect whether people are lying to themselves or to observers, when their verbal outputs disagree with their brain images. Neuroethicists and neurologists should re-think this lie-detector approach.

Geneticists are collaborating with neurologists and molecular biologists to chart the chromosomes and identify the genes that control the development of embryos, organize maps, determine sex, and endow susceptibility to metabolic diseases. Some researchers propose that specific genes shape the character of adults with respect to native intelligence, emotional disposition, proneness to violence, and sexual preference (Hamer and Copeland 1994). Others aim to work back from the anatomy and chemistry of brains of behaviorally disadvantaged adults in order to locate the genes that determine inherited behaviors, opening an opportunity to identify and deselect undesirable embryos, or to replace one or several of their genes with alleles expressing traits more in keeping with parental desires. Here again is an area needing more understanding before we are again overtaken by technological imperatives.

1.6 Too many brain data with inadequate metaphysics

These bodies of knowledge are hard won at high financial and emotional cost to taxpayers and research scientists. They have value far in excess of current usage, but the more we learn the more confused we get. Brains don't work the way we had supposed them to. There is small comfort in knowing that physicists and chemists are facing similar problems of complexity. In the early 1930's physicists had four particles in their stable (proton, neutron, electron, and photon), but before the end of the decade they had embarked on an extension into more particles and deeper layers that appears to have no end (Taylor 1994). Even worse, they are in danger of losing touch with experimental reality (Lindley 1993). Theoretical chemists are enthralled by quantum mechanics in both senses of the word, being enraptured with the power and beauty of the theory and bound to a mathematical structure they cannot understand or explain. Neurobiologists have similar combinatorial explosions in the proliferation of neurotransmitter chemicals, neuroactive genes, and remarkably varied classes of behavior of single neurons and networks in tissue cultures and brain slices.

Pragmatically, the modes of thinking that are necessary to make these discoveries differ from the modes that are needed to assemble data into holistic theory. Laboratory work proceeds most effectively within a framework provided by the simplistic, linear modes of circuits, nets, maps, alphabets, and bit maps from information theory. Construction of unifying hypotheses requires a more poetic, holistic turn of mind and more tolerance for ambiguity and uncertainty than reductionists care for. This appears to be why the concept of intentionality has virtually disappeared from contemporary brain science.

Numerous complaints about the limitations of reductionism have been lodged in the course of this century. For example, the pragmatist John Dewey (1896 p. 362) wrote that reflex theory is inadequate to describe intentional behavior, since

... the real beginning [of sensation] is with the act of seeing; it is looking, and not a sensation of light. The sensory quale gives the value of the act, just as the movement furnishes its mechanism and control, but both sensation and movement lie inside, not outside the act. ... More technically speaking, the so-called response is not to the stimulus; it is into it.

Merleau-Ponty (1945) also described the sensorimotor act as an "intentional arc" that completes an organic loop from action through the world and back into a brain, a conception that recalls the active intellect of Aquinas stretching forth into the world and shaping itself in the task of understanding. However, neither he nor Dewey offered workable alternative explanations or routes to find any. Gestalt psychology enjoyed substantial clinical success, but despite the remarkable achievements of Wolfgang Köhler (1940) in the analysis of animal minds, its practitioners failed to provide a physiological explanation for their findings and beliefs, and so, like the acupuncturists, were pushed aside by practicing neurobiologists. A rebuttal of reductionist views was written by Sir Frederic Bartlett (1932), who documented "remembering" in humans:

...some widely held views [of memory] have to be completely discarded, and none more completely than that which treats recall as the re-excitement in some way of fixed and changeless 'traces'. ... The picture is one of human beings confronted by a world in which they can live and be masters only as they learn to match its infinite diversity by increasing delicacy of response, and as they discover ways of escape from the complete sway of immediate circumstances. ... All this growth of complexity makes circularity of reaction, mere rote recapitulation and habit behaviour, often both wasteful and inefficient. ... A new incoming impulse must become not merely a cue setting up a series of reactions all carried out in a fixed temporal order, but a stimulus which enables us to go directly to that portion of the organized setting of past responses, which is most relevant to the needs of the moment. ... "There is one way in which an organism could learn how to do this. It may be the only way. ... An organism has somehow to acquire the capacity to turn round upon its own 'schemata' and to construct them afresh. This is a crucial step in organic development. It is where and why consciousness comes in; it gives consciousness its most prominent function [p. 206].

Plaintively, he added, "I wish I knew exactly how it was done."

1.7 A fresh start based in nonlinear dynamics

So do we, and here is the impasse. We do not now have an updated metaphysics that would enable us to interrelate our massive quantities of data and construct a comprehensive theory, by means of which to explain brains to ourselves beyond our capacity for introspection. We do not understand brain mechanisms for learning, memory, volition, consciousness, creative insights, and the genesis of meaning in our relationships with each other. We have learned how neurons work, and we can empathize with the victims of the exotic neurological diseases described by Oliver Sacks (1985), Calvin and Ojemann (1994) and Damasio (1994), but we cannot organize the facts and fit them together into a unified whole. The impasse is not resolvable with new techniques or more data. It is conceptual, not experimental or logical. Present thinking has formulated the mind-brain problem by a distinction between form and function (Table 1.1). Behavior is commonly regarded as the function of the body, and by analogy the mind is seen as the function of the brain. This formulation has been a disaster, and in the coming chapters, I hope to show why.

Table 1.1   Simplistic Relations of Brain and Mind

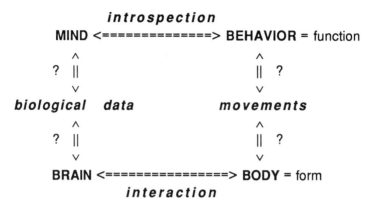

introspection
MIND <================> BEHAVIOR = function

? ‖   ‖ ?

biological   data   movements

? ‖   ‖ ?

BRAIN <=================> BODY = form
interaction

New advances in the physicochemical sciences and mathematics bring opportunities for fresh insights in neuroscience. The past two decades have seen explosive growth of nonlinear dynamics, including chaos (Glass and Mackey 1988), the lively performance of a class of equations that physicists and mathematicians had thought to be moribund. It is as though one's grandmother had risen from her rocking chair and won a prize for disco dancing. Much of the progress has come from the capacities of computers to solve nonlinear equations by using numbers instead of analytic methods with algebraic symbols. Chaotic dynamics has produced aesthetically pleasing color pictures and naturalistic background images of StarTrek movies, but whether chaos can now or ever be shown to exist in brains (Rapp 1993), and whether it might be an essential property or an unavoidable detriment (Schiff et al. 1994), are matters currently debated by biologists and engineers. The best introduction to nonlinear dynamics for nonscientists is by Abraham et al. (1990).

My view is that nonlinear dynamics despite its difficulties (Section 3.10) and limitations (Section 5.6) provides the best available new tools to explore brain function. It enables us to use deterministic equations to create novel patterns that are analogous to the novel patterns created by brains using neurons. Owing to the power of its tools, nonlinear dynamics may play a pivotal role in studies of intentionality by providing a language for making bridges between measurements of brain activity and observations of behavior, including introspection, falling in and out of love, and dealing with hatred as it comes.

However, in order to apply dynamics to brain function it is essential to define what it is in brains that constitutes brain activity, and to measure it (that is, to express it in numbers). Those things in brains that are changing with time are called variables, and because they characterize states of brains at successive instants, our representations of them in equations are called *state variables*. Most people assume that mind is the activity of brain and seek a direct relation between them. This doesn't work. In Chapter 2, I show why, and what does work by seeking a basis for defining state variables in brains.

1.8 Summary

Understanding minds through introspection has progressed from spiritual concerns through Greek logic, medieval mathematics, and continental metaphysics to the modern formulation in terms of symbol manipulation according to logical rules. Brain science has developed in close alliance with physics and chemistry. The concept of intentionality with properties of unity, wholeness and intent emerged from scholastic studies of medicine and philosophy as the basis for epistemology. It was lost in the Kantian revolution, which reversed intentionality by having brains shape their input to accord with inner categories, instead of having brains shape themselves to accord with input they get by acting into the world. This left a metaphysical vacuum at the center of analytic philosophy for biologists to reclaim and fill. Experimental neuroscience has been very productive of new data with the help of other sciences. Effective theory is still lacking. Recent developments in nonlinear dynamics and chaos offer new tools for building a new brain theory, which is centered in the concepts of intentionality and intentional structure.

Chapter 2

Nerve Energy and Neuroactivity

For the wayward sceptic ... will discard the dogma which an introspective critic might be tempted to think self-evident, namely that he himself lives and thinks. That he must do so is true; but to establish that truth he must appeal to animal faith. If he is too proud for that, and simply stares at the datum, the last thing he will see is himself.
George Santayana (1923)

The revolution in the 17th century with the emergence of dynamics as the science of change was truly comprehensive, owing to the abstractness that accompanied the use of equations. Euclid's geometry was one thing; calculus was quite another. The equations required novel concepts of space, time, and causality; brought much higher standards of numerical precision in describing and predicting phenomena; and forced scientists to define more carefully *that which changes*. In order for us to understand the assumptions on which modern neuroscience is based, we have to see them from the historical perspective of how they evolved into their present form, with emphasis on that which changes.

2.1 Dynamics and Descartes

Zeno's paradox in ancient times held that for an arrow to reach its target it had to cover half the distance, but half of that first, and so forth. By infinite regression it was inferred never to have started at all. This paradox was resolved in the 17th century with the invention by Leibniz and Newton of the calculus of infinitesimals (McLaughlin 1994). As the distance of travel decreased, so also did the time needed to cross it. In the limit, as the distance and time increments both approached zero, their ratio approached a finite value, the velocity. This brilliant innovation opened the development of dynamics to supercede the static physics of the ancient world.

The acceptance and success of this new way of thinking was solidly grounded in the new precision of prediction. The modeling of the solar system and the tides (Peterson 1993) was followed by a host of applications in military hardware and the mechanical devices that supported the industrial revolution, and later in analog and digital computers that support the Age of Information. The modes of describing change also found their way into the fields of literature and psychodynamics, but lacking the support of numbers and equations, the formulations were metaphors that gave the aura of hard science. The first application of the new concepts to the mind-brain problem was focused in hydrodynamics, particularly the relations of the higher faculties of the mind to the ventricles of brains. These are fluid filled cavities that make brains seem analogous to other "hollow" organs like hearts and stomachs, giving us some metaphors for thinking like "digestion" and "rumination".

Descartes (1637) compared the ventricles to the heart and the nerves to veins and arteries. He saw animal and human bodies as "automates, ou machines mouvantes", the difference being that humans had "*l'ame raisonnable ... logée dans le corps, ainsi qu'un pilot en son navire*" (p. 73, the rational soul lodged in the body, like a pilot in his boat), which operated the body by opening and closing valves, such as the pineal body, to control the flow of animal spirits, and which provided the faculties for thought, language and mathematics. Ryle (1949) found that Descartes attributed similar properties to souls and bodies, and called it a *category-mistake*: identifying objects or events with ideas, for example, momentum with motivation, an action potential with a binary digit, a pulse train with a word, or a molecule with a memory. Ryle's example most often cited is the confusion of a university with its buildings or faculties, a metonymic replacement of a function with a part of a system. The term is useful to distinguish that kind of mistake from scientific errors, such as phlogiston (replaced by heat) and ether (replaced by Einsteinian space-time), and from uncritical metaphors, such as seeing synapses as variable resistors, neurons as transistors, and cortices as neural networks.

The seminal importance for brain studies of the formulation of equations can be seen from the following standpoint. In a dynamic system some material quantity moves or changes with time. Since Newton and Leibniz the preferred description has been a differential equation, for example, $dQ/dt = \alpha Q + i$. In words this means that time t progresses independently and inexorably. At each moment the system has a state symbolized by the letter Q, which represents that which changes, a state variable. The rate of change dQ/dt at that moment is also a state variable. It is equal to the sum of an input i and the quantity itself, multiplied by a *parameter* α determined by the unit of measurement (Note 3.1). To use it we must define the quantity and then measure it twice in as short a time interval as possible. The ratio of the difference dQ divided by the time interval dt approximates the rate of change, as in meters/second or grams/year. By measuring the input quantity and its rate of change (sweeping the problem of infinitesimals, dQ and dt, under the rug), we can predict what value the quantity will have at some time in the future. This is the essence of dynamics; the rest is technology and computers.

In Cartesian studies of brains, the quantity Q would have represented the flow of animal spirits, had the equations been written. This was not to be. The difficulty was that there was no way to measure the flow of animal spirits through the nerves and express it in numbers. Descartes postulated that the muscles were shortened by being pumped full of the spirits like a balloon. That prediction was disproven by Swammerdam (in Fulton 1966), who invented the plethysmograph to measure changes in volume. He found that muscles did not increase in size like balloons but actually decreased slightly due, we know now, to the molecular mechanism of contraction. Nor, as shown by Borelli, did they bubble forth from the cut ends of nerves. These results showed that animal spirits had no volume to measure. Hence animal spirits could not be represented by a string of numbers in a model, revealing a category error, in this case the assignment of the properties of volume and inertia to an unknown entity. Subsequent machine models successively were clocks, telegraph nets, thermodynamic engines, chemical reaction systems, computers, and holographs (Pribram 1991).

2.2 The reflex as an input-output relation

A further elaboration of the machine hypothesis came from an unexpected source late in the 18th century, when a Bohemian ophthalmologist, Giri Prochaska, made a remarkable discovery. Until his time scientists assumed that brains were a source of animal spirits. Prochaska (1784) observed the behavior of anencephalics (newborns with no forebrain, due to a failure in embryogenesis) and found it was normal. (We now know that the human forebrain is not turned on before birth, which protects it from birth trauma.) His findings led him to propose that sensory receptors are the source of animal spirits, which are released by the action of stimuli from the environment. He drew on Newtonian optics to formulate a theory of appetitive and aversive reflexes based in a sensory commune in the brain stem:

> The reflection of sensory impressions into motor ... is not performed solely according to physical laws ... but follows special laws inscribed, as it were, by nature on the medullary pulp. ... The general law ... is that of our preservation: so that certain motor impressions may follow external impressions about to harm our body and produce movements aimed at warding off and removing the harm ... or sensory impressions about to be favorable to us, and produce movement tending to preserve that pleasant condition longer. [p. 116].

Whereas brains had been seen as creative, Prochaska opened the way to see them as a mirror. "Reflections" became reflexes, which have a central role in neurobiological thinking, despite repeated attacks by philosophers. Dewey (1896) wrote:

> But ... it will be urged, there is a distinction between stimulus and response, between sensation and motion. Precisely. ... We ought to be able to see that the ordinary conception of the reflex arc theory, instead of being a case of plain science, is a survival of the metaphysical dualism first formulated by Plato, according to which sensation is an ambiguous dweller on the border land of soul and body, the idea (or central process) is purely psychical, and the act (or movement) is purely physical. Thus the reflex arc formulation is neither physical nor psychological; it is a mixed materialistic-spiritualistic assumption. [p. 365]

Merleau-Ponty (1942) criticized reflex physiology on the basis of reports by Goldstein and Gelb (1939) on brain injuries in war:

> Thus the reflex - effect of a pathological disassociation characteristic not of the fundamental activity of the living being but of the experimental apparatus which we use for studying it ... - cannot be considered as a constituent element of animal behavior except by an anthropomorphic illusion. But neither is the reflex an abstraction; the reflex exists; it

represents a very special case of behavior observable under certain determined conditions.   But it is not the principal object of physiology; it is not by means of it that the remainder can be understood. [pp. 45-46]

Prochaska tried to define the quantity Q as a state variable to represent his "impressions", but he made a category mistake in identifying his sensory and motor impressions with electric current, after it was discovered by Galvani and Volta. The nerve action potential includes electric current along with metabolic activity, but its context is the mediation of behavior, which is not at all in the context of electric fields.   His hypothesis was disputed by Carlo Matteucci, who made a different category mistake in maintaining that nerves carried not electricity but a spiritual force that evolved a century later into Bergson's (1907) *élan vital.* Prochaska's contributions were swamped in a post-Napoleonic tide of clericalism.

2.3 Nerve energy replaces vis nervorum

Physics took the lead again with a new generation of materialists in mid-19th century.   DuBois-Reymond discovered the injury current and the "negative variation" (the nerve action potential).   Helmholtz measured its conduction velocity.   To study reflexes Sechenov developed an animal model for anencephalic humans by pithing a frog.   The centerpiece of this anticlerical and antivitalist movement was the experimental demonstration of the First Law of Thermodynamics, the conservation of energy.   In the grandest category error of them all, animal spirits were replaced with nerve energy, which flowed from the environment through sensory receptors into the brain and out again through muscles, after being stored in nerve cells and then "liberated".   The new doctrine was promulgated by Herbert Spencer (1863), Darwin's spokesman for evolution:

[It is] ... an unquestionable truth that, at any moment, the existing quantity of liberated nerve-force, which in an inscrutable way produces in us the state we call feeling, must expend itself in some direction -- must generate an equivalent manifestation of force somewhere. ... [A]n overflow of nerve-force, undirected by any motive, will manifestly take the most habitual routes; and, if these do not suffice, will overflow into the less habitual ones. [p. 109]

Charles Darwin (1872) continued:

This involuntary transmission of nerve force may or may not be accompanied by consciousness. Why the irritation of nerve-cells should generate or liberate nerve force is not known; but that this is the case seems to be the conclusion arrived at by all the greatest physiologists such as Müller, Virchow and Bernard, and so on. [p. 70]

The application of Newtonian dynamics was explicit in the work of J. Hughlings Jackson (1884), the founder of modern neurology:

...we speak of the dynamics of the nervous system.... A normal discharge starting in some elements of the highest centres overcomes the resistance of some of the middle, next the resistance of some of the lowest centers, and the muscles are moved. ... A fit of epilepsy is an excessive caricature of normal physiological processes during what is called a voluntary action. ... We have, in the case of 'discharging lesions,' to consider not only the quantity of energy liberated, but the rate of its liberation. ... *Resistances* will be considered later. [pp. 42-44]

A note in Jackson's handwriting was found in the margin of this text: "No more of this was published." It had become clear that while nerve tissue did have electric resistance, the barrier to the flow of "nerve energy" was not so simple. Conservation of momentum was used by Freud (1895) as a foundation for his project of a scientific psychology, in which he confused his "neuronic inertia" with electric current of dendrites:

This line of approach is derived directly from pathological clinical observations, especially those concerned with excessively intense ideas. ... These occur in hysteria and obsessional neurosis. ... What I have in mind is the principle of neuronic inertia, which asserts that neurones tend to divest themselves of quantity (Q). ... We arrive at the idea of a 'cathected' neurone (N) filled with a certain quantity. ... The principle of inertia finds expression in the hypothesis of a current, passing from the cell-processes or dendrites to the axone. ... The secondary function [memory] is made possible by supposing that there are resistances which oppose discharge

... in the contacts [between the neurones] which thus function as barriers. The hypothesis of 'contact-barriers' is fruitful in many directions. [pp. 356-359]

Two years later these barriers were named by Foster and Sherrington (1897): "Such a special connection of one nerve-cell with another might be called a synapsis." [p. 929]. Four decades later the hypothesis of "synaptic resistance" was disproven by the discovery of chemical neurotransmission, though it persists in treatments of electric synapses, in which it denotes electric current, not nerve energy. In principle, "nerve energy" is not constrained by the First and Second Laws of Thermodynamics, and the assumption that it was became a source of mischief.

2.4 Fields of nerve energy.

Another physical principle, the magnetic field of potential as visualized by Michael Faraday using iron filings, was introduced by Gestalt psychologists to explain their data from studies in perception. Koffka (1935) conceived the environment as a source of nerve force, which flowed through the sensory receptors into brains, with striking motivational consequences:

...things in our environment tell us what to do with them. ... Their doing so indicates a field of force between these objects and our Egos... which...leads to action. ... A handle wants to be turned,... chocolate wants to be eaten .... [p. 353]

Köhler (1940) studied field phenomena in perception:

Our present knowledge of human perception leaves no doubt as to the general form of any theory which is to do justice to such knowledge: a theory of perception must be a field theory. By this we mean that the neural functions and processes with which the perceptual facts are associated in each case are located in a continuous medium. [p. 55]

He pressed further into physics by identifying the perceptual fields with fields of the electroencephalogram (EEG) that was discovered after his behavioral studies. This hypothesis suffered the same category error and fate as Prochaska's, for it was quickly disproven by Roger Sperry (1958), who placed strips of mica and silver needles in the visual cortex of trained cats and monkeys and showed that the resulting distortions in electric fields had negligible effects on behaviors involving perception. The corpus of Gestalt theory was discredited among neurobiologists (though not among psychologists), and it is almost unknown to the younger generation. What a pity!

With continuing advances in the analysis of anatomical pathways in the cerebrum, it became increasingly obvious that the concept of fields of energy flow made no sense. What are all those axons for, if activity can flow diffusely? Karl Lashley (1942) brought the problem into focus:

"Generalization [stimulus equivalence] is one of the primitive basic functions of organized nervous tissue." [p 302] "Here is the dilemma. Nerve impulses are transmitted ... from cell to cell through definite intercellular connections. Yet all behavior seems to be determined by masses of excitation. ... What sort of nervous organization might be capable of responding to a pattern of excitation without limited specialized paths of conduction? The problem is almost universal in the activities of the nervous system. [p. 306]

He repeatedly noted his difficulty in finding useful concepts to capture the interesting aspects of behavior: "... expressions like mass action, stress patterns, dynamic effects, melodies of movement, vigilance, or nervous energy [are] all highly metaphorical and unproductive of experimental problems". Yet he continued to borrow contemporary engineering concepts such as "reverberatory circuits", "equivalent nervous connections", "systems of space coordinates", "wave interference patterns", "tuned resonating circuits ", and so on (Lashley 1942).

2.5 Information replaces nerve energy

The repeated failure of the energy metaphor opened the way for a new approach that came from the communication sciences. Basing his work on Golgi analyses of the entorhinal cortex by Lorente de Nó (1934), McCulloch (1969) introduced the concept of nerve cells operating as binary switches in neural networks to compute Boolean algebra. Hebb (1949) used the drawings of Lorente de Nó to derive his concept of the synaptically connected rings of neurons that he called "cell-assemblies". John von Neumann (1958) used the concept to develop programmable digital computers. Shannon and Weaver (Lucky 1989) developed the theory of information by *divorcing it from meaning*. This led to the replacement of energy by information as a descriptor of Q, that which neurons carry. Information and energy are both conceived as flows from environmental sources. They are transduced through sensory systems; transmitted by axonal tracts as channels; carried by action potentials (bits); transformed (processed) in brains by synapses working as binary switches; stored as fixed patterns (representations); recalled by read-out under constraints of finite channel capacities and entropic losses, like the content addressable memories in computers; and matched or correlated with new input patterns.

Information metaphors are found at four levels. At the level of nerve cells each neuron is seen as generating a pulse train that represents a meaning corresponding to a word or an object, such as a grandmother. Barlow (1972) proposed that the frequency of the pulse train represents the probability that the object is present. He thought it unlikely that a memory for a word could be entrusted solely to one neuron, which would control the entire brain as a "pontifical cell" (Sherrington 1951) for its brief moment during action such as speech, but would be lost forever if the cell died, so he proposed that the memory for a word is redundantly distributed over a collection of neurons he called "cardinal cells" (Section 3.5 and Note 2.1).

At the behavioral level, arising from the *intentional arc* of Merleau-Ponty and the perceptual field of Köhler, is the work of J.J. Gibson (1979), whose *affordance* denotes information that flows into a brain from the world through exteroceptors and from within its body through proprioceptors. The information is selected by behavioral actions that are controlled by the brain.

... the affordance, being invariant, is always there to be perceived. An affordance is not bestowed upon an object by a need of an observer and his act of perceiving it. The object offers what it does because it is what it is. ... [T]his does not in the least imply separate realms of consciousness and matter, a psychophysical dualism. It says only that the information to specify the utilities of the environment is accompanied by information to specify the observer himself. ... [E]xteroception is accompanied by proprioception ... to perceive is to coperceive oneself. [p. 139]

Subjects are embedded interactively in the environment, which contains information that is selected by their actions into the world (Shaw et al. 1990). That information goes into resonant circuits in brains, from which *effectivities* flow by the muscles as object-oriented actions that are complementary to the affordances. The sequential transformations of information in these closed loop actions form *ecological maps* (Note 2.2).

At the subneuronal level the discovery of DNA as the basis for transmission of genetic information has also stimulated search for stores of experiential information in the form of "memories" in RNA molecules and synapses. The search for a "molecular alphabet" of learning is a major area of neurobiological research (Alkon 1992), though studies of synaptic change have not yet progressed beyond habituation, facilitation, and simple go/no go reflex arcs (Section 6.2). Holger Hyden first demonstrated a change in RNA in brains of rats trained to climb a wire and suggested that it indicated the storage of a procedural memory in the neurons of the vestibular nuclei. This line of thinking culminated in attempts to transfer the memory of working a T-maze by feeding trained planarian flatworms to their naive, cannibalistic siblings. After initial success, this experiment failed repeatedly in the hands of trained scientists, but the result is still being "replicated" annually in high school science fairs across the country, which shows that scientific proof does not hinge on democratic vote and majority rule.

2.6 Extension of brain theory to the quantum level

Models based on transmission, reception, storage, and retrieval of information are explicitly computational (operating with numbers). Alternative models generating interest among scientists are *noncomputational* at the level of propositions (Globus 1992), molecules (Edelman 1987), or quantum particles (Herbert 1993). A lens, for example, does not compute a Fourier transform, though what it does can be described by Fourier's mathematical operation. Herbert wrote:

Though materialists agree that mind (defined as 'inner experience') is no more than a particular motion of matter, they differ concerning how complex matter's movement must be actually to produce a noticeable sensation, to generate what might be called a 'quantum of sentience' ... analogous to physicist Max Planck's famous quantum of action" [p. 26] "Most quantum models of consciousness are similar to Crookes's coherer proposal in that they consider the synapse to be a sensitive receiver of mental messages that originate outside brains. The main difference between the coherer model of mind and quantum consciousness models is that ... mind is somehow resident in Heisenberg's quantum potentia rather than in electromagnetic ether. [p. 248]

This view resembles a philosophy now called panexperientialism that Whitehead (1938) developed after the impasse he and Russell encountered with pure logic. He appears to have known Bergson's (1907) hypothesis of *élan vital* distinguishing living from nonliving matter. Recognizing its failure, he stripped *vital* and defined every particle in the universe as an "event" having an "objective aspect" of matter and a "subjective aspect" of "experience". This enabled him to overcome Cartesian dualism and an undesirable abstraction of matter into a "vacuous entity". He distinguished compound entities like brains having minds with unity of experience from aggregates like stones without minds that experienced only at the low level of particles. He extrapolated his "experience" from man to animals, bacteria, molecules and atoms. He had problems with plants.

A hypothesis by Penrose (1994) on consciousness distinguishes brains from computers by "the brain" being noncomputational in two senses. In his weaker sense a brain functions in a space-time continuum and *not* with discrete numbers as do digital computers, nor with analog voltages or distances used in analog computers, owing to their intrinsic noise and truncating limits on accuracy. Penrose does not (and cannot) rule out the possible future existence of machines based in continuous dynamics that could perform cognitive functions in accordance with existing physical theory but without numbers (Section 5.6).

In his stronger sense noncomputation includes "the quality of understanding" (1994 p. 372) that distinguishes a brain, which knows what it is doing, from a computer, which does not. He locates this quality in quantum coherence states, which he identifies with superconductivity in cold semiconductors. He speculates that water in neurons is bound into cold storage by microtubules (Hameroff 1987), which are the internal protein skeletons that give neurons their shapes. For Penrose the reticulum formed by the endoskeletons is the "real brain", and neurons are the "shadows" that "amplify the resonances" of the microtubules. I question how his "understanding" differs from Whitehead's "experience", but since he cites neither the later Whitehead nor panexperientialism, he has either overlooked his predecessor or hopes to avoid *aspectual dualism* (Note 2.3).

Most to the point, quantum models are new wine in an old bottle. The same properties are invoked as for nerve energy and information: environmental sources of input, sinks for output, receptors tuned to resonate with selected inputs, connectionist mechanisms for storage and retrieval, and matching of present inputs with retrieved past inputs. The elemental building blocks (reflexes, action potentials, bits, words, symbols, primitives, atoms, quanta, and microtubules) change with the centuries, but the underlying concepts of transmission and reception pass whole from one generation to the next. The qualities of consciousness, sentience, experience, comprehension, intent, and awareness are not conceived in terms of independent spirit, soul or Bergson's *élan* as in Cartesian dualism, but they are assigned as *aspects* of brains, neurons, and particles.

A main hope that drives these investigations in search of "new laws of physics" is that they will re-establish consciousness as primary in the cosmos, and that they will explain paranormal phenomena such as distance viewing (Targ and Putoff 1977), extrasensory perception, precognition, and psychokinesis. There is some confusion here, in that some parapsychologists cite quantum *nonlocality*, as manifested in simultaneous but spatially separated quantal events, to explain distant actions of minds, even though special relativity disallows transmission of information faster than the speed of light. I return to this topic in the Epilogue and interpret these beliefs as due to awareness of isolation, which leads to efforts to send thoughts directly across the solipsistic gulf in defiance of "normal" science.

2.7 Neuropil, Neuroactivity, and the "new laws"

Three properties of brains singly or in combination are missing from these several approaches. The first is that brains are creative. They do not wait passively like video cameras but actively stretch forth in search of input. The second property is that the tissue formed by neurons in brains is unique (Section 3.3). It is called *neuropil*. There is no other substance like it in the known universe. It has emerged by phylogenetic evolution three times, in molluscs (octopus), crustaceans and vertebrates, always as the basis for adaptive, goal-directed behavior. Being unlike anything else, it affords the opportunity to discover its "laws" as an alternative to the "new laws of physics" Penrose (1994) seeks, which might properly be called the "new laws of neuropil". The third property is that the functional state of neuropil evolves ontogenetically in small steps that are abrupt, unpredictable, and self-determined. The state is revealed by observations on the activity of neurons in awake brains.

While the activity of neurons is based in flows of transmitter molecules, inorganic ions, and electric currents fueled by metabolic energy, while it is controlled by conformational changes of proteins located in cell membranes and microtubules, and while it carries meaning and information, it is not defined by any one of these physical, chemical, and conceptual quantities. We can observe the potentials that manifest the activity ("signs" according to Adrian 1950), and we can see the metabolic expenditures with PET scans and fMRIs. We can also see the behavioral consequences of the activity of neurons, but only indirectly, like seeing a windstorm through a window and knowing that force is being exerted by the way the trees are bending, but not seeing the force.

Therefore I introduce a new term, *Neuroactivity* (Note 2.4). As *force* in physics is defined by a relation of mass to time and distance in Newton's basic equation, $F = ma$, Neuroactivity is defined by the relations between its electrochemical signs and overt, measured behaviors. Neuroactivity does not flow across the receptors, the muscles, or the blood-brain barrier as energy, matter and information do. Since meaning is created and carried by Neuroactivity, brains are closed systems with respect to meaning, whereas they are open to energy and information. The input boundary of brains is in the sensory cortices where meaning is created by Neuroactivity; the output boundary is in the brain stem where Neuroactivity shapes meaningful patterns of muscle contractions. Neuroactivity, not mind, mediates actualization of intentional structure. Neurobiologists measure its physical and chemical signs and construct models to explain these properties. Their studies culminate in differential equations, in which the state variables represent Neuroactivity. Psychologists measure the words and motions of bodies and describe patterns of behavior. Their studies culminate in formation of the concept of mind as the structure of behavior. Intentionality having unity, wholeness, and intent is the process by which mind is constructed. Neuroactivity, mind, and intentionality are ideas at a comparable hierarchical level of abstraction, whereas brains, bodies and the signs of activity are structures at the level of matter. A geometric way to see the issue is to change the square in Table 1.1 to that in Table 2.1.

Table 2.1   The Relations of Brain and Mind

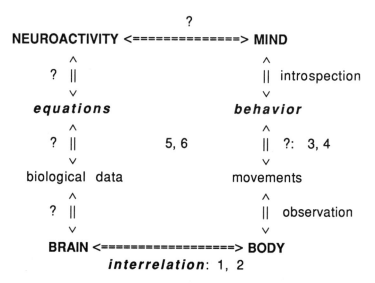

```
                        ?
NEUROACTIVITY <===============> MIND
        ^                        ^
    ?  ||                        ||  introspection
        v                        v
    equations                 behavior
        ^                        ^
    ?  ||          5, 6          ||  ?:  3, 4
        v                        v
biological  data              movements
        ^                        ^
    ?  ||                        ||  observation
        v                        v
    BRAIN <==================> BODY
         interrelation: 1, 2
```

Describing regular relations between brains and minds is not the same as assigning causal relations between them. The extra step of labeling an observed relation as causal can lead to profound difficulties, and I want to use this table to focus on the issue of causality. Given the two levels of function (mental and material), we commonly use four causal statements to express mind-body and brain-body relations:

1. My brain caused my lips (body) to contract (motor action).
2. My lip muscles (body) excited my brain (proprioception).
3. My joy (mind) caused my lips (face) to smile (experience).
4. My smile caused me to feel joy (the Lange-James (1922) theory of emotion).

These seem innocent enough, because they appeal to some traditional ways of thinking about our bodies and our emotions. The mind-brain relation can be expressed in comparable terms:

5. My brain activity caused me to feel joy (matter to mind).
6. My joy caused my brain to become active (mind to matter).

Whereas the relations (1, 2) are material and (3, 4) are mental, relations (5, 6) extend between the mental and material. I see them as examples of category errors that lead to intractable forms of the mind-body problem. However, they are useful, because they help to expose the deepest aspect of the problem, which attaches to the nature of causality. I agree with Searle (1990) that neural and mental events are different facets of the same entity, and I respect his efforts to bring brain functions into philosophy, as I believe he respects mine in coming in the other direction. However, I disagree with his claim that each facet "causes" the other. He wrote:

I believe that the key to solving the mind-body problem is to reject the system of Cartesian categories in which it has traditionally been posed. And the first step in that rejection is to see that "mental", naively construed, does not imply "non-physical" and "physical" does not imply "non-mental". ... So on this view, which seems to me a kind of common-sense view, mental processes are caused by "objective" microprocesses in the brain but are at the same time "subjective" macro-level features of the brain. [pp.127-128]

This accords with Whitehead in combining the material and conceptual aspects of brains and their functions. It echoes the physicists who attribute to particles experience (Whitehead 1938), sentience (Herbert 1993), or understanding (Penrose 1994), the psychologists who attach hedonic motivation to neurons (Klopf 1982), and the shamans who attribute intentions to objects. Concerning Cartesian dualism Dewey (1896) wrote:

Purposive behavior exists and is given as a fact of behavior; not as a psychical thing to be got at by introspection, nor as a physical movement to be got at by physical instruments. It *is* and it *exists* as movements having specific qualities characteristic of them. ... But to ascribe independent complete existence to the movement, to say that *is* deliberate behavior, behavior having meaningful or conscious quality, is a fallacy of precisely the same kind as ascribing complete and independent existence to purpose merely as a psychical state. And it is a fallacy that flourishes only in an atmosphere already created by the belief in consciousness ... . [pp. 510-511]

Overt dualism (Sherrington 1940; Eccles 1994) is not at issue, because it is clearly placed. Aspectual dualism is harder to target. Merleau-Ponty (1942) put the fallacy concisely in his belief that consciousness is not a cause and it is not an effect; it is a relationship between cause and effect. He emphasized "relationship" as prior to either cause or effect [pp.176-179]. My proposal is to interpolate Neuroactivity between mind and brain and to search first for relations between brain and Neuroactivity (Chapter 3), next for inferred relations between movements and behavior as the structure of mind (Chapter 4), and then for relations between mind and Neuroactivity (Chapters 5 and 6). Finally, I propose to return in Chapter 7 to the nature of cause and effect, in order to explore how causality arises in brain function, and how it works in social relations.

2.8 Neuroactivity and neurodynamics

In order to find an alternative to stimulus-response approaches to brains, we must recognize that patterns of Neuroactivity are endogenous. They are constructed from within, not imposed by flows of energy, information or quanta from outside brains. Nonlinear dynamics (Abraham et al. 1990) enters, since it offers techniques for describing conditions required for the emergence of self-organized patterns (Skarda and Freeman 1987; Freeman 1992a) and the creation of information (Shaw 1981). The idea of self-organization (Section 3.10), which is as old as Aristotle, has been recast by Prigogine (1980), Haken (1983), and cognitive psychologists. For example (Brown 1977) wrote:

The structural organization of cognition is no less dynamic than the psychological systems it supports." ... "The incessant flow of cognition, the continual appearance and disappearance of new form at each moment of our waking and sleeping life, are manifestations of the activity of the structure as a whole as it achieves one or another level of realization. ...Affect is not an energy that invades and charges an idea. .... There is no need for the concept of psychic energy (instinct, motivation) as a motivating force in cognition. The orderly sequence and unfolding of cognitive levels repeats and extends the phylogenetic and ontogenetic pattern. The progression from depth to surface, the incessant repetition of developmental form, and the striving toward higher levels are all part of an evolutionary trend that leads in a forward direction simply because it is in the nature of the organization to unfold in this manner. [pp. 127-133]

This is an expression of *wholeness* (Section 1.4), comparable to the "self-actualization" of Maslow (1968). The question persists: How do brains do it? Given a defined state variable, Neuroactivity, Q, we can model it as an *activity density function* (Freeman 1975) in our equations.

2.9 Summary

In order to use dynamics to analyze and model the changes in brain activity that accompany behavior, it is essential to define what it is that the state variables in the equations represent. For the past 300 years what neurons transmit has been successively defined as animal spirits, electrochemical energy, field energy, information, and quantum coherences. Each is a part or component of transmission in either material or conceptual aspects, but it is not the whole, nor does measurement of a sign of activity suffice to determine what a neuron does. In my view *Neuroactivity* is like *force* in physics, being apprehended only by relations between matter, time, and distance. The material manifestations of active neurons in electrochemical fields are related to sensory stimuli and motor actions. Neuroactivity provides one of two essential links between brain and mind, the other being behavior. Models of Neuroactivity are constructed by use of differential equations from observations of chemical and electric brain activity (Section 3.9). The solutions are numerical patterns called activity density functions, which represent our best approximation to Neuroactivity. There is no direct path between minds and brains. At the core of the mind-brain problem, like a spider in a web that can cause paralysis, lurks the inveterate concept of causality (Section 7.3).

Chapter 3

Sensation and Perception

There are more things in heaven and earth, Horatio,
Than are dreamt of in our philosophy.
William Shakespeare. Hamlet, Act I, Scene v

3.1 Remarks on the use of dynamics

Neurodynamics is a tool for simulating how brains and neurons change with time. Effective use by dynamicists requires plodding routines, meticulous attention to experimental detail, a talent for fruitful speculation, and an ability to turn mistakes and bad luck into good insights. An application is made in steps:

1. We choose or delimit a system for study (Chapter 2).
2. We give it an input, which we measure (Note 3.1).
3. It gives an output; we measure it for an *input-output pair.*
4. We collect input-output pairs until there are no surprises.
5. We construct an operation, a rule to change input to output.
6. We derive an equation to express the rule.
7. We put the set of numbers that describes the input into the equation, solve it, and fit the solution to the output.

The observed and calculated outputs never match exactly, so we re-assess each step and modify it to reduce the disparity. These steps give all we can know of neurodynamics. The equations are a mathematical skeleton of neuroscience. It is the best method we have to describe formal relations among the widely differing physical and chemical properties of neurons. It serves to describe function in neurons, in their parts down to the atomic level, and in their assemblies up to whole brains (Freeman 1975; Basar 1980; Nunez 1981).

Dynamics degenerates into curve-fitting, if the equations serve to match the observed outputs without modeling the global processes that generate the outputs. What avoids degeneracy is including the behavioral context in which a neuron or population functions. Each variable and parameter in a set of equations must represent an experimental quantity or condition in the parts of a system, and the system must be chosen and analyzed as a part of a larger system in brain and behavior. Simulation of axonal and dendritic potentials of a neuron is a necessary step toward understanding brains (Bower and Beeman 1994), but it is incomplete unless the neuron is modeled as embedded in an intentional structure. Neurodynamics is used as a bridge between brains in societies and Neuroactivity as their mode of operation (Table 3.1) by simulating their measured signs of Neuroactivity, the fields of axonal and dendritic potentials.

Table 3.1   The Relations of Brain and Mind

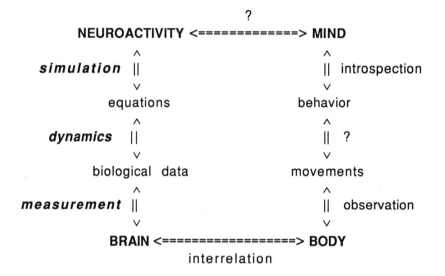

```
                          ?
        NEUROACTIVITY <=============> MIND

                  ∧                    ∧
    simulation  ||                    ||  introspection
                  ∨                    ∨
             equations             behavior

                  ∧                    ∧
      dynamics  ||                    ||  ?
                  ∨                    ∨
          biological  data         movements

                  ∧                    ∧
  measurement  ||                    ||  observation
                  ∨                    ∨
           BRAIN <==================> BODY
                      interrelation
```

Dynamic operations take place in serial stages through brains. The input-output pairs of whole brains are stimulus-response relations, which are studied by psychophysicists and behavioral psychologists. The serial operations are the transformation of stimuli into receptor activity at sensory receptors (transduction), transformation of the receptor activity into sensory cortical activity (sensory physiology), transformation of sensory activity into motoneuron activity (motor physiology), and transformation of motoneuron activity into patterns of muscular activity (kinesiology). Between these sensorimotor shores the feedback operations within brains form a largely unknown continent. These serially forward operations are child's play. Dynamics comes to maturity in modeling feedback, by which the outputs of parts within brains provide internal inputs to the sensory cortices. Nonlinear neural feedback, as it is found in animal and human brains, quite suffices to account for the logical indeterminacy of epistemological solipsism.

3.2 Input-output of neurons: Forward transmission

A sensory receptor is a specialized neuron that converts some chemical, mechanical, or electromagnetic energy locally into a continuous flow of electric current and re-expresses the intensity of the current in the frequency of a train of action potentials on its axon. These are staccato pulses like clicks or points of light. The receptors operate in arrays in body surfaces and send their axons in bundles forming pathways into the spinal cord and brain, where the axons terminate in synapses onto central neurons. Apart from their selective sensitivity to one kind of external energy, all receptors operate in essentially the same way, so it is reasonable to speak of the "code" (see Note 3.2) of a sensory system. Quality is expressed by which axons are *firing* (starting pulses at the root of the axon, the *trigger zone*), and quantity is expressed by the frequency (how often firing occurs). Most of the sensory pathways transmit through synaptic relays to a sensory cortex, where the transformation from sensation to perception begins, but a simplified exception is found in the olfactory pathway, where the receptor axons end directly on neurons in a specialized form of cortex.

All organs in bodies are composed of cells. Each cell is completely enclosed by a membrane, which regulates its interactions with its neighbors. A cortical neuron is the proper unit to begin modeling brains with. We assign to the cell an input, an output, and a state of activity. Initially this is easy, since most nerve cells have well-defined input structures (the dendrites) and output structures (the axon). As in the receptors the dendrites generate electric current with a continuously varying amplitude, and the axon generates pulse trains. Each neuron receives pulses at synapses from other neurons, transforms the input pulse frequencies to electric currents, sums the currents, and transforms the amplitude of the sum into its own output pulse frequency at its trigger zone. By far the most common kind of neuron has one axon as its singular output channel that cannot signal which dendritic input led it to fire or not to fire. While dendrites can easily combine the currents from their many synapses by adding them, they can only sum over short distances. Axons can be very long, and once a pulse is started, it travels reliably to the end of every branch of the axon. Dendrites integrate their synaptic inputs. Axons transmit the sum as a pulse frequency (Note 3.3).

Neurons have three basic actions on other neurons. One is to increase the activity of others at excitatory synapses. The second is to decrease the activity of others at inhibitory synapses. The third is to modulate the efficacy of the synapses between other neurons. Measurement of activity from neuron A tells us whether it has been excited or inhibited by its input, but only measurement of the activity of another neuron B that receives from A will tell us the action of A. If neuron B is excited, A is excitatory, and if B is inhibited, A is inhibitory. If the activity of a third neuron C goes to B and only changes the response of B to input from A, then neuron C is *modulatory*. The great neurochemical systems of brains that give the unity of intentionality secrete neuromodulators (Sections 4.7, 6.4).

Another simplifying assumption that makes dynamics possible is that the system under study is not changing its structure during the period of observation, analysis and modeling. It is well known that neurons undergo continual changes in the growth and retraction of their axonal and dendritic branches, in availability and turnover of chemicals, and in the sensitivities of operations for generating waves and pulses. Dynamicists construct time scales with varying rates of change (Table 3.2).

Table 3.2   Form and Function *versus* Time

fast		neurophysiology		thoughts
medium	**NA**	neurochemistry	**MIND**	affects
slow		neuroanatomy		instincts
fast		electrical events		reflexes
medium	**BRAIN**	chemical reactions	**BODY**	learning
slow		morphogenesis		growth

When they are analyzing in one time scale, they assume that changes in properties holding for faster or slower processes are negligible. The difference between form (anatomy) and function (physiology) of a neuron is determined by the time scale of observation. Experiments are often repeated as rapidly as possible in one time frame, and then they are repeated in multiple time frames at stated intervals, in order to capture both fast and slow changes. Each time scale requires its own equations and unit of time, and state variables in the slow-time equations become parameters in the fast-time equations.

3.3 Neuron populations: Feedback transmission

Seeing an individual neuron as it is represented in textbooks is like looking at a model of a whale in a museum. The object is singularly difficult to construct from observations, breath-taking in its size and beauty of form, and totally out of its normal context. Neurons, like brains, are designed by evolution to work together in large numbers. The basis for cooperation is revealed by their cellular architectures (trees, bushes, spindles) and by the anatomical structures their assemblies form (sheets, clusters, tubes, barrels, and columns). The main neurons in cortex are aligned like divisions of soldiers with their apical dendritic trunks pointing outwardly to the cortical surface and their main axonal trunks pointed inwardly to other parts of the brain. Their cell bodies form layers; their dendritic and axonal side branches go in all directions, most prominently parallel to the cortical surface. The branches intertwine at unimaginable density, so that each neuron makes contact with 5,000 to 10,000 other neurons within its dendritic and axonal arbors, but those neighbors so contacted are less than one percent of the neurons lying within the radius of contact. The chance of any one pair of cortical neurons being in mutual contact is less than one in a million (Sholl 1956; Braitenberg and Schüz 1991).

A useful name for the tissue of dendrites and axons of neurons and their supporting glial cells is *neuropil*. The specialized variety found in cortex is called *laminated neuropil*. Like a hemisphere it has few boundaries or edges. A local zone of neural interaction corresponding approximately to the mean diameter of the dendritic arbors is called a *column* (Mountcastle 1978). It does not represent a piece in a mosaic or colonnade, but a flexible, adaptive field of cooperative activity, like air vortices and dust devils on a broad plain. Discrete areas of cortical neuropil are identified by mapping the terminals of axons, which carry input from sensory receptor arrays and from other areas of cortex, but these subdivisions refer to the streaming of inputs by channels like the doors to a stadium, which within itself holds the unity of a crowd.

The neuron population is not merely an aggregate of nerve cells. The cells must interact at high speeds in large numbers, without giving up their local autonomy. The interactions are supported by the long threads that extend from the cell body in all directions and engage in widespread synaptic transmission. The extensively branched dendritic trees provide a large surface area that accepts synapses from thousands of other neurons in its neighborhood. The synapses act as batteries, and the current is fed by the dendrites to the trigger zone of the axon, where it is summed over time in *spatiotemporal integration*. An axon, too, is like a branching tree, which diverges the neuronal output to thousands of other neurons in the neighborhood. It multiplies its pulse output by the number of its branches and transmits it rapidly to its many targets without attenuation over distance. The synaptic influence of any one neuron on any one neighbor is small, but the innumerable, weak interactions among the many create a population from an aggregate, an entity transcending its neurons. The cooperative feedback is between each neuron and its embedding population, not between pairs of neurons.

3.4 Transfers of activity across hierarchical levels

This brings us to a fresh distinction, which is between the microscopic activity of the neuron and the macroscopic activity of the neural population. The neuron and the population can each give observable forms of energy in both the wave and pulse modes, and there are level-specific rules, and therefore equations, by which activity in each mode is transformed into the other mode. The activity of the population wave mode is observed in local field potentials, also known as the EEGs (electroencephalograms), which accompany the summed electric current of masses of dendrites. Magnetic, optical, and thermal fields of observable energy also accompany the massed activity. Macroscopic activity in the pulse mode sounds like the roar of surf when it is played through a loudspeaker, owing to the density of the pulses from innumerable neurons (Note 3.4).

The microscopic and macroscopic activities co-exist, just as each molecule in a liquid has its kinetic energy and elasticity, while the ensemble has a temperature, pressure, and viscosity. So, also, each citizen in a society has a life as an individual but contributes to the activity of the collective by voting and being taxed, writing and reading, which in the integration support the political and economic life of society. The transfers of activity from the microscopic level to the macroscopic level and back again have been the subject of intensive study and remarkable new insights through nonlinear dynamics over the past 30 years. Three contributors are particularly noteworthy.

Hermann Haken (1983) coined the term *synergetics* to denote dynamic processes in physical systems, in which macroscopic spatial structures emerge from the disorderly behavior of a large number of microscopic particles, when energy is pumped into the system to bring it to a threshold for change. His favorite example is the laser, in which erratically vibrating particles in a container can be induced to jump suddenly into a global interactive state of harmony, by which a brilliant beam of coherent light is emitted. He uses his principle of *circular causality* to describe the manner in which the particles cause the sudden emergence of coherent behavior, and the macroscopic pattern, which he describes as an *order parameter,* imposes itself on the particles in accordance with his *slaving principle.*

Here is another major concept, that of the *state transition*, in this case from incoherence to coherence or *vice versa.* The classical example from physics is the change of water from ice to liquid to steam with heat. Examples from brains include sleeping to waking, walking to running, chewing to swallowing, looking to listening, and thinking to dreaming. In each case the system of neurons, muscles and bones jumps globally from one spatiotemporal pattern of activity to another. Though the equations are the same, the parameters are different, and the forms of the solutions differ accordingly. We say that the entire collection of patterns that a system can display exists within its *state space*, and that a state transition is a jump from one *state* to another. The dimension of the state space is given by the number of state variables, and the size is given by the permissible ranges of the state variables.

Ilya Prigogine (1980) coined the term *dissipative structures* to contrast the orderly spatial patterns of dynamic systems with the inert structures of crystals. The prerequisites are a large collection of independent particles, each weakly interacting with many others, a continuous source of energy to drive the system far from equilibrium, a sink for disposing of waste heat and entropy, and a nonlinearity. When such a system is brought close to its threshold for change, erratic local fluctuations appear, and when threshold is reached, one of the microscopic fluctuations is enormously amplified, so it appears in a macroscopic pattern. A favorite example is a dish of wax heated uniformly from below, which at some temperature develops a hexagonal spatial pattern of convection cells, and at a higher temperature begins to boil, both manifesting state transitions. He describes this as the appearance of order from disorder through small fluctuations. Most fluctuations are damped and smoothed. Only those that carry the system across the threshold can take it to a new form. Typically the new form drifts, oscillates, scintillates, then suddenly disappears to be replaced by another form, then another, and another in a dazzling sequence of unfolding order. Prime examples of the wholeness of intentionality are the stages of the growth of a brain in an embryo from a fertilized egg, the blooming of an adolescent beauty, and the emergence and maturation of a pair bond.

These concepts are directly relevant to brain dynamics, and to the evolving structure of behavior. Brains are obviously open systems with a continuous supply of energy from the liver and oxygen from the lungs brought by arteries, and with continuous removal of waste heat and carbon dioxide by veins. They operate far from equilibrium and keep themselves, when awake, close to thresholds for making sudden state transitions when sensory inputs are being sought. A sensory stimulus arriving at a sheet of receptor cells such as the skin, retina and nose is re-expressed in a spatial pattern of pulses on a selected subset of receptor axons. The pulses are transmitted simultaneously by the massive array of receptor axons in parallel. Among the millions of receptors available, the stimulus typically activates a small selection. This microscopic input induces a state transition in a population of cortical neurons. A macroscopic spatial pattern of cortical activity emerges, which is imposed on the entire cortical population. It is sent to the targets of the cortex by the axons of cortical cells, which convert the output to microscopic pulses for transmission. The targets must undergo their own state transitions to macroscopic patterns when their microscopic inputs arrive, in order that the transmission be successful. Each cortical pattern is a dissipative structure emergent from a microscopic fluctuation.

The analysis by Michel Foucault (1976) of *power* and the emergence of *knowledge* in the context of society provides a useful analogy for the analysis of Neuroactivity and the emergence of intentionality in masses of neurons. He writes that by power he does not mean state sovereignty, law, police, courts and armies (analogous to neural connections, transmitter potencies, electric currents, etc.), for these are "the terminal forms that power takes". Power (and Neuroactivity) must be understood "...as the multiplicity of force relations immanent in the sphere in which they operate and which constitute their own organization; ...as the support which these force relations find in one another, thus forming a chain or a system...; and lastly as the strategies in which they take effect, whose general design or institutional crystallization is embodied in the state apparatus..." (pp. 92-93). So Neuroactivity arises initially in the developing brain in the absence of mature structure, and thereafter structure (connectivity) is shaped by activity as much as the converse, giving the Neuroactivity-intentional structure duo that is a counterpart to the power-knowledge duo. He advances four rules as "cautionary prescriptions" rather than as "methodological imperatives" (all quotes from pp. 98-101):

1. The "rule of immanence" advises starting from "local centers" of power-knowledge, which he conceives as pairs and groups of actants and reactants, and which have their parallel in pairs bound by synapses and masses of neurons, a "society of cortex".

2. The "rules of continual variations" mean that "the 'distributions of power' and the 'appropriations of knowledge' never represent only instantaneous slices taken from processes..."; they are "'matrices of transformations'", that are analogous to Neuroactivity patterns that evolve by serial state transitions resembling the steps between Stephen Jay Gould's "punctuated equilibria" (Gould 1987).

3. The "rule of double conditioning" means that "no 'local center,' no 'pattern of transformation' could function if, through a series of sequences, it did not eventually enter into an over-all strategy. Inversely, no strategy could achieve comprehensive effects if it did not gain support from precise and tenuous relations, serving not as its point of application or final outcome, but as its prop and anchor point." In equivalence to Haken's "principle of circular causality" the macroscopic

patterns of neural mass action feed on the totality of neurons, "local centers" and neural circuits within them. In turn they reinforce the whole by imposing order onto ("enslaving") the parts. This macroscopic whole enters as a part into yet larger interactions by the global systems of brains (Section 4.7).

4. The "rule of the tactical polyvalence of discourses" addresses the process by which "power and knowledge are joined together. And for this very reason, we must conceive discourse as a series of discontinuous segments whose tactical function is neither uniform nor stable." By analogy, Neuroactivity evolves along complex trajectories, with discontinuities that mark the transitions among transiently stable states. We seek the markers by which to define times at which Neuroactivity is divided into stable segments by endogenous state transitions.

These rules neither predict nor explain, but they reflect an attempt to grasp in words what we encounter as we move conceptually from the local neural network and its clearly defined properties out to the limits of its utility, multiply the network to infinity, and then awaken into a new local network, in which the infinities of components are collapsed into the emergent elements at the next higher hierarchical level. This transcendence is among the most difficult passages to negotiate in science, because it goes across the boundaries that separate levels of understanding, and it requires a leap of intuition that cannot be reduced to formal logic or causality (Wimsatt 1976). The passage is a separatrix, watershed, or continental divide, confining reductionists and logical positivists to the barnyards of concrete detail, and preventing them from conceiving the existence of the palace of global process. Some researchers try to by-pass the watershed by proposing that neural populations form by a soup of neuromodulators, or by the extracellular electric currents of dendrites. Neither has the spatial texture and speed that action potentials provide to construct patterns of Neuroactivity. In any case EEG currents are 100-fold too weak to drive cortical neurons (Freeman and Baird 1989).

3.5 Observation, analysis at the microscopic level

The unique character of neuropil was discovered over a century ago by neuroanatomists, among them Golgi, who learned how to impregnate the long filaments of neurons with silver, and Ramón y Cajal (1911), who used Golgi stains to demonstrate the unity and integrity of neurons. Fortunately, the Golgi method stains only one in a hundred neurons; otherwise the neuropil would be opaque. But the cortical neurons falsely appear to exist in nets. The development fifty years ago of techniques for recording pulses of single cortical neurons leads to the interpretation of neurons as connected by synapses in networks like transistors joined by wires. Each neuron is described by its Sherringtonian (1906) *receptor field*, referring to the area of a receptor array in which stimulation excites or inhibits the neuron, and its place in a *topographic map*, referring to the orderly relations between neighboring sites in the arrays of receptors and the activated cortical neurons they project to.

A new metaphysical basis for interpretation was laid by Lettvin and his colleagues in their classical paper, "What the frog's eye tells the frog's brain" (1959). They introduced the concept of the *feature detector* neuron, in reference to an observer-determined object to which each neuron was tuned by learning in developmental processes. This conception was revolutionary in the same sense that Kant turned intentionality upside down (Section 1.4), because it put meaning from the mind of the observer into the mind of the subject, instead of the other way around. In the view from neurodynamics, neurons that respond to edges, lines, and moving spots are manifesting the local topological properties of neuronal maps, which extract local time and space derivatives in automatic preprocessing for spatial and temporal contrast enhancement. No objects or features are manifested at the level of the single neuron, assuredly not those used by an observer. Other neurobiologists had found *on-center* and *off-center* receptive fields in retina. Hubel and Wiesel (1962) found *simple cells* (edge detectors), *complex cells* (line detectors), and *hypercomplex* cells (line segment detectors) in visual cortex. Their hypothesis, that hypercomplex cells took their input from complex cells and these from simple cells in a sequential process, was nullified when others showed that the predicted order of latency did not hold. This could have been expected from the topology of the visual pathways. Detectors for "hands" and "faces" were found in nearby cortex, but the search for detectors of curves, angles and other geometric primitives for construction of complex feature detectors was unsuccessful.

This shift in viewpoint, unnoticed and unacknowledged, has led the neurobiological theory of perception deep into difficulties. The view has been caricatured by the term "grandmother cell hypothesis", in reference to the neuron that fires once a year at a family Christmas, but it still provides a main foundation for interpretation of pulse trains from single neurons. An object in the visual field is thought to be decomposed by retinal receptors into points, which are reassembled by cortical neurons into features represented by pulse trains. The feature hypothesis requires a next stage in which to combine the feature detector outputs so as to represent the object. This is known as the *binding problem.* A solution to it (Milner 1974; von der Malsburg 1983) has been promulgated with the discovery in the olfactory system of oscillations around "40 Hz" (Freeman 1975). If feature detector neurons fire at different frequencies, or if they fire at the same frequency but are not locked in phase, so that the firings are not synchronized, then the sum of inputs from an array of feature detectors to a target neuron is a featureless blur. If the array fires at the same frequency and phase, then the target should also fire at that frequency. Pulse recordings from visual cortical neurons have shown (Gray and Singer 1989) that presentation of a visual stimulus like a moving line to either of two line detectors may excite each of them, but they do not fire synchronously, whereas if a single line stimulus is given to both detectors, they fire in synchrony. They are said to be *phase-locked,* or to be "synfiring" (Abeles 1991) and their outputs are thought to sum to represent the object, in this case the extended line.

The biggest difficulty with this solution to the binding problem is the feature hypothesis on which it rests. It is a metaphysical proposition, not a biological inference. The synaptic connections by which features are extracted are inferred to develop ontogenetically between the neurons in visual cortex, but they have not actually been seen. The output connections are virtually unknown, and no one has found *object detectors* receiving input from phase-locked feature detectors, other than for faces and hands. The source of repetitive firing is unexamined. Receptors and other single neurons are *relaxation* oscillators (Llinàs 1988), like heart muscles, which flush, drain, and refill periodically. Cortical neurons fire irregularly and unpredictably. The *probability* of firing in cortical neurons oscillates at a common frequency, and that frequency does not appear in *observed*   pulse trains of single cortical neurons (Freeman 1975).   There are other difficulties with hypotheses to avoid or resolve them (Note 3.5), but they concern the experts.

3.6 Observation, analysis at the macroscopic level

A single neuron firing repeatedly by itself can fire periodically like a clock. Cortical neurons are never "on their own", and they rarely fire periodically, but they do fire continually at seemingly random time intervals, like crackles of lightning in a storm.   Single neurons are dominated by their own receptor or dendritic currents, which can hold them far above their thresholds, so that they regularly "flush, drain, and refill". Cortical neurons are held just below their thresholds by mutually exciting each other (Freeman 1975, 1992a).   Their cooperative actions create an excitatory bias, which is mainly smooth, but which has a noisy ripple that takes now one, now another above threshold, but only briefly, and not in coordination with other neurons' firing.   They give steady, unstructured noise, which is stationary, autonomous, and spatially homogeneous.

When the excitatory neurons transmit also to inhibitory neurons and receive from them, dendritic waves can emerge.   The process is negative feedback, and the waves are *oscillations* manifesting alternating periods of excitation and inhibition. Sometimes the oscillations are nearly periodic, in the traditional (Barlow 1993) *theta* range of 3-7 Hz, the *alpha* range of 8-12 Hz, the *beta* range of 13-30 Hz, or the *gamma* range of 30-80 Hz, but more typically they are *aperiodic*, that is, broad spectrum from 20-100 Hz.   The waves are macroscopic properties of cortical populations.   Dendritic potentials in EEG waves reflect macroscopic Neuroactivity of columns of cortical neurons, which establish fluctuations in the probability of firing of individual neurons within the population at a frequency of 30-80 Hz, even though the single neurons typically fire at less than 10 Hz, meaning once every three to eight cycles, or once during presentation of a stimulus (Tovée and Rolls 1992).

Most significantly, the frequency of oscillation tends to vary continually, either smoothly or abruptly, and when it changes, it changes in the same way over an entire area of cortex on all the channels in simultaneous recordings from an electrode array, though at different amplitudes (Freeman and Schneider 1982).

This spatial coherence indicates that the oscillation is a macroscopic property of the whole area, that all the neurons in the neuropil share it, and that the same frequency holds at each instant everywhere. This cooperation provides the basis for selective transmission of self-organized cortical patterns (Section 3.8). Also, there is always highly irregular *background activity* before and after a stimulus. The possibility that these seemingly random wave forms could occur by chance almost simultaneously on all channels is vanishingly small. In the olfactory system I searched for sources that might impose this activity onto the whole bulb, either from receptors, the forebrain, or the brain stem. I found unequivocal evidence that no external source produced the observed commonality of wave form. I conclude that the oscillations are endogenous (Note 3.6).

My macroscopic observations were focused on the olfactory EEGs from small animals, which is phylogenetically the oldest sensory system (Section 4.1) and the most important of the senses for cats, rabbits and rats. In the crucial experiments (Viana Di Prisco and Freeman 1985) rabbits were surgically implanted with an array of 64 electrodes in an 8 x 8 grid on the surface of the bulb, giving a window onto the spatial patterns of Neuroactivity. They were trained to respond by licking to one odorant, such as amyl acetate (banana oil) that was accompanied by a reward (water), and merely to sniff in response to another odorant such as butyric acid (goat sweat) as an unrewarded stimulus. On each trial a set of 64 EEG traces was recorded for 6 sec, half a control period and half a test period. Brief EEG segments lasting 0.1 sec were selected during the times of inhalation of the background air in the control period and the periods of the two test odorants given on randomly interspersed trials. Several hundred of these EEG segments were analyzed for each animal. We knew which of the three odorant stimuli each segment came from. The crucial question was: What aspect or aspects of the segments would enable us to classify the segments correctly to the three odorant conditions?

Each olfactory receptor cell responds selectively to an odorant chemical in a narrow range of concentration (Kauer 1987). The *tuning* is broad, in the sense that each cell is excited or inhibited by some chemicals and not others in a *profile*, with extensive overlap of profiles of different cells. Cells that are sensitive to any one odorant are scattered in clusters over the array of receptors in the nose, so sniffing an odorant   activates a spatial pattern of firing like a constellation of twinkling stars, though it is never twice identical.   This pattern is sent into the bulb by receptor axons which excite bulbar neurons in a similar pattern, due to an orderly mapping of the axons onto the bulb (Freeman 1975).   My hypotheses were that between the time of inhalation and the performance of a correct response, a spatial pattern of bulbar Neuroactivity would exist as the basis on which the animal could make its behavioral discrimination, and that this Neuroactivity pattern would be manifested in EEGs.

The results showed that odors which the animal identified (as distinct from odorants which the observer presented) were indeed accompanied in the EEGs by spatial patterns of oscillations in the gamma range (Bressler and Freeman 1980). The odor-related patterns were not directly observed.   They were extracted from the 64 raw EEG traces by calculating a *carrier* wave form in each segment and estimating its numerical amplitude embedded in noise on each channel (Freeman 1987b). The spatial pattern of amplitude of the carrier tended toward a reproducible shape each time within a recording session that the background or a test odorant was present.   The patterns were monotonous to look at and were poor in meaning for observers, because they had no more symmetry than swirls of clouds.   Yet they were unique for each animal.   The patterns corresponded (Section 5.1) to the odorants on repeated sniffs. In principle this form of "central code" is   a sequence of frames like a black-and-white movie, in which the carrier wave is the light, and the patterns are formed by the highs and lows of the light intensity.   In an information theoretic sense the capacity could be very high, owing to the thousands of columns in parallel.   However, the odor information content could not be measured (expressed in numbers) on any precise scale.   It must be modest in rabbits, as inferred from odor psychophysics, for they can tell only a few odors at a time, unlike cooks, perfumers and tea tasters who use language (Rabin and Cain 1984).

3.7 Distinguishing reception and perception

Spatial "coding" for olfactory stimuli was predicted by Adrian (1950) from his pioneering studies in central olfaction.   The role of the receptors forming a sheet in the nasal cavity is to transform an incident chemical species into a spatial pattern of pulses, much as a pattern of light on the retina, a sound in the cochlea, or a touch to the skin is transmitted as a spatial pattern of pulses to cortex. Evidence for microscopic sensory patterning has been found in all sensory systems by electrical recording and metabolic labeling (e.g., Lancet et al. 1982). In olfaction a spatial pattern of pulses is sent with each inhalation, and it induces a burst of oscillation emerging from the background activity. In contrast to microscopic patterns, which are carried by a few sensory neurons that differ with each smell, the macroscopic spatial patterns are distributed over the entire olfactory bulb for every odorant (Note 3.7). By inference every neuron participates in every discrimination, even if and perhaps especially if it does not fire, in that each spatial pattern requires both action and imposed silence. This finding was demonstrated by repeating the classification test while deleting randomly selected groups of channels. No channel was any more or less important than any other channel in defining the patterns (Section 5.3). I concluded that the process for behavioral discrimination of odors was done by the entire bulb, not by a specialized part for each odor (Notes 3.2, 3.8).

Unlike the stimulus-locked activity, the macroscopic bulbar patterns did not relate to the stimulus directly but instead to the meaning of the stimulus. We showed this in several ways, the most direct being to switch the reward between the two odorants, so the previously rewarded stimulus was no longer reinforced and vice versa. Both spatial patterns changed, though the two odorants had not. So also did the spatial pattern for the control segments in background air, so that all the patterns changed whenever a new odorant was added to the repertoire. We trained rabbits serially to odorants A, B, C, D, and then back to A. The A pattern did not return; a new one appeared (Freeman 1991a). This is to be expected in a true associative memory, in which a new item is connected to every other, thereby changing them all. The regularities that we found in patterns of cortical activity had no fixed relations to the patterns of sensory stimuli that induced them, but instead changed with evolving experimental contexts. The findings gave us an essential clue to the unity of intentional structure, because they implied that there is no mosaic of compartments in the olfactory "memory" in the bulb. It is the seamless store of the synaptic web of neuropil.

3.8 Neural mechanism of read-out of bulbar patterns

The discovery of behaviorally related spatial patterns in bulbar EEGs is not in itself convincing, in that the two kinds of spatially patterned activity co-exist in the bulb with each inhalation concurrently. One kind consists of the global spatial pattern of cooperative bulbar activity, which expresses the meaning of a stimulus in a small covariant fraction of the total variance of the population. The other kind is stimulus-evoked activity, which takes the differing form of spatial patterns of pulses in sparse networks of interconnected neurons, and which expresses the properties of the stimulus. Both kinds of patterns can be observed and measured only in part, but they can be inferred to exist in their entirety: the global pattern by spatial ensemble averaging and the pulse pattern by time ensemble averaging (Freeman 1987b). How can we know which of these patterns is accepted and acted upon by the olfactory cortex?

Clearly the global pattern that is transmitted from the bulb is accepted by the cortex, for the EEGs of the olfactory cortex are highly correlated with those of the bulb in the gamma range at which the bulb is driving the cortex (Bressler 1988). But the stimulus-evoked activity pattern is removed, due to divergence in the transmission pathway and integration performed by the cortical neurons that receive the bulbar output. Each bulbar axon branches and distributes its output broadly over the cortex. Conversely each cortical neuron receives input from many thousands of widely distributed bulbar neurons, and its dendrites sum that input continually over time. The only portion of the output from the bulb that survives this operation of integration in space over time as the input to the cortex is the common wave form, which is the product of the global cooperativity in the bulb. The stimulus-evoked pulse pattern is localized spatially, and it is uncoordinated temporally, so that even though it is transmitted to the cortex, as recordings from the pathway have demonstrated, it is minimized by the smoothing process of integration in the receiving neurons, a *laundering* operation in the second stage of perception (Freeman 1991a, b). Hence the olfactory system determines for itself what is signal (the percept) and what is noise (the recept) automatically, without use of filters, yet nothing is thrown away at this early stage. The sensory traces continue to exist in the bulbar output, so that if some aspect of an odor is made significant by further reinforcement, the bulb and cortex can modify their sensitivities and amplify that aspect.

More complex discriminations of odor are achieved by transmission of olfactory cortical output by a pathway from the olfactory cortex directly to the thalamus (Heimer 1969). Thalamic lesions in rats cause no change in thresholds for odor detection but impair the capacity for odor discrimination (Slotnik and Kaneko 1986). Most animals can discriminate only a few odors (on the order of 16). What gives humans, especially perfumers and tea tasters, the ability to discriminate large arrays of odors is language (Rabin and Cain 1984), showing that higher cortex participates in olfactory discrimination.

I predicted that a similar process would be found in all sensory cortices (Freeman 1992b). Evidence for it has been accumulated for the olfactory system in rabbits, rats and cats; for the visual system in monkey (Freeman and van Dijk 1987) and cat (Gray and Singer 1989; Eckhorn 1991) and for the visual, auditory, and somatosensory systems in the neocortex of rabbits (Freeman and Barrie 1994). The results are discussed in Section 5.2.

3.9 Modeling neural dynamics from pulses and EEGs

Our results indicate that the proper node with which to model perception is the population, not single neurons (Freeman 1975). I group synapses by type and assigned a connection weight to the bundle of axons connecting two populations, and I model the dendrites of neurons in a local neighborhood by a linear sum over weighted inputs. I convert each sum to a pulse density output with a nonlinear function that limits amplitude excursions in both directions by bilateral saturation (the *sigmoid* curve, Note 3.4). I simulate the gamma oscillations in our *Katchalsky sets* (Freeman 1975) by coupling an excitatory node with an inhibitory node in negative feedback to make an oscillator. The bulb has several thousand oscillators synaptically coupled with one another, giving a common frequency. Our model is limited to 64 nodes, which suffice to demonstrate cortical cooperativity.

The EEG oscillations are not random, because the same scribbled wave form is found across distances of a centimeter or more. We have simulated these strange wave forms and their spatial patterns with our Katchalsky sets without having to put in any noise. Engineers call such solutions *chaotic* (Note 3.9). Chaos arises in the olfactory system when the bulbar oscillators are interconnected with oscillators in the olfactory cortex to form a long loop, so that each excites the other (Freeman 1987a; Yao and Freeman 1990). Each has its own characteristic frequency, but they differ and cannot agree. Neither can escape the other, so there is endless, aperiodic oscillation. If the two parts are separated surgically (Note 3.6), the chaos disappears and all neurons go silent, showing that the *background* activity is an emergent property of the whole olfactory system. If they are separated chemically with an anesthetic, the chaotic activity returns after the anesthetic wears off, showing that the chaotic background state is stable.

The global origin of the background activity is what enables a microscopic stimulus to send the entire system through a state transition in a unified jump from one pattern to another. This unitary action is characteristic of chaotic systems. However, the jump is not simultaneous at all points in a distributed medium like neuropil. It begins at one point and spreads radially, like a wave from a stone dropped in water, to a spatial extent that depends on the densities of synaptic connections in the neuropil. The velocity in the olfactory bulb is slow enough to be measured (Freeman and Baird 1987). It appears to equal the conduction rate of axons parallel to the bulbar surface. It is fast enough that the spread of a state transition is complete within a quarter cycle of the oscillation in the common wave form. This is necessary, because the read-out mechanism only works if the coupled oscillators have nearly the same phase as well as the same frequency (Note 3.10). The radial spread of the wave in each burst is from a different site of nucleation. This is our best evidence for the endogenous origin of successive frames of Neuroactivity with respiration. Such phase gradients cannot be imposed by pattern generators outside the bulb.

3.10   Basin-attractor   theory

Populations are coupled neurons, oscillators are coupled populations, and systems are coupled oscillators. The millions of neurons interact in ways beyond number. A sensory or motor system might seem unwieldy and its performance indescribable. However, systems tend to enter into preferred modes of activity and stay there until driven out, as though that way they can minimize their expenditures of metabolic energy. They tolerate jostling by input, but after the perturbation ceases, they fall back into one of their preferred modes, and in this falling back reveal the stability of that mode. The spatial pattern of wave form of a mode provides our means for identification of the mode. Examples of a motor system are from the spinal cord of the lamprey, which has been studied in isolation and in the intact eel (Grillner, Wallén and Viana Di Prisco 1990) and of cats, which have been modeled as neural populations coupled into oscillators (Collins and Stewart 1993). The spinal cord and model can both generate patterns of output corresponding to classical gaits of swimming, walking, trotting, galloping or running. The same synaptically coupled neurons generate different patterns, depending on synaptic weights that are under neuromodulatory controls from the brain stem and forebrain. Each pattern is stable under perturbation by sensory input, as when an animal is progressing over rough terrain or through turbulent water, but the entire set of coupled oscillators can jump in an instant from one gait to another (Kelso et al. 1988).

Dynamics offers a useful language to describe these properties (Abraham et al. 1990). A stable mode of activity in a self-organizing system manifests an *attractor*, so called because the system returns to that mode after it has been perturbed. There are four classes of attractor. The simplest is a point attractor, which is a rest state, like that of a chandelier after an earthquake or a neuron after an action potential. For position control the motor system in the spinal cord is guided by point attractors (Bizzi et al. 1992). Next is the periodic orbit of a limit-cycle attractor, which is like a clock and the periodic firing of sensory receptors (Bullock and Horridge 1965). If there is more than one frequency like the precession of a top or the sound of musical instruments the attractor is quasiperiodic. Neurons can generate quasiperiodic trains of pulses in groups, which are *bursts* at intervals (2 frequencies). If a system flutters like a butterfly, it may have a chaotic attractor.

Rhythmic motions during locomotion come close to being regular, but close observation shows that even skilled runners are not robots and do not run like clocks. They wobble, and the wobble worsens when they tire. Each gait manifests a chaotic attractor, or, alternatively, a global attractor that has a set of states for the gaits, including the states of rest and motionless readiness, which are point attractors.   Amit (1989) calls these states *metastable* due to the ease of transit from one to another.   I call them *wings* by analogy to the wings of a butterfly, or to the rooms in a hotel off a central lobby, which can be accessed one at a time by moving through doors.   A jump between basins is a state transition, which takes place either when the system is forced into one of its wings by a sensory stimulus (an *input-dependent state transition*), or when some synapses are changed by neuromodulators (a *bifurcation*) and open a wing or create a new one.   A person going after a bus switches from a walk to a trot in a metastable state transition; the same person learns a new dance step in a bifurcation.

The starting point at which a system begins a new course of action upon a state transition need not be specified precisely, because for each wing or attractor there is a range of starting points that is equivalent.   The set of equivalent points defines a domain of input that is called the *basin* of attraction, in analogy to a ball rolling to the bottom of a container, no matter where it starts from within the container.   The concept of basin is particularly useful in sensory physiology, because it defines the extent of variation in a stimulus over which the same response occurs, which is a generalization gradient.   In the olfactory bulb the array of coupled oscillators generates a reproducible spatial pattern of amplitude of a common chaotic wave form, whenever an example of a learned class of stimuli is presented to the receptors, because for each learned class of stimuli the olfactory system maintains a wing of a chaotic attractor with its basin of attraction.   The wing is accessed by a state transition that is forced by receptor input on inhalation.   The excitatory input that does this is called a *forcing function*.

The generated pattern is transmitted to the olfactory cortex, where it provides the basis for identification and classification of the stimulus presented.   With each inhalation of an odorant a selection of receptors sensitive to that odorant is activated, but owing to turbulence in the nose and to the small number selected from the large number of appropriate receptors available, the selection is never twice the same, so the starting point (the *initial condition*) for each state transition is different.   The basin of attraction enables convergence to a reproducible pattern, which is generalization over equivalent receptors.   The equivalence of the receptors is determined by the selection of the receptors during the learning process when the animal is trained under reinforcement to respond to examples of the odorant (see Section 6.2). Hence the basin of attraction offers a solution for Lashley's (1942) dilemma, which is described in Section 2.4.

Attractors and their basins in biological systems are elusive. Point, limit-cycle, and even quasiperiodic attractors are relatively easy to define, measure, and validate by modeling, when the systems settle quickly enough (Abraham et al. 1990), but the activities of neurons and populations can only be approximated by them. Recordings from them are invariably mixed with noise, which is difficult to describe, looks like chaos, and distorts and obscures the appearances of attractors. In order that an attractor be unequivocally defined within it, the system must be *autonomous*, which means to be isolated from input and allowed to organize itself, and it must be *stationary*, which means to be unchanging within itself (Grassberger and Procaccia 1983). Biological systems are continually buffeted by their environments, and they continually adapt themselves accordingly. Chaotic activity requires energy, which systems continually draw from the environment while disposing of their wastes into their surrounds. Modeling of chaos is made difficult by component drift and noise in analog computers and by numerical instabilities in digital computers. Attempts by biologists to measure the geometries of attractors, the dimensions of the spaces they are embedded in, and the fractal boundaries of their basins have yielded variable results (Mayer - Kress et al. 1988; Rapp 1993). What makes basin-attractor theory usable is reliable clusters of distinctive spatial patterns in aperiodic EEG wave forms and our computer simulations of the patterns with differential equations (Freeman 1992a).

Development of the theory of chaos beyond basins and attractors has taken several directions. One is the theory of *itinerancy* (Section 5.4). Another is complexity theory (Lewin 1992), which subsumes chaos as a region between rigid order and total disorder. For example, an ordered system like an ice crystal and a homogeneously disordered system like still water are *simple*, whereas a mix of stormy water and melting icebergs is *complex*. A collection of silent neurons under deep anesthesia is simple and rigid. The state of a population in an awake, unmotivated animal is also simple, since every neuron fires randomly, uncorrelated with others and with no global pattern. In a state of arousal and expectancy (Section 4.7) the normal synaptic interactions within the population maintain an ever-changing cooperativity among the neurons, that constitutes its partially ordered chaotic macrostructure. This state is complex. When a familiar stimulus arrives and forces a state transition, a spatial pattern emerges as order *replacing* disorder. If the stimulus is novel for the animal, the population becomes more disordered, which may be essential for the process of learning to identify the stimulus (Section 6.3). According to complexity theory, an adaptive system ranges between order with rigidity and disorder with flexibility, and it controls its degree of order: hence "life at the edge of chaos". The states of the olfactory system show that its degree of chaos is set to the task at hand by the dynamics of the forebrain. Chaos is *controlled* disorder.

3.11 Implications of neurodynamics for solipsism

These experimental data and dynamic models have profound consequences for understanding how sensory cortices work at the interface between brains and the world. The crucial finding is made by tracing the course of a stimulus into the receptor layer, where it is transduced into a pattern of action potentials, and then into the cerebral cortex, through the thalamus to cortex for other systems, but directly for olfactory input. This is precisely the stage at which conventional neurobiologists lose the thread in the labyrinth. What happens is a sudden destabilization of an entire sensory cortex, so that it makes an explosive jump from a pre-existing state, expressed in a spatial pattern of activity, to a new state that is expressed in a different spatial pattern. The new pattern is triggered, not selected, by the stimulus, and it is determined by prior experience with this class of stimulus. The pattern expresses the nature of the class and the meaning for the subject rather than the particular event, though a "class of one" in forming an *eidetic* image in one-trial learning is admissible, though not testable by current techniques. The identities of the particular neurons in the receptor class that are activated are irrelevant and are not retained. The activated receptors need only to have been assigned to a class of equivalent receptors by activation during prior learning trials. The entry into the basin of attraction for the class by each specific input is the basis for generalization over the particulars of a learning set of inputs.

Sensory data merely serve to trigger the structuring of the Neuroactivity that overtakes them. Here is a beginning explanation of the gulf that separates people from the world and from each other, as Rilke saw, no matter how close they might come. Construction through chaotic dynamics is needed at the first stage of olfactory perception because the environment is infinitely rich in odorants (Section 4.2), only a small portion of which forms the basis for actions, and that portion is different for every subject. One might conclude that smell offers a weak basis for comprehending perception. On the contrary, as I will try to show, olfaction is the main entrance to vertebrate brains, and smell is the prototype for perception through other senses.

3.12 Summary

Dynamicists collect input-output pairs from unfamiliar systems in order to understand them. They determine rules to map the inputs into the outputs, which is easy for feedforward single neurons. Indeterminacy arises with feedback, for which dynamics comes to flower in descriptions of neural populations. Diffuse and global synaptic interactions support the continual emergence of macroscopic Neuroactivity patterns, which undergo abrupt changes manifesting state transitions in neural populations. Microscopic sensory stimuli activate receptors that trigger the state transitions in sensory cortex, leading to the emergence of endogenous activity patterns at the first stage of perception. According to dynamics the stimulus places the cortex in one of its basins of attraction, and the form of the output is determined by the attractor. The finding that perceptual patterns are created by the sensory cortices implies that the cortical dynamics is nonlinear and chaotic, because neither linear operations nor point and limit cycle attractors can create novel patterns. Having played its role in setting the initial conditions, the sense-dependent activity is washed away, and the perceptual message that is sent on into the forebrain is the construction, not the residue of a filter or a computational algorithm. A requirement for this process of "laundering" is for spatial coherence, which arises from cooperativity over the cortical populations. This process of replacement of sensory inputs by endogenous constructions in perception constitutes the basis of epistemological solipsism in brains.

Chapter 4

Intention and Movement

Don Juan: May I add,..., it is inconceivable that Life, having
once produced [birds], should, if love and beauty were her
object, start off on another line and labor at the clumsy
elephant and the hideous ape, whose grandchildren we are?
The Devil: You conclude, then, that Life was driving at
clumsiness and ugliness?
Don Juan: No, perverse devil that you are, a thousand times
no.   Life was driving at brains - at its darling object: an
organ by which it can attain not only self-consciousness
but self-understanding. ...
The Statue: Why should Life bother itself about getting a
brain. Why should it want to understand itself?   Why not
be content to enjoy itself?
Don Juan: Without a brain, Commander, you would enjoy
yourself without knowing it, and so lose all the fun.
The Statue: True, most true.   But I am quite content with
brain enough to know that I'm enjoying myself.   I don't
want to understand why. In fact, I'd rather not.   ...
Don Juan: That is why intellect is so unpopular.   But to Life,
the force behind the Man, intellect is a necessity, because
without it he blunders into death.
George Bernard Shaw (1903)
Man and Superman: Act III Don Juan in Hell

The sensory input and the perceptual output of sensory cortex
are carried by microscopic pulses in arrays of neurons, while
integration is done by the cortex at the macroscopic level
(Chapter 3).   We derive equations to describe the operations by
which the cortex uses input to construct its macroscopic
activity, and how that construct is transmitted as a message to
the targets of cortex.   This is the essence of cortical dynamics,
through which the cortex influences and is influenced by the
world, using its microscopic messengers on sensory and motor
axons, while the central mass of neurons broods like an empire
over its roads and boundaries.   Chapter 4 addresses further
questions: Where does the sensory message go?   What makes it
a message?   How did it arise in the first place?   How is it
shaped by advance preparation from other parts of the

forebrain? Where and how does it become a perception, and what might that be? The answers go beyond modeling with differential equations, so they are more tentative, but they offer a framework in which to pursue modeling of intentionality.

4.1 Brain architectures

The animal kingdom offers diverse brains and behaviors from which to draw samples for consideration. An evolutionary perspective gives the best insight into the essentials of brain organizations, particularly in respect to elementary structures of behavior (Herrick 1926). Brains come in three basic types of architecture (Bullock and Horridge 1965; Berkowitz and Tschirgi 1988). First and simplest, a circular network of neurons surrounds the cylindrical gut in hydras and jellyfish, embedded in the layers of longitudinal and radial muscle fibers. The same types of networks in ourselves control comparable peristalsis of tubular organs like the intestinal tract and arteries.

Second, two chains of neurons with their cell bodies in clumps called ganglia are found in those invertebrates that have the capacity for well directed locomotion. The chains form a ladder owing to axons running longitudinally parallel to the body axis and transversely at segmental intervals to coordinate the two sides of the body. We have neurons forming similar chains of sympathetic and parasympathetic ganglia beside our vertebral column inside our chests and abdomens. They control smooth muscles, glands, and circular neural networks in our digestive, circulatory, respiratory, and genitourinary systems. They are largely self-regulatory, whence their collective name, autonomic nervous system, in that they receive information from the viscera regarding temperatures, pressures, volumes, and a broad range of chemical concentrations in the watery internal milieu of the cells comprising bodies, and they initiate corrective actions by the viscera to maintain these quantities automatically near predetermined set points. This is the regulatory process by negative feedback that biologists refer to as *homeostasis*. The desired set points are adapted to changing needs by commands from the front end of the chain, where the largest collections of neurons in ganglia form a brain.

The reason brains are found up front is that animals have receptors for light, sound, and chemicals most typically at the end in the direction of locomotion where the mouth is. They are called *distance receptors* from their capacities to detect objects from which physical energies are being radiated. Brains are devised by evolution to identify weak energies as signals from these objects, classify the recepts, determine the direction and distance of probable source, plan an appropriate action sequence of attack or evasion, put it into effect, monitor the on-going sequence, and evaluate its degree of success. The front-end collections of neurons form lobes or bodies. The upper lobes receive bundles of axons coming from sheets of distance receptors and interpret the sensory input. The lower lobes program actions and emit bundles of axons into the chains, from which axons go to the muscles of the trunk and limbs to carry out the movements. The ganglionic chains and lobes for programming are located below the gut near the limbs, whereas the interpretive lobes are located above the gut, near sensory receptors on top. Bundles of axons interconnect the interpretive and executive lobes on both sides of the gut, so the esophagus runs through the middle of the invertebrate brain. Remarkably, invertebrates with large lobes, sophisticated brains and intelligent behavior, such as bees, spiders and octopuses (Young 1971), have liquid diets ingested by sucking, perhaps because swallowing a bolus of solid food might rupture their brains.

The third type of architecture, that of vertebrate brains, is entirely different. The central nervous system starts as a longitudinal groove on a plate of embryonic cells, which deepens and then closes over by folds from the two sides, with Henson's node running like a zipper from front to back to close the *neural tube*. This is a thick-walled cylinder filled with cerebrospinal fluid, which normally closes at both ends. Failure at the back (posterior) end results in spina bifida (the central cavity of the spinal cord drains its fluid out onto the rump), and failure of closure at the front (anterior) end results in anencephaly (no forebrain). The neural tube is later surrounded by a row of articulated bony rings forming the vertebral column; the brain is encased in plates of bone derived from skin.

The hind tube develops into the spinal cord, which receives sensory axons on its upper *dorsal* side and gives motor axons from its lower *ventral* side. The front end is the site of especially vigorous cell division, where the tube balloons into the brain stem and forebrain. The dorsal brain stem bulges into a fold that becomes the cerebellum. In other primates this segment of the neural tube bends down (ventrally) during the first month of gestation, which will bring the eyes forward, but in humans there is also a second, upward bending (dorsally), so instead of leading to the slouching posture of a gorilla, further growth gives the erect stance of proud men and women.

The forebrain merits a subdivision into the diencephalon (*betweenbrain*) and the telencephalon (*endbrain*). The neurons carrying sensory input are relayed through a dorsal diencephalic nucleus called the thalamus (Greek for "vestibule"). The lateral diencephalon has another bulge on each side that thrusts toward the skin to induce formation of the eye and the retina. Neurons in the ventral diencephalon, the hypothalamus, send axons down into the brain stem and spinal cord for regulation of the autonomic nervous system. Its most ventral bulge joins with the roof of the gut to form the pituitary gland, which controls the endocrine system in tandem with autonomic regulation.

See also p. 76

The telencephalon has a symmetric bulge on each side that becomes a cerebral hemisphere. Its outer shell is a continuous sheet of laminated neuropil called cortex (Greek for "tree bark"), and its interior is filled with ganglionic neuropil called *striatum*. It is laced with axons going to and from cortex, whence "striped". The hemispheres make contact with the skin at the front of the head and induce the formation of an olfactory receptor layer on each side of what becomes the nose. The receptors grow axons into the hemispheres and induce formation of the olfactory bulb. Odors have privileged access to the forebrain, which reflects the dominance of olfaction in primitive vertebrates, particularly the function of the forebrain.

4.2 The architecture of intention

Telencephalic function in its most general form is revealed by surgical removal of the forebrain in experimental animals at any level in the vertebrate phylum. The animals thus deprived retain all of their autonomic and endocrine regulatory machinery and their mechanisms for essential actions, such as feeding, maintenance of posture, locomotion, and clearance of the airway by sneezing, gagging, coughing, and yawning, but they fail to attend to stimuli or to initiate goal-directed movements. They can walk and run, but they don't go anywhere. Like Prochaska's anencephalic humans (Section 2.2) they lack the structure of intentional behavior, which is what we seek (Table 4.1).

Table 4.1   The Relations of Brain and Mind

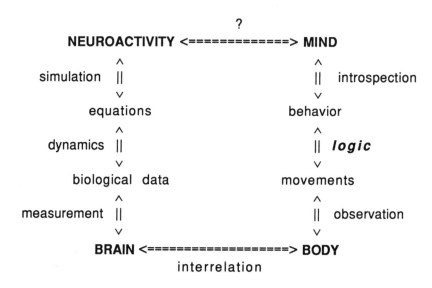

Destruction of the bulbs and their connections in rats and humans leads to profound, intractable depression (Freeman 1993), indicating a fundamental role for the bulbs in vertebrate intentionality, going well beyond the sense of smell.   Its elemental structure can be comprehended by an analysis of the properties of behavior in a normal animal using its nose to find food.   The search begins with emergence of a state of hunger that is manifested by movements of the head and body to bring the receptors into contact with a plume of odorous substance in the water or air.   When contact is made, the odor must be identified as coming from an edible object and not from a predator or from an irrelevant source.   Another movement is made, and a new sample is taken.   The forebrain must keep a record of the previous sample and compare it with the new one to determine whether it is stronger or weaker.   It must also have a record of what motor command was issued, and a report on whether the action that was ordered actually took place, which comes from receptors in muscles and joints in the somatosensory system, to determine if the action succeeded.

reafference

A sequence of samples from the olfactory and somatic systems must be combined over time in a trajectory, which provides the basis for predicting where the source of the odor plume is located, and where the animal is located within its own field of action. Behavioral testing by Tolman (1951) and his colleagues has shown that animals maintain a *cognitive map* in their forebrains (Tolman 1948; O'Keefe and Nadel 1978), which gives them a picture of their spatial field of action and enables them to go directly to sites of interest, instead of merely retracing past trajectories from point to point. Beritashvili (1971) has shown that the time span over which the sensory information can be integrated ranges from a few seconds in fish and salamanders to minutes in mammals, hours in higher primates, and indefinitely long in humans.

The forebrain that generates goal-directed behavior is found in its simplest form in the salamander (Roth 1987), which Herrick (1948) thought to be the form closest to a generalized vertebrate brain like that of the remote ancestor of surviving species of vertebrates (Note 4.1). He wrote: "... the tiger salamander ... is appropriately named, for within the obscurity of its contracted world it is a predaceous and voracious terror to all humbler inhabitants" (1948 p. 3) Each hemisphere is the size of a small pea, yet it contains all that is needed to generate intentional (goal-directed) behavior of the kinds essential for feeding, reproducing, attacking and defending.

In the following I extrapolate to olfaction from Roth's work on vision. Hunger is an emergent pattern of Neuroactivity in the forebrain that expresses the requirements of brains and bodies for metabolic fuel and building material. It manifests a state transition in the neural populations of the forebrain under the influence of sensory stimuli from the gut and its own chemoreceptors for the chemical state of the blood. It is also shaped by neurohormones from nuclei in the brain stem (Section 4.7) The emergent pattern impacts the brain stem and spinal cord, leading to stereotypic searching movements that are adapted to the immediately surrounding world. However, success in acquiring food depends on identification of minute traces of classes of appropriate chemicals that are embedded in a rich organic stew, the olfactory environment we all share and contribute to with the excreta of our bodies, which carries molecules from live and dead animals, plants, furnishings and

noxious machines.   It is infinitely complex, with no stable or
countable number of odorous chemicals in the background.   The
selection of foreground odor is subject to continual variation
and need for update.   An odor being tracked is continually
changed by aging and by masking or by combining with other
chemicals in the background, in the manner that butter and
vanilla combine to give the odor of cake.   Moreover, with each
sniff the input pattern is equivalent but different.   The
olfactory sensory layer has about a hundred million receptor
cells of at least a thousand different types, so for each odorant
there are about a hundred thousand receptors to capture a few
molecules.   Due to turbulence of air flow in the nose, the subset
of receptors that get the odorant on each sniff is never twice
the same.   Devices have been built by engineers that simulate
the chemical detection of odorants by receptors, but the bulbar
capacities   for   adaptiveness,   selective   sensitivity,   and
generalization have not yet been matched with machines.

The same problems of identifying and classifying infinitely
complex sensory stimuli have to be solved at the interface of
brains with the other sensory portals onto the world outside.
The visual system has marvelous mechanisms for edge
enhancement, color decomposition, and tracking of moving dots.
The auditory system has mechanisms for tonotopic pitch
discrimination, binaural sound localization and temporal
integration.   Bats and dolphins emit vocal sounds for echo
ranging and identification of objects, analogously to deep sea
fish that emit light to see with, and electric fish and platypuses
that emit electric current to "see" with.   These kinds of
preprocessing and signal emission have been simulated with
sonar, radar, and signal detection algorithms, but what has not
been achieved is the fast, reliable extraction of rapidly changing
figures in uncontrolled backgrounds, which salamanders do with
alacrity.   Their forebrains have something that our devices don't.
What is it?   Furthermore, for all animals the problem of
obtaining food ends with odor classification, since at last they
sniff before they eat, so it is no accident that olfaction is the
dominant process in vertebrate brains.

The structure of salamander brains shows that it is primarily an
olfactory analyzer, and that visual, auditory, somatic, and taste
inputs coming up from the brain stem to the cortex through the
thalamus, where more complex preprocessing is required,

constitute minor additions to the heavy neural traffic of the forebrain during the search for food. The evolutionary history of vertebrate brains suggests that the problems of generating intentional behavior were first solved in olfaction, and those mechanisms were then adapted to visual and auditory worlds. If so, we cannot expect to understand seeing and hearing until we comprehend our sense of smell.

4.3 Objective orientation in space and time

Beyond the complexity of odor recognition is the problem that point fixation by a few olfactory receptors of a few molecules of food odorant in itself tells the searcher nothing about where the source of the molecules is to be located, whether it is fixed or moving, where it might be expected to move to, or what the searcher is to look for and listen for. That is the work of the forebrain. Each sensory modality must have access to a short-term memory in a cognitive map. Each must also have access to the motor commands that move the sense organs through the world and modify its sensory input. The architecture of salamander brains and the persistence of its basic form into mammals and humans make it clear that, in intentional behavior, multimodal sensory convergence takes place first, and the combined sensory input is then integrated over time and located in space. There is only one cognitive map with memory that serves this function for all of the senses, not one for each sense, and it is located in an area of association cortex called the *hippocampus*. Operations of the cognitive map are revealed by simultaneous recordings of pulse trains from up to 100 neurons in the hippocampus in behaving animals. The trains of pulses from the neurons occur in spatial patterns distributed through the hippocampus that change as the animals move through their spatially structured world (O'Keefe and Nadel 1978; Rolls et al. 1989; Wilson and McNaughton 1993). It is not a literal map in 2 dimensions. It is Neuroactivity in a dynamic space of unknown dimension that emerges in textured neuropil with an immediacy that implies continual change and update.

We don't know where in the undivided web of neurons forming the forebrain neuropil the patterns of Neuroactivity in behavior begin. Most likely, the question is inappropriate, since it is the entire structure, or all of it that is available at any one time, that creates the patterns. Nevertheless, for heuristic purposes

76   Societies of Brains

we need some place to begin our analysis. In the salamander brain the best place is the hippocampus, when it is interacting with a deeper lying mass of neurons forming the striatum. The laminated neuropil of cortex in the outer wall of the neural tube maintains constant two-way traffic between itself and masses of ganglionic neuropil in the inner wall of the neural tube near its central cavity, the ventricle. In particular the hippocampus interacts with two parts of the striatum, the septum (in humans the nucleus accumbens) having two-way connections with the hypothalamus for autonomic regulation, and the amygdaloid nucleus having two-way connections with the motor nuclei in the brain stem for regulation of the musculoskeletal system. The septum and amygdaloid work closely together (Kirkpatrick 1994; Kalivas and Barnes 1993). No intentional behavior is begun without prior and concomitant activation of the cardiovascular, respiratory, and endocrine systems that provide the necessary set, tuning, fuel and oxygen. This explains the sympathetic discharge upon threat of danger, whether or not physical action is engaged in.

Each hemisphere of the salamander cerebrum can be viewed from above as a "pie" with three "slices" (Freeman 1984, 1990a). The hippocampus constitutes the medial third and can be called an *association* cortex. Its emergent pattern of Neuroactivity is transmitted in parallel by axons to the septum, hypothalamus and amygdaloid nucleus. It is sent also to the lateral one third of each hemisphere, which is a motor cortex. Here Neuroactivity patterns are formed under the influence of hippocampal input and in cooperation with underlying masses of neurons constituting the rest of the striatum. The patterns shaped by cortex are delivered to the motor systems in the brain stem and spinal cord to initiate search movements of the head, eyes, trunk and limbs. I propose that the hippocampal pattern is also transmitted to the anterior third of each hemisphere comprising a sensory cortex (Section 4.6), mainly the olfactory bulb, where it poises the cortex to transit into a basin of attraction (Section 3.10) previously formed by learning (Section 6.2), so that if a sought stimulus is present in the air flow induced by search movements, the bulb generates the appropriate activity pattern for that class of input.

Unlike search operations in engineering and AI, the hippocampal transmission does not select input for the bulb by filtering, nor tune the bulb to act as a filter, nor provide a "top-down" stored pattern of previous or expected input to correlate with the present observed input. I propose that it shapes bulbar *output* (Section 4.6). It biases the bulb so as to move in an appropriate direction of pattern construction, if the input contains the receptor activity that the command has predicated. This is essentially a mechanism of attention. It is a process of motor control, by which the sensory outflow is subordinated to an action toward a desired goal. *It is the output and not the input of sensory cortex that is arranged by the hippocampus.* This is not filtering or template matching. The bulbar pattern is transmitted directly to the motor cortex, which is why it is called the olfactory cortex, and also back to the hippocampus.

Another property that distinguishes brains from computers, which wait for input before working, is the tight circle from cortex to spinal cord, muscles, receptors, and back to cortex after it goes through the world. More importantly, brains move their bodies through the world. Knowledge of space and time is constructed by combining the messages sent to the muscles with the subsequent changes in receptor activity. This is the basis for brains knowing when things happen and where things are outside, including their bodies, which are outside brains. We have all forgotten when our brains learned to construct space and time, because they did it in infancy when they functioned intentionally at the level of the brains of salamanders.

4.4 The limbic system

The sensory, motor, and hippocampal cortices form a ring of interconnected neuropil, having what Herrick (1948) called a *transitional zone* in the center, where somatic, visual and auditory pathways send the first trickle of sensory axons through the thalamus, a trickle that becomes a torrent in higher vertebrates, as the transitional zone expands first into general cortex in reptiles and birds and then into neocortex, the exclusive property of mammals. This ring maintains its topological form and functional integrity through all the transformations found in diverse species of vertebrates (Note 4.2 on Paul Maclean). It constitutes a belt ("limbus" from Latin) surrounding the stalk of each ballooning cerebral hemisphere, hence "la grande lobe limbique" of Paul Broca.

The limbic system takes many forms and has been given many
definitions, but however it is conceived, it provides for the
central operations of vertebrate behavior. The hippocampus,
which is crucial for temporarily holding Neuroactivity patterns
and for referring patterns to neocortex for short- and long-term
modifications (Eichenbaum, Otto and Cohen 1994), and the
amygdaloid, which is the main striatal nucleus for output, have
a central location in the limbic lobe. It expresses the metabolic
and hormonal needs of bodies in its self-organized patterns of
activity, which are translated into motoneuron activity that
supports directed body movements. It receives inputs from all
the sensory cortices as the body moves through the world, and
shapes the autonomic and endocrine support systems. Here are
the mechanisms for assembling activity patterns that embody
and sustain the integrated past, serving to express the whole of
the messages that inextricably intermingle in space and time,
thereby to construct and maintain short-term memory and the
cognitive map of personal space where events are taking place,
and to mix new inputs into an evolving store. Everything is
buried in the flood of messages, until the end of the working day
or night, when the system shuts down to sort itself in sleep, but
usually with one eye, ear or nostril open and, metaphorically
speaking, on guard (Hobson 1994).

The knowledge gained in this process exists as latent
possibilities in a seamless web of synaptic connections in the
neuropil of the entire forebrain. It is brought to the fore by acts
of construction that are instigated by the chemical milieu of the
neuropil and shaped by the constructs that emanate from the
sensory cortices. The knowledge is not stored locally in the
limbic lobe (Note 4.3 on Wilder Penfield), but the additions many
times each second and through the years are done there by
behavioral actions continually under construction, which bring
new environmental input to the receptors, and which shape the
sensory constructions that are continually folded in by the
limbic dynamics. Some idea of the nature of the constructive
process in humans is afforded by the effects of bilateral
surgical removal of the hippocampus and adjacent structures
(Milner 1972). Bloom and Lazerson (1988) summarize:

Some items from short-term memory get transferred to
long-term memory, where storage may last for hours or for a
lifetime. We know that one brain system necessary for

making this transfer is the hippocampus. This function of the hippocampus was discovered when a patient, referred to as H. M. in the literature about postoperative capacities, underwent brain surgery. There is one hippocampus in each of the brain's temporal lobes, and, in H. M.'s case, both hippocampi were removed in an attempt to ease his violent epileptic seizures. (After the discovery of H. M.'s subsequent incapacity, this procedure was never again performed.)

As a consequence of his surgery, H. M. lives entirely in the present. He can remember events - objects or people - only for the time they remain in his short-term memory. If you chat with him and then leave the room for a few minutes, when you return he will have no recollection of ever having seen you before. [p. 254]

This passage gives the story of H. M. and also the contemporary framework in which it is interpreted, in the assumption that a register for temporary storage of information analogous to core memory in a computer exists in brains, not in the hippocampus, since bilateral lesions from natural diseases that are restricted to the hippocampus do not give this syndrome, nor do lesions restricted to adjacent structures. The hippocampus is described as transferring information to a storage site of a knowledge base, like the hard disk of a computer, from which it can be retrieved intact by readout (Eichenbaum et al. 1994). The transfer is called the *consolidation* of long-term memory.

This interpretation fails to address the functions of temporal and spatial orientation, and most especially the rich texture of associative meaning in declarative memory. H. M. has no impairment of intelligence, as measured by standard tests, or loss of recollections for events prior to his surgery. His capacity for emotion seems unimpaired. For example, each time he learns of the death of a favorite uncle after his operation, he keenly experiences fresh grief. He has no loss of motor skills but has difficulty finding his way to where he lives. What H. M. lost is his mechanism for updating intentionality, which gave him the capacity for continuing construction within himself of his life history by his actions embedded in time and space. It is a parody to think of this dynamic process as a knowledge base of information in long-term storage, like books in a library, with look-up tables to consult before taking each new step.

4.5 Subjective orientation in space and time

The center of the "pie" of the salamander hemisphere (the
transitional zone of Herrick, which receives thalamic input),
expands with phylogenetic evolution like a squash from a bud.
The cortical surface area increases so much faster than the
volume that it wrinkles.   The convexities (gyri) and fissures
(sulci) vary in detail from one brain to another, but their main
features are landmarks for the four main lobes of the cerebrum:
temporal, parietal, occipital, and frontal.   Many aspects of the
perceptual and motor functions we are concerned with have been
localized within these lobes.   The temporal lobe with the
hippocampal formation receives input relayed through the
thalamus from the ears to its *auditory* cortex.   It also has areas
that provide recognition of hands, faces, and rhythmic patterns
in dance and music.   The parietal lobe maintains *maps* of the
same and opposite sides of its body in the *somatosensory*
cortices, serving the sensory receptors in the skin, muscles and
joints through gates and relays in the spinal cord and thalamus.
The occipital lobe has the *visual* cortex with thalamic input
from the retinas in numerous specialized areas for classifying
patterns of color, motion, and texture.   The frontal lobe has the
motor   cortex with its neurons arranged in a map of connections
to motoneurons in the brain stem and spinal cord.

The primary sensory or motor area is a small fraction of each
lobe in humans.   The immense frontal cortex provides the neural
machinery for constructing patterns of behavior shaped by
understanding of the personalities of others (insight) as the
basis for socialization, and foresight, the ability to plan
(Freeman & Watts 1950; Fuster 1994).   Recordings of electrical
potentials from the scalp of humans engaged in complex tasks
reveal participation of the frontal lobes in anticipating their
own actions in response to sensory stimuli (Gevins et al. 1989).
The rapid enlargement of the frontal lobes in evolution over the
past half million years has made humans transcendent over
other species (Spatz 1967).   Here is located the capacity for
imagination and also for anticipating pain and death.   Most
frontal lobe output goes to the limbic lobe, from which it is
returned through the amygdaloid; to other parts of the striatum
from which it returns through the thalamus; and to the
cerebellum, from which it returns by the thalamus.   The

enormous feedback paths between cortex, striatum, and
cerebellum indicate that the cortex uses them to prepare
movements prior to execution by imagination and mental
rehearsal, constituting practice with continual additions to
procedural memory by learning (Squire 1987).

The cerebellum and striatum do not set goals, initiate
movements, coalesce temporal sequences of multimodal sensory
input, or provide orientation to the spatial environment. These
functions are performed by the limbic system. Its front door is
the entorhinal cortex (Lorente de Nó 1934), which gets input
from all the sensory cortices and sends it to the hippocampus,
where it is integrated over time. Hippocampal output goes back
to the entorhinal cortex, which returns it to all of the sensory
cortices, and updates them to expect new sensory input
(Freeman 1990a). The entorhinal cortex is the key part in human
brain architecture for multisensory convergence (Note 4.4).

A remarkable property of perception is that sensory inputs are
localized not to the receptors, where transduction takes place,
but to points in the cognitive map that express the relation of
the perceiver to an inferred distant source of the input. This
assignment in space is based on prior action of the perceiver
into the world, and it is essential as a basis for planning and
orienting future action in respect to perceived stimuli. It takes
place automatically, in concert with postural and kinematic
adjustments of bodies to the accelerations imposed by gravity
and by the animals and vehicles we use for transportation.

Part of the assignment must take place within the parietal lobe,
because recordings of pulse trains from parietal neurons in
monkeys show that firing in response to an object can depend on
whether the object is within reach of the subjects within their
"personal space" (Mountcastle 1978). Perhaps this is a site of
action of the hallucinogen mescaline, which shrinks the sense of
personal space (Fischer 1971). Parietal lesions can result in
loss of comprehension of the personal space inside or adjacent
to the body (Sacks 1985). People with damage to the right
parietal association area may neglect events and objects on the
left side of their bodies, as by hitting the edge of a door with
the left arm as they walk through. This agnosia may be separate
from or combined with loss of body image, such that half the
body may be perceived as belonging to someone else (Note 4.5).

No, we learn to do it & then forget having done so —
Freeman is just cutting corners in his explanatory work here

Libet (1994) has found evidence for a comparable neural system for orientation with respect to time. Neurosurgical patients were given electrical stimuli directly to the left somatosensory cortex (which gets input from the right hand) and also to the left hand. They were asked to report the time at which they perceived the stimuli. In both cases approximately half a second elapsed before their brains initiated a perceptual report, but the stimulus to the hand was automatically back-dated to its time of occurrence. The neural basis for this operation is provided by the two ascending sensory channels. The axons in one (*lemniscal*) system are fast and unbranched. They can report in 30 milliseconds exactly where and when a fly is biting the skin. The axons in other (*spinothalamic*) system are slow and widely branched into the reticular formation all along the neural tube. The cumulative activities they induce are the basis for perceiving a fly half a second later, but perception of the time and place is based on lemniscal input. Lesions of the lemniscal path bring loss of fine discrimination and the ability to identify objects by manipulating them. Spinothalamic lesions bring loss of pain and temperature sense. Curiously, when physiogists cut all spinal tracts in rats except that for the lemniscal system and tested its function, the rats ignore all stimuli below the level of the cut (Melzack and Wall 1983), leaving the question: What does the system do? Libet's work gives an answer.

Experimental psychologists commonly use a *double threshold* technique to detect events in noisy time series, a high threshold to determine that an event with gradual onset has occurred, and a low threshold to back-date the time at which it began. In constructing a mechanical model of learning Walter (1963) used two electronic circuits, one with a step output to report "that an event happened", the other with a pulse output to report "when it happened". According to Libet, "... dissociation between the timings of the corresponding 'mental' and 'physical' events would seem to raise serious though not insurmountable difficulties for the prevalent theory of psychoneural identity" [p. 222] Indeed, his data show that there are no simple relations between bursts of Neuroactivity and mental content (Section 5.7). However, only Cartesian dualists could believe that "this antedating procedure does not seem to be explicable by any neurophysiological process" (Popper and Eccles 1977 p. 364). The view in dynamics is that Libet's delay is the time needed for propagation of a global state transition through a forebrain to update the state of the intentional structure by learning. It is longer than the time required for state transitions in olfactory bulb (Section 3.9, Note 3.10), but it appears to correspond to a putative delay in awareness of decisions, after they are taken (Section 7.4). All that is needed is some short-term memory.

4.6 Reafference and motor control

The facts have been mentioned that motor axons leave the spinal cord only by the ventral roots, and sensory axons enter only by the dorsal roots. After surgical section of only the ventral roots to a limb, physiologists unsurprisingly found paralysis of the limb, but they were astonished to find paralysis also after cutting only the dorsal roots. They went on to find that muscles and tendons have sensory receptors for length and force that provide *muscle sense*. Brains cannot operate muscles without continuously monitoring their states and positions by receiving reports from their receptors. Sherrington (1906) called this input *proprioception* to distinguish it from *exteroception* from body surfaces and *interoception* from the viscera. Its existence had not been suspected beforehand, because proprioceptive input is passed through the cerebellum and is integrated into movement patterns before it is sent to the thalamus. No one can directly experience either blood pressure or muscle sense, in that brains are protected from overload by raw sense data. Proprioceptors work beside mechanoreceptors in bone, joint, and connective tissue (Kandel, Schwartz and Jessup 1993, Ch. 35), which send input directly into the thalamus concerning limb position as distinct from limb motion. Two sets of muscles have no muscle receptors: the tongue, which is controlled by sensory input from the ear in speech; and the muscles of the eye, for which the direction is controlled by the frontal cortex to fix gaze on targets identified by the visual cortex. In neither of these organs is muscle tension an important factor, but in locomotion and manipulation of objects, sensory data on muscle lengths, tensions, and rates of change are essential. Also, axons descend from the cerebral cortex to the sensory relays in the thalamus and spinal cord, which amplify, diminish, and gate the flow of Neuroactivity to the cortex in a process referred to as *centrifugal control* of sensory input. The role of the motor cortex in mammals is to position the limbs so as to optimize the sensory inflow in respect to search (stereognosis). The same holds for the frontal eye fields located close to the motor cortex, which control the conjugate movements of the eyes in search and fixation.

But there is much more. Hermann von Helmholtz, Army surgeon, neuroanatomist, biophysicist and as close to a Renaissance Man as the 19th century offered, in the course of his monumental studies on vision made a remarkable observation. Patients with paralysis of the eye muscle for lateral gaze reported that, when they tried unsuccessfully to move the affected eye laterally, the visual field in that eye appeared to move oppositely. He concluded that visual perception has three components: the input from the retinas, the motor control of the eyes, and a sense of effort or volition, by which subjects distinguish apparent motion that is caused by the subject moving the head and eyes from real motion, in which objects in the visual field change their locations. He showed further that when an eye is moved passively by applying pressure with a finger on the half-closed eyelid, the visual field appear to move, which it does not when the eyes are moved by its muscles. He wrote (1879):

> The sensations, which enable us to perceive changes of position of the parts of the body through muscular action are known as the muscular feeling. This term includes, however, several essentially different sensations that have to be distinguished. Thus we may perceive: 1. The "intensity of the effort of will" ... whereby we endeavour to bring the muscles in action; 2. The "tension of the muscles", that is, the force by which they try to act; and 3. The "result of the effort" ..., which, regardless of its being perceived by other organs of sense, such as sight and touch, makes itself felt in the muscle by a contraction which actually takes place. ... [O]ur judgments as to the direction of the visual axis are simply the result of the effort of will involved in trying to alter the adjustment of the eyes. ... The sole action of the impulse of the will ... is the change of position of the eye. [A]s a matter of fact, these variations of the image are being continually utilized to regulate the proper relation between the impulse of the will and its effect. [p. 294]

This finding illustrates the general principle for every sensory system, that part of its centrifugal control compensates for the changes in sensory input, which must take place when the body is moved in the process of observation. Another example is being able to distinguish one's own voice when speaking from the voices of others. Some individuals terrorized by explosions, falls, and other violent events, have reported hearing repeated screams, and only later realize that the cries were their own, indicating that, under stress, the limbic system can come apart.

The concept was re-formulated by von Holst and Mittlestädt (1950), who introduced Das Reafferenzprincip (the reafference principle) in the context of cybernetics by feedback control of movement in insects. According to their theory, a movement is carried out by specification of an end state that differs from the present state. A motor center issues an "efference" by which a limb is moved, and at the same time maintains an "efference copy". The proprioceptors return an "afference" to a sensory center, which is relayed to the motor center and compared with the efference copy. A difference between the two messages constitutes an error, which is initially large, so, in accordance with predictive control theory, the motor system changes its output until the error is minimized.

von Holst and Mittlestädt conceived the process as taking place in conjunction with proprioception during automatic, reflexive adjustments and corrections of actions with the immediate environment, well below the level of attention and perception. It gave important insights into motor control through sensory feedback. It has now been experimentally shown to exist as predicted in the oculomotor control system of vertebrates, as a neural mechanism for storing and matching patterns, and calculating errors from the set points already defined (Bizzi et al. 1992) in an error reduction system. However, cybernetics is not a good context in which to understand intentionality by which set points are chosen; synergetics is better (Haken 1983).

Roger Sperry (1950) developed the concept of "corollary discharge" in his studies on the circling motion of fish produced when one eye was covered or blinded, the other eye was rotated 180 degrees, and the muscles were reattached. Thereafter, the forward motion of the fish was registered as backward motion in the optic lobe, so the fish circled. He removed various parts of the brain either separately or together, but only removal of the optic lobe belonging to the inverted eye stopped the circling. If the other eye was not blinded but merely covered, circling stopped when the cover was removed. The normal eye with its own optic lobe was able to compensate for the incorrect apparent motion registered by the rotated eye. He concluded that the optic lobe is the primary integrating center for the optokinetic response by which the eyes track moving objects.

[A] ... kinetic component may arise centrally as part of the excitation pattern of the overt movement. Thus, any excitation pattern that normally results in a movement that will cause a displacement of the visual image on the retina may have a corollary discharge into the visual centers to compensate for the retinal displacement. This implies an anticipatory adjustment in the visual centers specific for each movement with regard to its direction and speed. A central adjustor factor of this kind would aid in maintaining stability of the visual field under normal conditions during the onset of sudden eye, head, and body movement. With the retinal field rotated 180 degrees, any such anticipatory adjustment would be in diametric disharmony with the retinal input, and would therefore cause accentuation rather than cancellation of the illusory outside movement. ... [the central kinetic factor] would provide a neural basis for what Helmholtz called the sensation of the "intensity of the effort of will". The need for some kind of central mechanism to eliminate blurring of vision between fixations in eye movement has long been recognized. [p. 488]

Error detection and compensation for movement-induced changes in sensory input are important aspects of reafference, but transcending these, I propose (Freeman 1990a), is its putative role in expectancy and selective attention. When an animal undertakes a search by eye movement or a sniff, it is guided not just by a prior odor or glimpse but by inputs from all of its senses, which have converged into the entorhinal cortex and combined in the hippocampus. The anatomical basis exists for returning that output to all of the sensory cortices. Updated entorhinal output may act to bias every sensory cortex in a direction appropriate for the predicted input coming from its own exteroceptor array, but in the context of recent input from all sensory arrays, thus maintaining the unity of intentionality.

An experimental study of reafference in this sense is being undertaken in my laboratory by Leslie Kay (1994; Kay and Freeman 1994). Promising results show that, just prior to a sniff, the entorhinal cortex sends a burst of activity to the olfactory bulb, which registers there just before the receptor input arrives in response to the sniff and changes the bulbar state. After the bulbar burst has been transmitted to the olfactory and entorhinal cortices, another entorhinal burst travels centrifugally, as though in acknowledgement. If these experiments can be replicated, they will give the first demonstration of a reafferent message, and they will help to explain how reafference can be modeled as a form of spatially textured bias control over selective access by a sensory cortex to one or more of its learned basins of attraction. This would offer a neural mechanism for selective attention and the unity of brain function, and go far to explaining *state-dependency* of responses to stimuli (Section 5.4). So much is riding on these EEG recordings from hungry rats trained to press a bar for food.

4.7 The reticular formation and arousal

The importance I assign to the limbic system may seem to neglect the importance of the major neocortical systems and their thalamic gateways and brain stem controls. That is not my intent. I wish to explain the structure of behavior as the genesis of purpose within the limbic system, followed by constructions of actions to reach the goal. The constructions require continual merging of percepts from all of the sensory portals and the continual updating of the sensory cortices, where percepts are constructed to be shared across modalities.

The brain stem also supports multisensory convergence. The vertebrate neural tube begins as a cylinder of neuropil with a central canal. Laminations in the outer shell emerge to form cortex. Nuclei in the thalamus, hypothalamus and striatum emerge as clusters or ganglia. They remain embedded in the all-encompassing neuropil, which has a central, nuclear-free zone: the reticular formation. The reticular formation in the brain stem sends axons into the spinal cord that impose excitatory and inhibitory modulations on the motoneurons that facilitate rhythmic activities, such as breathing and locomotion. It activates the entire cerebral cortex by its extension through the thalamic reticular formation, in which the relay nuclei are embedded, whence its name, the *reticular activating system* (Magoun 1958). All sensory axons send side branches into the reticular formation as the basis for arousal. Direct electrical stimulation with electrodes implanted in the brain stem suffices to awaken sleeping animals. Bilateral lesions in the brain stem reticular formation lead to permanent coma with EEG waves that are characteristic of deep sleep. Gastaut (1964) has proposed that normal arousal acts upwardly and downwardly, but that imbalances may occur. He suggests that descending activation results in sleepwalking, in which locomotion, as in decorticate animals, occurs with no goal, whereas ascending activation alone is accompanied by nightmares, particularly those involving difficulty in breathing, a "cannonball on the chest", and paralysis of limbs. His thesis is unproven, but it illustrates the broad control that is exercised by the reticular formation. However, to call it the seat of consciousness (Penfield 1975) is to confuse the light switch with the lights.

The thalamus exchanges input with the hippocampus, so it participates in constructions induced in cortex by the input it relays from the skin, ears and eyes. Perhaps the limbic system helps the thalamus to select the portions it sends on to the somatic, auditory and visual cortices. It has major janitorial tasks to perform, such as dynamic range compression; normalization of input to improve signal-to-noise ratios at all levels of intensity; batch gating of input by control of oscillation (Dempsey and Morison 1942; Andersen and Andersson 1968; Sillito et al. 1994); turning cortices on and off by neurohormonal bias controls; controlling sleep, as shown by Hess (1957), who induced normal sleep by electrical stimulation of the thalamus; and optimizing the frequency ranges for thalamic transmission of bursts of oscillatory inputs to cortex (Singer 1994). A special role is proposed for the "NRT" (nucleus reticularis thalami) by John Taylor (1994) for his "relational mind". Neurons in the NRT are mutually inhibitory, and thereby they are capable of a flexible and competitive "winner-take-all" gating of thalamocortical output in the process of selective attention, but the intentional hand on the gate is unspecified. His model provides a mechanism to implement the attentional "searchlight" of Crick (1984), but leaves unanswered the question: What mechanism selectively aims the searchlight?

Likewise, the genesis of intention is not the exclusive domain of the frontal lobes, which occupy half of each hemisphere and appear as the crown jewels of human brains. Bilateral frontal lobotomy has no effect on performance in standard tests of intelligence, but it destroys capacities for imagination, creative play, and experiencing nuances of emotion. The impoverished mind is no longer capable of constructing empathic hypotheses on the thoughts and feelings of others, and it is unable to construct plans that require flexible timetables of sequential actions to bring about future states. There is also loss of anxiety, fear of pain, and a thanatic drive to suicide, which is why frontal lobotomy was performed for depressions and obsessive compulsive disorders prior to the discovery of effective chemical treatment. The frontal lobe elaborates goals into plans but does not generate them *de novo* and embed them in space for execution and update in time. Those are the roles of the limbic system. Moreover, it should not be supposed that the limbic system in human brains was finished first in evolution and then put on hold while the rest of the forebrain caught up. The human hippocampus is the largest of any and would appear like the engine of a commercial jet aircraft in a sport plane, were it transplanted into brains of lesser primates.

4.8 Communication between brains

Communication is priming and enaction of cooperation between solipsistic brains. Its primordial role is to support sexual reproduction. A pregnant fish searches for a suitable place in which to deposit her eggs, and in the laying gives off an odorant chemical that diffuses into the surround. The donor male detects the scent, identifies it against the background, tracks it to its source, positions its body suitably, and releases its sperm over the eggs. In terms of communication, the odor is the signal, the dispersive medium is the channel, the female is the transmitter, and the male is the receiver. The same paradigm holds for most animals with elaborations involving visual and auditory signals, including humans who apply perfume to attract mates. The process uses the main features of intentionality in vertebrates, including the distance receptor systems for sights, sounds and odors, the hippocampal system for localizing targets in space and sequencing events in time, the limbic system for generating actions and expectancies by reafference, and the intentional structure of cortical neuropil that provide attractor basins for generalization and classification during multimodal convergence into the limbic system (Note 4.6). Invertebrate brains have comparable functions (Young 1966; Griffin 1992).

Basic neural connections within the motor and sensory systems are laid down under the control of genes to generate *fixed action patterns* and *autoshaped responses* that are appropriate for each species at each stage of reproductive processes (Griffin 1992). Mechanisms by which genes are expressed in the division and sprouting of neurons, the selective formation of connections, and the later actualization of self-organized firing patterns are under intensive study, particularly in favored species such as song birds that grow new neurons with each new breeding season. But animal communication is too often conceived in narrow terms of an alphabet of signs that forms a "code" and a repertoire of behaviors, for example the dance steps of bees that signal the kind, direction, and distance of food to other worker bees, the grunts and howls of apes, and the chirps and whistles of dolphins. In order for communication to occur between animals their intentional mechanisms must be tuned, so that the limbic system can access the attractors by which the motor systems send reproductive signals, and sensory cortices can be biased to attractors that classify reproductive signals. The neuromodulators that facilitate the organization of Neuroactivity patterns are discussed in Section 6.4.

Animals that live in packs and herds have more elaborate systems that are designed to communicate internal states across the solipsistic gulf. It is important for the welfare of the group, as well as for each member, to have distant early warning of the probable intended behaviors of other members, particularly the alpha males. In human groups we read the signs of dominance and submission in terms of anger and fear, and of pursuit, territoriality, and loss in terms of desire, pride and grief. Charles Darwin (1872) catalogued and illustrated the signs of these states in his classic work, "The Expression of Emotion in Man and Animals", showing the postural and autonomic actions that are homologous across mammals in their social interaction. The ravages of viral encephalitis and related diseases of the basal ganglia such as Parkinson's disease (Sacks 1985), have shown that the capacities to express emotions and even to experience them involve neural assemblies that extend well beyond the limbic system, especially into the frontal lobes. The existence of homologous signs of emotions and our automatic responses to them in our feelings and actions when we are faced with a cringing dog or a posturing male gorilla with its gaze fixed on us, gives evidence for some commonality of intentional structures across the range of social mammals.

Where humans break new ground is in language (Note 4.7). In a narrow sense, Critchley (1979) wrote:

Speech has been called a socioeconomic device for saving effort in the attainment of objectives. One of its earliest and most fundamental purposes is to orientate the individual within the community. This socializing effect operates early in childhood, and in a phylogenetic sense it was perhaps one of the greatest factors in the origin of speech in primitive man. [p. 45]

Most of what we know about speech mechanisms has come from studies of diseases of brains, including locating Broca's area in the frontal lobe, where damage is associated with loss of coherent speech but not understanding, and of Wernicke's area in the parietal and occipital lobes where damage leads to selective loss of understanding of speech. Critchley observed:

Language, being a built-in aspect of one's personality, is therefore something specific. No two persons possess identical systems of communication. Loss of language ... is never uniform in pattern. The anonymous coterie of uncommunicating inaccessibles holds no two of a kind. Put more simply, no two aphasiacs are absolutely alike. [p. 83]

Given this lack of reproducibility, the prospects for a neuroscience of language based on rules of grammar seem dim, even with images by PET and functional MRI. We need to learn the mechanisms of intentionality as the embedding medium of communication. Critchley regards speech:

... as the utilization of symbols. The sounds emitted by animals are in the nature of signs, while man's speech is made up of symbols. Signs *indicate* things, while symbols *represent* them. Signs are announcers of events; symbols are reminders. In other words, symbols are not restricted to the confines of immediate time and place. ... When an ape utters a cry of hunger, it can be looked upon as perhaps making a declaration, perhaps an imperative utterance, or even an exclamation of discomfort. No ape, however has ever uttered the word "banana," for such a word is a concrete symbol, a tool of thought which only man can employ, and he can do so in a variety of ways, irrespective of the barriers of time and space. [p. 23]

Researchers who have taught sign language to chimpanzees will no doubt take issue with this view. The critical point is that some apes can learn to use symbols, but only humans can make them, which leads us to consider representation in Chapter 5.

4.9 Summary

The basic architectures of brains are revealed by studies in comparative neuroanatomy, together with topological analysis of the breakings of the radial symmetry and global connectivity of primitive nerve nets, and of the emergence of connections between the clusters of ganglionic neuropil in the striatum and areas of laminated neuropil in the cerebral cortex. Basic behavior emerges as movement directed into the world that manifests the metabolic needs of brains for building materials and fuel, which must be predicted, searched for, found in the world, and ingested. The search requires an internal structure of mind for orientation in space and time, which we represent as a *cognitive map*, and which brains construct through their directed actions into the world. The sensory environment is infinitely complex, and the messages that emerge from the sensory cortices on being triggered by stimuli are shaped by the synaptic structure of the neuropil and the reafferent messages that express expectancy and attention. The emergence of directed motion is conditional on neurohumoral controls, that are exerted on the forebrain by brain stem nuclei, the most basic being the action of the reticular formation to induce arousal. All these intentional mechanisms are brought into play in the interactions that take place between brains as the pre-logical basis of communication. In humans the process is crowned by the construction and use of symbols and language.

Chapter 5

Intentional Structure and Thought

The certainty of ideas is not the foundation of the certainty of perception but is, rather, based on it - in that it is perceptual experience which gives us the passage from one moment to the next and thus realizes the unity of time. ... In this sense all consciousness is perceptual, even the consciousness of ourselves.
Maurice Merleau-Ponty [1947 p. 13]

The role of reafference in shaping the constructs of sensory cortices offers a challenge to the phenomenological view of Merleau-Ponty. In my view, ideas are a basis for perception in the context of intentionality. I approached this view in steps. I defined Neuroactivity as a set of regular relations between the physical properties of neurons and observed movements of bodies (Chapter 2). I measured some manifestations of brain activity and modeled neural function with state variables, Q, representing Neuroactivity (Chapter 3). In the context of evolution I analyzed the behavior of animals to show how the wholeness of intentionality grows by continuous action into the world (Chapter 4). The coming three steps are to relate Neuroactivity to thought and representation in the context of shared knowledge (Chapter 5), to review the stretching forth of intentionality in the context of learning (Chapter 6), and to reformulate the mind-brain problem by relating patterns of Neuroactivity to feelings derived by introspection (Chapter 7).

5.1 Classification by multivariate statistics

My approach to closing the loop in Table 5.1 is to use multivariate statistics so as to classify many EEG patterns into a few antecedent sensory conditions. This is not a *mapping* of brain states onto mental states envisioned by Dennett (1991) and others, nor is it a form of *psychoneural identity*, by which brain and mind, neuron and psychon, are "events" (Whitehead 1938; Russell 1948) having objective and subjective "aspects" (Section 2.6). That is a metaphysical belief that I cannot verify, because I cannot adequately observe my own brain waves while thinking, and I cannot know what rabbits think.

Table 5.1   The Relations of Brain and Mind

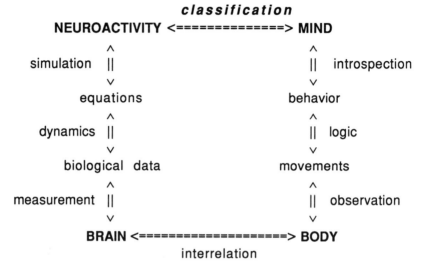

classification

NEUROACTIVITY <===============> MIND

simulation ‖ ⌃
                ⌄   ‖ introspection

equations   behavior

dynamics ‖ ⌃
              ⌄   ‖ logic

biological data   movements

measurement ‖ ⌃
                  ⌄   ‖ observation

BRAIN <===================> BODY

interrelation

My students and I train rabbits to discriminate two odors from
the background odor and from each other (Section 3.7). We find a
new spatial pattern of EEG oscillation for each of the three
odors, when the animals has been motivated by thirsting and
either odor is present. The EEG patterns for each odor are never
twice the same in any one session and any one animal.   There
are always differences, and the experimental question always
is: Are the three EEG patterns *significantly* different?

This question is right at the core of the mind-brain problem, so
a description is worthwhile of what experimentalists actually
do to get an answer.   We find the common wave form of a
pattern in the window made by our electrode array in a time
frame corresponding to where and when we believe a perceptual
event is taking place.   We measure the amplitude of the carrier
wave on each electrode, so the pattern is expressed in a set of
numbers (Note 3.1).   We express the amplitude as a point on a
line.   If there is one electrode, the difference between two
patterns is given by the distance between two points along the
line.   We repeat the recording with 20 presentations of each
stimulus, plot the two distributions of points in a graph, and
show that they fall into bell curves (normal distributions).   We
calculate the mean and standard deviation of each distribution.
If the difference between the means is more than three times

the average standard deviation, we conclude that the difference between the two patterns is not due to chance.

One electrode does not suffice. With two electrodes there are two lines at a right angle in the pattern space, forming a plane. The distance between two points on the surface is given by Euclid's theorem: the square of the distance is equal to the sum of squares of the amplitudes. The same rule is applied for any number of electrodes, 64 in our system. The spatial pattern of each burst is measured by the 64 values of amplitude of the common wave form. This gives a 64x1 column vector, and a point in a vector space with 64 coordinate axes, whence *multivariate*. We set a criterion for significance by measuring 20 patterns for each odor in each session in each animal. Each pattern consists of a cluster of points. As stars in the three dimensions of space appear as clusters in the two dimensions of the sky, the points in 64-space are projected onto a piece of paper. We show that the mean of a distribution is the same as its center of gravity, and its probable size is taken as a circle with the radius derived from its standard deviation.

The two separated distributions of points give us a start on pattern classification. In its general form, our procedure is called *cross-validation*. A data set is divided in two parts. One part called the *training set* is used to determine the centers of clusters, and those centers are used to classify the other part, the *test set*. The roles of the two sets are then reversed, and the classification is repeated. The question is: How well do the centers generalize to classify data that were not used to derive them? We randomly divide the 40 trials into 10 training trials and 10 test trials for each odor, A and B. If a test point for odor A is closer to the training mean for the A cluster than to the training mean for B, it is classified as *correct,* and so also for test points for odor B. When the likelihood that the number of correct classifications by chance is less than 1 in 100, we conclude that the patterns for A and B are *significantly* different. We obtain the same outcome by cross validation in every session and every rabbit tested, and thereafter we conclude that we have established a relation between the stimulus conditions and the spatial patterns of Neuroactivity in the rabbit brains (Freeman and Viana Di Prisco 1986; Freeman and Barrie 1994).

5.2 Context dependence and pattern variability

We repeated the test with electrode arrays placed on the visual, auditory, somatic, or olfactory cortices. The largest Euclidean distances were found between subjects. Each rabbit had its characteristic pattern, never twice the same like a handwritten signature. The smallest distances were between the centers for stimulus clusters. The standard deviations of stimulus clusters were smaller than the clusters for the background from the same session and subject. There was a substantial difference from each session to the next, often in see-saw fashion, so that rabbits seemed to have off days when their performance was poor (Barrie, Freeman and Lenhart 1994), but we found an unequivocal trend of increase in distance between session means with an increasing number of sessions while keeping the trial conditions constant. The average daily step was only 2% of the variance within each session, and this was about a quarter of the step when a new stimulus or reinforcement was introduced (Freeman and Grajski 1987). We think that the mean daily change reflected the phenomenon of *perceptual drift*. Its daily magnitude was so small that it was difficult to measure.

The pressing question was whether Neuroactivity patterns in the same session could be correctly classified with respect to two discriminated stimuli by the distance method. Given the limitations of the EEG analysis the best we could do was about 75% correct classification for both stimuli in each of the four sensory cortices. This was about the same as the animals' rates of success in identifying stimuli, as shown by their conditioned response rates (Viana Di Prisco and Freeman 1985).

Among the properties of the Neuroactivity patterns revealed by the multivariate statistical analyses, the most salient feature was a lack of invariance of the EEG patterns with respect to the stimuli, which was found in olfaction (Section 3.7) and replicated in the other modalities. The variations for stimuli within a session could easily be explained by noise or random variation of the selection of sensory receptors on successive trials. The fluctuations in mean patterns over sessions could be explained by uncontrolled variables relating to the degree of arousal, affect, hunger, or thirst of the animals, good days and bad days. The underlying trend might be accounted for by the growth and aging of the animals. These are all normal factors in long-term biological experiments involving brain and behavior.

What can't be explained away by uncontrolled variables is the dependence on context of the Neuroactivity patterns. Examples are given for olfaction (Section 3.7) of experiments with serial discriminative conditioning and reinforcement contingency reversal. The same variability with these manipulations is found in the other sensory cortices. With each new stimulus or change in reinforcement, the existing pattern changes slightly to a new form. This outcome is inconsistent with a hypothesis by which a stimulus is selectively filtered by neural networks and compared with stored templates for best match in a classification algorithm, but it is entirely compatible with the performance of a dynamic system in which the connectivity is modified with each successive training to a new stimulus in a cumulative manner. The stimuli are not different, but the circumstances in which the discriminations are done are evolving. The forms of the responses are not different, but the relative frequency (number of responses out of the total number of trials) characteristically decrease over sessions, indicating that the context as uncontrollably changing. The fact that the form of the conditioned response is not altered is explained by the hypothesis that the output pattern of the cortex changes by only a small fraction of the total variance (Freeman and Grajski 1987), so that the output falls within the basin of attraction in the motor system for that percept. Moreover, synaptic weights are changed in both sensory and motor systems during learning (Section 6.2). When a new stimulus is introduced or when an animal makes a mistake by trial and error, it is reasonable to believe that learning may re-shape the basins of attraction in the motor system to accommodate the new perceptual pattern. This is another aspect of the unity of intentionality.

5.3 Other aspects of Neuroactivity and behavior

The EEG-derived representations of Neuroactivity in paleocortex (bulb, olfactory nucleus and cortex) reveal a sequence of bursts that are created by state transitions with inhalation and exhalation. The respiratory *frame rate* is about 5/second in rabbits, much faster than human sniffing. Oscillation within the bursts has a dominant frequency in the high gamma range, typically "40 Hz" in cats and humans, 50-80 Hz in rabbits and

70-110 Hz in rats (Bressler and Freeman 1980), but that frequency is different for each burst, and even within bursts the frequency tends to vary. This dominance holds only for stimuli the animals have learned to identify. Stimuli that are not known by the rabbits or mistaken for known stimuli elicit a broad band oscillation without a dominant frequency, along with an orienting reflex (sniffing, searching, "What is it?", a "double take"). The repetitive driving of the paleocortex by respiration makes it easy to divide the continuous EEG records into segments lasting about 100 milliseconds, which correspond to bursts recurring at intervals of about 100 milliseconds from the end of the preceding burst to the onset of the next one.

We find that in neocortex (Freeman and Barrie 1994) there are no dominant frequencies at which identifiable bursts occur. The spectra show continuous distributions of energy in which the logarithm of the power declines linearly with the logarithm of frequency. (This "1/f" spectral pattern is characteristic of chaotic systems but also of non-chaotic systems like operational amplifiers driven by thermal noise.) The neocortical EEGs reveal continuously emergent fluctuations with no bursts, and no slow wave like that with respiration in olfaction, which forces the bulb into state transitions. We therefore make our comparisons across sets of discriminated stimulus trials in time windows of 120 milliseconds that we shift along the EEGs of 6-second trials in steps of 20 milliseconds. In each window we extract the common wave form and determine its spatial pattern of amplitude. We find no significant difference between the EEG traces taken from the pre-stimulus control period, but in the stimulus-response period there is a rapid sequence of two to four time segments in which reliable differences in spatial pattern distinguish the trials with differing sensory stimuli.

As in the olfactory recordings, the differing segments last about a tenth of a second and are separated in time by about the same interval. The first segment starts about 30 milliseconds after the onset of a stimulus, the next about 200 milliseconds later. They are seen so early only for stimuli in the appropriate modality. Cross-stimulation from other modalities leads to EEG segments that differ with respect to stimuli in other modalities start more than a half-second after stimulus onset (Barrie, Freeman and Lenhart 1994), suggesting that this is the order of time lag that is required for reafference. The information in the amplitude patterns was broadly distributed over EEG spectra. It was homogeneously distributed over the 64 EEG traces; none was more or less important than average. Spatial patterns of amplitude varied from each trial to the next, and they changed when the context of the stimulation was modified, showing the same lack of invariance with respect to stimuli as in olfaction.

The sequence of two to four distinctive frames of Neuroactivity after the arrival of a stimulus occurs in about half a second, which is approximately the time delay reported by Libet (Section 4.5) for perception to take place. It suggests that perception leading to awareness (Section 7.4) requires a staccato of frames, perhaps enlarging spatially by serial stages from sensory cortices into the entorhinal cortex (Note 4.4) at a rate corresponding to global state changes that are found in scalp EEGs of waking humans to occur on average at 5/second (Lehmann and Michel 1990). The frames are also seen in brief episodes of coherence between areas of sensory and motor cortex in monkeys during the performance of a conditioned response (Bressler, Coppola and Nakamura 1993).

5.4 Forced state transitions and cortical itinerancy

I conclude that the context dependence is an essential property of the cerebral memory system, in which each new experience must change all of the existing store by some small amount, in order that a new entry be incorporated and fully deployed in the existing body of experience. This property contrasts with memory stores in computers, libraries, and telephone books, in which each item is positioned by an address or a branch of a search tree. There, each item has a compartment, and new items don't change the old ones. Our data indicate that in brains the store has no boundaries or compartments, and that it comes into play wholly with each cortical state transition, in olfaction with each inhalation and exhalation. Each new state transition in a sensory port initiates the construction of a local pattern that impinges on and modifies the whole intentional structure to a degree, depending on conceptual distances in time, modality, and neuronal propagation delays. Each event has its focus in the intentional structure with its relations fanning in the surround, attenuating with conceptual and neural distances.

I conclude that each observed pattern manifests a meaning, which I define as a focus in a region in an evolving landscape that is provided by the intentional structure of the subject. The meaning is not the pattern, nor is it in the pattern. It is the set of relations that is expressed by the pattern and enacted by the neurons sustaining it, which may include the entire forebrain, if one allows that neurons participate not only by discharging but also by actively remaining silent under inhibition, when that is required of them to form a pattern.

As inferred for the olfactory system (Section 3.10), each neocortex may have one or more global attractors with multiple wings. State transitions may occur as brief confinements to a wing of an attractor, followed by release to another. We have, at present, insufficient evidence to determine the mechanism or form of neocortical forcing functions equivalent to that working in olfaction. The concept of an attractor and its attendant basin is too rigid, because neocortical dynamics progresses through time by continual changes in state that adapt the cortices to the changing environment. The change constitutes a trajectory in cortical state space, which never returns exactly to a prior state, but which (on receipt of a stimulus, for example) returns sufficiently close to the prior state that cortical output places a target of the transmission into the same basin of attraction as did the prior output. By generalization over the basin of a wing in the target attractor, the activity pattern expressed by the target is indistinguishable from its prior pattern, so the behavior is the same. Yet the prior and present patterns are not identical, and with continuing evolution by learning in both transmitting and target cortices, the differences on repeated visitations to that part of the cortical state space accumulate, sooner or later making an overt difference, reflecting perceptual drift (Section 5.2). This mode of change is described as chaotic *itinerancy* (Tsuda 1991), by analogy to the seasonal progress of a peddler or farm laborer, continually revisiting former sites but finding them never twice identical. It differs from Stephen Jay Gould's (1987) "punctuated equilibria" in its emphasis on the recurrence of similar states.

Also coming into play in each sensory cortex are reafferent messages, putatively from entorhinal cortex (Section 4.6), and neuromodulators from brain stem (Section 6.4). We postulate that entorhinal bursts can bias the bulb and cortex rapidly to facilitate access to a wing corresponding to expected stimuli, and that modulators can slowly shape olfactory dynamics by bringing up or replacing whole attractor systems. Thus both fast reafference and slow modulation set the states of sensory cortices and implement the *state-dependency* of behavior, which is the controlled variation of behavioral responses to stimuli and drugs (Section 7.6) in differing *internal* contexts that are established by intentionality.

State-dependency also includes adaptation of generalization gradients for sensory sensory input and the range of flexibility in motor output, as discussed in terms of complexity theory (Section 3.10). The idea of a sliding scale of chaos, which runs from the stability of rigid order to adaptiveness in disorder but with loss of predictability, is clear in principle but difficult to verify and simulate in the laboratory, owing to present limitations on our methods for measurement and analysis of chaos (Notes 3.1, 3.9). For example, given a chaotic state in the olfactory bulb, is the degree of chaos a controlled parameter? What other part of the forebrain might monitor the bulbar output to measure it? What aspect of the output is used by the monitor? How is the control implemented? These questions are opened for exploration by neurodynamics (Schiff et al. 1994), and the answers may lead to a larger question addressed in Section 7.5. When a person experiences the "Eureka" reaction upon getting an idea with a sense of closure, some global increase in spatiotemporal coherence of Neuroactivity may emerge, that mediates the neurochemical basis for hedonic satisfaction and conviction. Experimental use of complexity theory may offer a route to explore this intentional phenomenon.

5.5 Neural activity patterns and representations

The spatiotemporal patterns of Neuroactivity, as I have described them, are like swirling clouds in a thickening sky. Do these same patterns constitute representations within the brains of the animals that generate them? Different answers are given by *classical* and *situated* cognitivism. A classical cognitivist would interpret my data as showing that a rabbit maintains a knowledge base in its brain to guide its actions into its world. Both brain and world are dynamic systems, and each goes through a succession of states - day, night, wake, sleep, hunger, satiety, and so on - so he infers that there is a mapping between brain states and world states. When a world state impinges on a rabbit as a stimulus, a corresponding brain state ensues as a response to the stimulus. When he looks at brain data, he finds a pattern of sensory activity that exists only after the stimulus and only briefly. The physical stimulus has not gone past receptors into the forebrain, so he says that the activity *represents* the stimulus. On the motor side of the brain he sees a pattern of activity that precedes and accompanies a movement, which changes the body by adapting it to the stimulus. The brain activity has not spilled out into the world, so he says that the neuromotor activity *represents* the response.

Since the neurosensory and neuromotor activity patterns differ, he infers that the rabbit's brain transforms the sensory pattern into the motor pattern in the operational manner of a dynamic system. An equation is a rule for making such a transformation, so he concludes that the sensory representation is operated on in accordance with a set of equations as rules to give the motor representation. The task of the neuroscientist is to learn the rules by which the rabbit makes representations (symbols) from pulse firings in receptor activity and transforms them into motor representations (commands). The task of a cognitivist is to construct a dynamic model that simulates the performance of rabbits by operating on inputs to give outputs according to the same or similar rules. A successful program for a robot that can at least get around in the world the way rabbits do is essential to validate the theory. It would include tables of representations playing the roles of brain activity patterns and a set of rules to manipulate the symbols as needed to simulate observed stimulus-response transformations. In his view a brain gets a stimulus, makes a representation of it (a symbol), draws on its memory store of past representations to match and classify it, and does whatever is necessary to select a motor representation from a table or to reshape the perceptual representation into a motor command to carry out the action.
The situated cognitivist avoids introducing "the brain" as a third party, that is making and manipulating symbols and commands, by embedding the brain in the world as a part of the world dynamic system (Slezak 1994). In his view brains act by inner states that are *internal representations* of the world and other brains. Objects in the world are *external representations* such as odors that signify food, predators and mates. Internal representations in brains have functional, meaningful relations

to the external representations as the basis for adaptive behavior. A Neuroactivity pattern that reliably recurs upon odor presentation to a rabbit trained to drink in response represents the odor and the water in its brain. In other words, the odor is an external representation of a reward for the animal, and the Neuroactivity pattern is an internal representation of the odor for the brain, so that the animal can find and drink the water.

5.6 Continuous *versus* discrete operations: Graining

The *descriptions* of brain states as internal representations or "mental images" (Chomsky 1975; Fodor 1981) and the *descriptions* of world states as external representations or material objects are both symbolic, so in principle they can be mapped onto each other. That is what dictionaries and glossaries are for. Neither of these symbol systems can be mapped onto the world or onto brains, in that material systems in the world are infinite, not merely in the mathematical sense of continuity, but in the sense of boundless complexity that is exemplified by the olfactory environment (Section 4.2). This incompatibility has been a barrier faced by AI for half a century. Representations in models of Neuroactivity (Table 5.2) are made with a finite set of numbers on digital computers.   In mathematics a continuous line segment of real numbers can't be mapped into integers or floating point numbers, so the digits in a computer can only approximate continuous world dynamics. Efforts to compute with real numbers instead of digits (Blum, Shub and Smale 1989) and to use infinitesimals that are located between the finite numbers (McLaughlin 1994) are in progress, but the theories cannot yet map the world onto mental images.

Table 5.2   The Relations of Brain and Mind

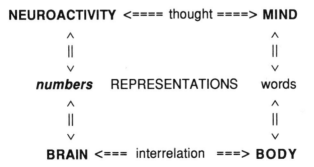

NEUROACTIVITY <==== thought ====> **MIND**

numbers   REPRESENTATIONS   words

BRAIN <=== interrelation ===> **BODY**

The problem is really two-fold. There is the ontological question: What do brains do? What is the relation between the infinite world and a unitary brain, both being dynamic systems? That is an engineering question: How can we build a device that simulates what brains do, as a way to understand their function? Three prior attempts at answers have failed (Note 5.1), because none has incorporated a hierarchy of macroscopic state transitions induced by microscopic fluctuations (Section 3.4). And there is the epistemological question, which must be answered before an artificial brain can be built: How do we *represent* what brains do? What is the relation between human brains and the descriptions of themselves and the world that brains make by shaping discrete bits of matter into symbols? If a brain starts and ends a task each time it makes a symbol, is it not working in discrete steps? Is the fact that a brain is a continuous-time dynamic system irrelevant to its intentional function, as the comparable fact about a digital computer is irrelevant to its computational function?

When a quantity enters a computer it is digitized and expressed in bits. The bits are gathered into a register as a frame, which is gated into a sequence of frames by a clock. When the quantity enters a brain it is discretized and expressed in pulses, which exist at points moving through and from the receptor surface. The pulses are grouped in the time dimension into volleys by respiration and movements of the fingers, head, or eyes (rapid flicks of gaze called microsaccades), and by neurogenic oscillations in the olfactory bulb or thalamus (Section 4.7). In digital computers the operations are kept discrete by representing binary numbers with voltage steps and pulses large enough to cross the thresholds of the nonlinear components reliably. In brains further action is transferred to the macroscopic level by induction of a global state transition, which is expressed by pulse densities (Note 3.4) in an activity density function, Q, of Neuroactivity over sensory cortex. The transition, too, has a threshold, and crossing it requires a strong push like the respiratory forcing function (Section 3.10).

Whether the Neuroactivity can be treated as continuous in space and time depends on whether the grain is fine enough. EEG fields of potential (Mitzdorf 1984) manifesting Neuroactivity can be so treated, because the grain is given by ions flowing across the tissue resistance, but Neuroactivity is transmitted between and from neurons in cortex by axonal pulses. The temporal and spatial *coarse-graining* of the macroscopic state variables by the microscopic activity composing them is not negligible. It may be comparable to the round-off and truncation errors in digital computations. In round numbers each neuron receives 10,000 synapses from other neurons. At average pulse rates of 1/second, the neuron receives 10,000 pulses/second, each pulse lasting 1/1000 second. In the time window of decision on whether to fire, input may average 10 pulses, so that the grain may be coarse. The high precision of digital computers may be misplaced in simulating brain function. A problem we have found in our efforts to simulate chaotic EEG time series with pseudotrajectories (Hamel et al. 1987) by numerical integration is a tendency of the computation to fall into a limit cycle, which it cannot escape, due to use of floating point numbers for calculation. There is no possibility for an infinitesimal variation to emerge at a macroscopic scale, to give *sensitivity to initial conditions*. Chaotic tangles have an infinity of limit cycles; a digital representation may lock on to one (Note 5.2).

At macroscopic levels each perceptual pattern of Neuroactivity is discrete, because it is marked by state transitions when it is formed and ended. It is bounded spatially by the anatomical distribution of cells that have been *enslaved* (Section 3.4) into its spatially coherent activity. I conclude that brains don't use numbers as symbols, but they do use discrete events in time and space, so we can represent them epistemologically by numbers in order to model brain states with digital computers, even though ontologically we cannot make artificial brains that way.

5.7 Thoughts and idols   Cop-out ?

Operational discreteness is essential for communication in dialogue. A pair of brains can act, sense, and construct in alternation with respect to each other, not merely as dogs sniff, but as two humans speak, listen, and hear. Consider Brains **A** and **B** interacting, where **A**-**B** are parent-child, wife-husband, philosopher-biologist, neuroscientist-rabbit, rabbit-dog, etc. **A** has a thought that formulates some meaning M(a). In accordance with this meaning **A** acts to shape a bit of matter in the world (a trace of ink on paper, a vibration of air, a set of keystrokes on e-mail, movements of the face, etc.) to create a representation (a sign or symbol for humans, merely a sign for

animals) directed at **B**, R(ab). **B** is impacted by this shaped
matter and is induced by thought to create a meaning M(b). So **B**
acts to shape a bit of matter in accordance with M(b) in a
representation R(ba), which impacts on **A** to induce M(a+1).

And so on. Already by this description we have recognized a
discrete ebb and flow of conversation like the tabulation of the
tides, so that meanings M(i)'s as constructions of thoughts
become the internal representations, and the R(ij)'s as
attributes of matter become the external representations. By
its nature an external "re"presentation can be used over and
over. It cannot be said to contain or carry meaning, since the
meanings are located uniquely in **A** and **B** and not between them.
Moreover, the same R's induces different meanings M(i) in other
subjects **C** who intercept the representations. The objects that
are used to communicate are shaped by meanings that are
constructed in **A** and **B** iteratively, and they induce the
constructions of meanings in **B** and **A** alternately. If the
communication is successful, then the representations will
come into harmony such as by dancing, walking in step, shaking
hands, exchanging bread, etc. Symbols can persist like books in
libraries, while minds fluctuate and evolve until they die. When
a representation replaces that for which it stands in the minds
of respondents, then in the words of Owen Barfield (1965):

... a representation, which is collectively mistaken for an
ultimate ought not to be called a representation. It is an idol.
Thus the phenomena themselves are idols, when they are
imagined as enjoying that independence of human perception
which can in fact only pertain to the unrepresented. [p. 62]

Table 5.3   Comparison of thoughts and idols

M(i)	R(ij)
Internal representation	External representation
Thought <==> meaning	Idol <==> information
subjective	objective
private	public
ephemeral	reproducible
evanescent	fixed, stable
lacking edges	delimited
immaterial	reified

I think it is a category error to put the same word on idols and thoughts (Table 5.3), even if the word is qualified as 'mental' *versus* 'physical' or 'internal' *versus* 'external', as analytic philosophers have done since Kant. For a biologist the spectacle is like watching a finite dimensional crab (Churchland 1986) wrestle with an infinite dimensional octopus (Young 1971), knowing the octopus always dines on crab, its favorite food.

I propose that Neuroactivity patterns in rabbits are not representations, but that EEGs seen through the small window available to us gives a glimpse of the physical manifestations of Neuroactivity in thinking. There is a chasm between electric traces from a rabbit brain and something about which it may be thinking. Some scientists and philosophers deny that animals can think at all, or that anyone can define the process well enough to correlate any physical quantity with it. There is good reason to try to bridge the chasm and seek a way out of the enclosure of introspection (Note 5.3). Thinking is a process by which some pattern is actualized from the intentional structure into meaning and deployed into the world. Thoughts differ from meanings in being the fleeting, unstable, dynamic operants by which meanings are constructed and carried. They enact the emergence of meaning as a set of relations in a place in an intentional structure, in accordance with which representations are shaped by action into the world. A representation formed and sent by one brain evokes thought that leads to the construction of meaning in a brain receiving the representation. Three classes of entities to interrelate are listed in Table 5.4.

Table 5.4 Thoughts, meanings, and representations

expectancies	aims	equations
feelings	beliefs	features
hallucinations	goals	models
intuitions	ideas	numbers
intents	ideals	symbols
recognitions	reasons	words

We can elevate concepts, hypotheses, postulates and theories to the status of organized collections of meaning, just as we treat books as organized collections of words. When we define thought as Neuroactivity by which meaning is constructed internally, and representation as an external construction by an act that is intended to elicit thought in others, it follows that in itself a representation has no meaning. Many examples can be found, but three suffice.

Concerning pictures, archeologists on discovering hieratics and petroglyphs are led to ponder what the markings mean. They infer that the tracings were made in order to express meanings, and by assembling information from many sources they construct new meanings in their minds, which they represent in texts with pictures in order to induce thought in other archeologists. As writers, they soon become aware that other writers find differing meanings in the same symbols and they may conclude that they can never be certain what the meanings may be or may have been. In the neurodynamic view they should conclude that there never were any meanings.

Concerning writing, most readers assume that a poem or a novel has meaning put there by the author, but deconstructionists seek alternative meanings. An instructive example is Umberto Eco (1992) as an author defending his intended meaning before critics who perceive other meanings in his novel "The Name of the Rose". In the view from neurodynamics, deconstructionists do not go far enough. A tract, poem or novel has no meaning whatever, though it was constructed in accordance with meanings in the writer, and has the potential for inducing construction of meanings in readers. When we read, we are unaware of the neural process of spatial localization of percepts (Section 4.5) by which brains automatically locate percepts as events in the world, not in themselves or in their sensory receptors, so that readers who are experiencing the construction of meanings naturally assign the meanings to the texts and not to their own minds.

Concerning reading, Derrida (1972) noted: "Reading is writing" (pp. 63-64), by which both involve intentional construction. However, their sites of nucleation differ, one being perceptual (Chapter 3) and the other motoric (Chapter 4). In his words, "If reading and writing are one, ... this oneness designates neither undifferentiated (con)fusion nor identity at perfect rest; the *is* that couples reading with writing must rip apart." Moreover, no two readers have the same intentional structure, so each induced meaning of a text is unique. Owing to the cumulative modification of an intentional structure by the Neuroactivity of thought (Section 6.2), each re-reading induces new meaning in the same reader, the "eternal sliding of the signified under the signifier" (Lacan 1966 p. 109). This continual opening of new vistas is a familiar source of delight to inveterate readers.

5.8 Age, rigidity, and wisdom in brain function

Thus far I have emphasized the variability of Neuroactivity patterns with respect to stimuli, by which the stimuli are fixed but their context differs. Another kind of discrepancy occurs with varying context and fixed Neuroactivity patterns, when we change the reinforcement contingency and neither the behaviors of the subject nor its EEGs undergo changes. Our observations of Neuroactivity patterns in conjunction with behavior show that, despite continuing local variations, the long-term trends may slow and even stop altogether as a subject ages or has been over-trained in one task. When we fail in our attempts to train a rabbit in a new task, we find that its Neuroactivity patterns are fixed, giving small clusters of points in measurement space.

This outcome indicates that an intentional structure can become rigid, no longer capable of shaping itself in conformance with the changing world. Decline in flexibility seems characteristic of aging brains in humans, dogs, and other species. While it may have tragic consequences for individuals, a case can be made that in old age (Hayflick 1994) survivors give substantial value to their societies by holding the tribal memories necessary to orient the young, who can then rebel rather than drift. This guidance is especially needed by illiterate youth in primitive tribes with no access to writing and by modern youth who have been stultified by television. Thus the tyranny of recollections in an old brain from a long gone past may reflect the flagging of brain chemistries or the irreversible growth into a cul de sac of complexity, but it may also reflect the involution of a rigid intentional structure, that has been genetically programmed into the survivor according to sociobiological rules for the good of society. Thus again, human brains are designed by evolution as agents for social constructions, not merely as epistemic engines for the intelligentsia. My teacher, Paul Yakovlev, conceived his own image as an old man, bereft of hair, teeth, hearing, speech, and ability to walk, riding on the shoulders of a warrior of his migrating tribe, silently pointing the way.

If aging brains get it right, the rigidity is tempered by tolerance and detachment. With advancing years and the accumulation of experience, at some point brains reach a threshold and undergo a state transition, such that on passage there is a remarkable coming together of all that is past, an awareness of global interconnectedness between the accumulated recollections and understandings over the years. This is the state of wisdom. It cannot be directly sought or striven for, but it is recognized when it comes, and it brings a serenity and graciousness of knowing how small the sense of self is, how transient are its aims and impacts, and how broad is the range of interconnection with other selves by influences too small to be singled out and labeled, yet undeniably acting within, in the way that a single neuron in cortex "knows" what is to be done from the field of activity within which it is embedded, without the need to know "why" or "what the big picture is". It is enough for a neuron to perform as a neuron is designed to do, and for a man or a woman it is enough to know that one has met a challenge or passed a test without realizing that a test was in progress. Not everyone achieves this state of mind, and it is not communicable in words or by teaching, but it is *there* and has been written about, and when one arrives, one knows that the future has joined with the past to make a circle outside time. One needs nothing more, for this suffices, reaching the mature wholeness of human intentionality.

5.9 Summary

The Neuroactivity that is extracted by statistical analyses of EEGs from behaving rabbits reveals flickering spatial patterns that are like frames in a movie. They are endogenous constructs from repeated dynamic state transitions, which correspond to meanings or thoughts about stimuli, and not to representations of stimuli. The selection of patterns by input-dependent state transitions depends also on reafference and neuromodulation. The patterns evolve over time erratically, giving the appearance of perceptual drift and chaotic itinerancy, but may become rigid in old age. Evidence for spatial and temporal coarse graining of Neuroactivity indicates that epistemological models of cortical dynamics can be implemented on digital computers. Building a brain based in digital computation may be impossible, owing to the need for a continuous medium in a noncomputational system to amplify microscopic states by global state transitions.

Chapter 6

Learning and Unlearning

We may thus well raise the question whether our "civilized" sexual morality is worth the sacrifice which it imposes on us, the more so if we are still so insufficiently purged of hedonism as to include a certain degree of individual happiness among the aims of our cultural development.
Sigmund Freud [1908 p. 40]

Measurements of the electrical activity of brains show that dynamical states of Neuroactivity emerge like vortices in a weather system, triggered by physical energies impinging onto sensory receptors, drifting in time, and changing with the context of the subjects. These dynamical states determine the structures of intentional actions and the patterns constructed upon destabilization of the perceptual systems when expected sensory input arrives. In Chapter 5 I concluded by statistical inference that Neuroactivity patterns provide the physical basis for thoughts and meanings. In this Chapter I explore the manner in which Neuroactivity in brains acts back onto the intentional structure, and changes it in accordance with the three basic properties of intentionality: to stretch forth and modify the self in conformance with the world; to seek wholeness in growth; and to maintain the unity of the self.

6.1 Learning and self-organization

In the educationist view a person learns by gaining knowledge, skills, and understanding. In the behaviorist view a system learns by changing its response upon repeated presentations of the same stimulus to elicit a reflex response. If the response strengthens, the system is *sensitized*; if it gets weaker the system is *desensitized*. In order to apply this rule to people and dogs behaviorists devise other rules. In behavioral terms desensitization is called *habituation*. The criteria are that the change in the system is in response to a narrowly restricted, specific form in which the stimulus is repeated, that it is easily and suddenly reversed when the stimulus is slightly changed unexpectedly, and that it is more quickly induced again on resumption of monotonous repetition. Sensitization is called *conditioning* or *associative* learning when the change in the system is selective for one stimulus that is repeatedly paired with another stimulus. The first one is called the *conditioned stimulus* (CS). It is selected as one that normally does not cause a response, or if it does, the response is nonspecific and easily habituated. The second one is called the *unconditioned stimulus* (US). It is selected as one that is pleasant or painful and reliably gives an *unconditioned response* (UR). The US is also known as a *reinforcement* in either negative (aversive) or positive (appetitive) conditioning.

If the US is given after the CS on repeated trials, irrespective of whether the CS elicits a *conditioned response* (CR), the procedure is called *classical* or Pavlovian conditioning, and the association is said to be *sensory-sensory*. If the second stimulus is given only if the system gives a CR (now called an operant) to the CS, the procedure is called *operant* conditioning, and the association is said to be *sensory-motor*. If the sensitization is not selective for the CS, and the system gives a response to background stimuli not paired with the US, the change is called *pseudoconditioning*. If the US is omitted while the CS is continued, and gradually the CR disappears, the CR is said to undergo *extinction*. If the range of variation in the CS is systematically expanded by repeated trials of pairing the US with the CS while varying the form of the CS, the procedure is called generalization. If the range is narrowed by giving the US only with one form of the CS and not others, it is called discriminative conditioning. This procedure of associative learning always requires habituation to unimportant or uninformative stimuli. They are called CS-, and they are given without the US on trials that are randomly interspersed with trials having the US paired with the CS+.

6.2 The neural basis for learning

When behaviorists apply these rules to a laboratory animal, they can approach reliable control of the animal's behavior without ever having to understand its aims, its desires, and other aspects of its mind. This simplicity makes it possible for cell biologists to apply the same rules not to a whole animal but to a neuron or part of a neuron as a system. The focus for studies of learning by cells is the modifiable synapse between two neurons. As Freud said, the logical place to look for cellular changes with learning is at the "contact barrier" (Section 2.3). The criterion for learning is that the conditions of a change in the synaptic strength must conform to the behaviorists' rules. The method is to find and analyze a synapse in which repeated stimulation of a presynaptic neuron leads to a *use-dependent* change in amplitude of the response of a postsynaptic neuron.

An increase is called *potentiation,* and a decrease is termed *depression.* For nearly a century biologists have known that brief application of an urgent stimulus called a *tetanus* to a single neuron or path can induce *post-tetanic* potentiation (PTP) or depression (PTD). However, these changes only last for a few minutes. In the past two decades a more sophisticated procedure of giving a tetanus to two neurons or paths converging onto a third has been found to induce *long-term potentiation* (LTP) or depression (LTD) that can last for days or even weeks. The robustness of the change makes it a favored paradigm for research on the neural basis of learning. Some questions being debated (Rose 1992) are: Does it occur in conditions that conform to the behaviorist rules? What chemical changes occur in the membranes of the two sides of the synapse? Does the amount of transmitter substance released presynaptically with each incoming pulse change, or is the postsynaptic sensitivity to action of transmitter substance altered (Malinow 1994)? Is the genome involved in permanently changing the synapse?

Chemical and structural changes almost certainly occur in both neurons that form a modifiable synapse, because chemical messengers travel in both directions to modify the strength of the channel between them. Two animal preparations are favored (Alkon 1992; Mpitsos and Burton 1992). One is the isolated ganglion from the brain of a mollusc (*Aplysia* or *Hermissenda*), because the simple animal can be conditioned according to the accepted rules, and the ganglion can be made to function in accord with the rules after it has been removed from the animal for study. The other preparation is the isolated slab of hippocampal cortex from mammals, usually rats or rabbits, because it can be kept alive and made active *in vitro*, and because the hippocampus is thought by most neurobiologists to be a site of memory and learning in vertebrate brains.

The reductionists have a Sisyphean task in attempting to construct an "alphabet" (Alkon 1992) of cellular and molecular

events with which to write the neural words of learning. An
increase in efficacy or sensitivity at a synapse may (or may not)
require an increase in amounts or rates of release of
transmitter, or in number of synaptic vesicles, or in membrane
locations or conformations of postsynaptic receptor proteins. It
is certain to require increases in synaptic membrane surface
fluxes, rates of turnover in lipids and proteins, replication of
the mitochondria to meet increased energy demands, sprouting
of new spines on dendrites and new axon terminals, and growth
of supporting glia and capillaries to increase the blood supply.
All these changes require activation of the genome, which
increases RNA production and protein synthesis with learning.

Learning also requires that discrimination be attended by
habituation, which may include atrophy of axonal and dendritic
branches and the programmed death of whole neurons
(*apoptosis*). Too many synaptic connections are as bad as too
few. During development the neurons sprout their branches
profusely and make connections indiscriminately. Intentionality
then prunes and shapes them. Other changes with learning, that
are not yet known, must occur in respect to maintenance of
long-term stability of cortex. Cumulative changes in excitatory
or inhibitory synapses must be regulated in some way to avoid
growing imbalances, and some kind of homeostatic feedback
mechanisms must serve this need. We have no idea what the
mechanisms might be or how to recognize them, but we surely
will encounter them, if we have not already done so in LTP and
related phenomena such as *kindling*. Among these mechanisms,
which are "essential" for learning? It would appear that all of
them play essential roles, even if they are merely janitorial.
New theory is needed to organize and interpret the data.

6.3 Artificial neural networks and digital computers

That need for theory appeared to have been met with emergence
of neural networks as an alternative to conventional AI Digital
computers that are used in AI had their origin in a mistaken idea
widely held in the first half of the 20th century that all
communication among neurons is done by action potentials,
which represent a "0" or a "1" in an array of neurons forming a
net (McCulloch 1969). The crux of a digital computer or Turing
(1950) machine is a central processing unit (CPU), which has a
register to hold a binary number, an input channel for taking in

numbers, an output channel for giving out numbers, and a memory for storing the numbers. The memory also stores instructions in numerical form for operations on the numbers. In each cycle of operation the CPU takes an input number into its register, combines it arithmetically with a number from the memory, and puts the new number back into memory or into the output channel. It does this rapidly but serially, so that the register is a bottleneck that limits the overall speed of a long sequence of operations. Engineers are trying to overcome the limitation of a *serial machine* by using an array of registers in parallel, but have not fully solved problems of coordinating and scheduling the parts of a *parallel machine* to make it flexible and easy to use. Moreover, as remarked by John von Neumann (1958), who invented the programmable computer, brains are "characterized by less logical and arithmetical depth than what we are normally used to" in machines. "Thus the outward forms of *our* mathematics are not absolutely relevant from the point of view of evaluating what the mathematical or logical language *truly* used by the central nervous system is" [pp. 81-82].

Artificial neural networks have an architecture that more closely resembles that of cortex than computers. It consists of a large number of simple components that are connected in parallel. A component occupies a *node*, a point of convergence and divergence of connections to other components. Each node resembles a neuron in receiving input from many other nodes simultaneously in parallel, multiplying each input by a number assigned to each input line (a connection weight), adding the products from all lines, putting upper and lower bounds on the sum by use of bilateral saturation (the sigmoid curve, Section 3.9, Note 3.4), and distributing its output to many other nodes.

The interesting properties of artificial neural networks lie in their patterns of connection between nodes. In a feedforward net the nodes are arranged in layers with the flow of numbers going from an input layer through one or more *hidden layers* to an output layer, so that each node in a layer receives input only from a preceding layer and sends its output to a next layer. These nets are also known as *parallel distributed processors* and as *multi-layered perceptrons* (MLPs, Anderson and Rosenfeld 1988). The operations they perform are equivalent to those done by fuzzy logic (Kosko 1993) and in statistics by nonlinear regression for gradient descent. In a feedback net each node has input lines from a layer of sensors. It transmits output to other nodes in the same layer, and to an output layer that conveys the state of the middle, computational layer (Amari 1977; Hopfield 1982). The feedforward nets operate as filters on their inputs, whereas the feedback nets operate as dynamical systems, maintaining a set of basins each with an attractor for a class of input, and constructing a pattern of output that serves to represent the class to which each input belongs. The feedback net based in cooperativity is more closely related to brains.

Artificial neural networks learn in one of three ways. In learning with a *teacher* a desired output is stored as a matrix of numbers. A "training" pattern (Section 5.1) is put into the net, and the difference is calculated between the observed and desired outputs. Then each of the connection weights is changed by a small amount, and the input is repeated. If the difference decreases, the weights are changed in the same direction, and if it increases they are changed oppositely. By repeated steps the difference between observed and desired outputs is minimized. Then test inputs are given to find out how well the network generalizes. The algorithm is known in statistics as error minimization by gradient descent. The neural network eases the task of finding solutions by automating the weight adjustments.

In learning without a teacher the desired output is not set in advance as a pattern to be simulated, but instead the network is made to seek out clusters of similar patterns in a data set. This algorithm is known in statistics as cluster analysis. Typically the clustering is done blindly, because it isn't known in advance how many clusters there are. An arbitrary cutoff is made between one extreme of a single cluster that contains all the items to be classified and the other extreme of as many clusters as there are items. In the third type, learning by reinforcement, a network is not given patterns to match but, instead, examples of patterns to be classified, as behaviorists do in training animals. The model forms its own criteria by which to extract features of the examples, and if it works, it generalizes from training patterns to test inputs (Section 5.2).

The key element in artificial neural networks is the modifiable connection, which is an entry in an N x N matrix of connections. In a globally connected net all of the strengths may be nonzero, while in a sparsely connected net resembling neurons in cortex most of the strengths are zero. A widely used rule governing use-dependent change is that the connection strength between two nodes increases, up to a limit, in proportion to the correlation of activity of the two nodes. A connection assigned this rule is called a Hebbian synapse, in recognition of Donald Hebb (1949), who understood that perception requires the formation by learning of groups of neurons that selectively strengthen their synaptic connections to form a "cell-assembly" when repeated firing of one cell accompanies firing of other cells. The Hebbian synapse is the element by which theorists in artificial neural networks and experimentalists in long-term potentiation (LTP) can understand and interact with each other.

The theory of neural networks is inadequate for the simulation of biological learning, mainly because the nets don't interface effectively with the world (Sections 1.6 and 5.6). The greater part of the work of building and using artificial neural networks resides in preprocessing input data from sensors by hand to get them into a form a network can use. This is precisely the role of sensory cortex: to serve as the interface between the infinite environment and the interior of unitary brains. Some hope is attached by engineers to the use of analog systems in optics and electronics, which, instead of numbers, use continuously varying currents and light intensities to transmit and integrate. This is a likely route by which machine intelligence will evolve. Working prototypes exist in Walter's (1963) turtles (Section 1.2) and Ross Ashby's homeostat (1960). Perhaps success is only a matter of time, insight, and grant money. Unsolved technical problems include drift in components with age and temperature, uncontrolled noise, nonlinearities leading to local instabilities and unwanted chaos, and the indeterminacies of distributed nonlinear feedback. The mathematics to handle large systems of nonlinear differential delay equations, which are dimensionally infinite, does not exist. Study of intentional brains and behaviors still provides the best hope for new theory.

6.4 Arousal, motivation, and reinforcement

In neurodynamics *learning* is defined as a directed change in an intentional structure that accompanies Neuroactivity. There is no other way to distinguish it from the hypertrophy of a muscle under weight training. Study of an isolated ganglion or slab of cortex is a good way *not* to find it, because intentional change is nonlocal. This biological premise is reflected in the existence of global neurochemical systems in brains. In all vertebrates, from the simplest to the most advanced, the brain stem has collections of neurochemically specialized neurons that send their widely branched axons throughout the forebrain. The nuclei form a double chain resembling the architecture of invertebrate brains (Section 4.1), but they are within the wall of the neural tube. Typically their axons form no synapses. The chemicals that they release diffuse widely through the neural tissue and bathe the neural populations in cortex and striatum.

The actions of brain stem chemicals are to modify the synaptic efficacies of conventional transmission (Section 3.2), so they are *neuromodulators* as distinct from *neurotransmitters*. In a double row of chemical factories each nucleus makes its own neuromodulator, which interacts with other neuromodulators in complex ways. The constancy of the architecture of this system throughout the phylogenetic tree and its global nature in each brain indicate that it appeared early in evolution to provide the essential neurochemical basis for intentionality. Evolutionary processes acted on the whole of the system, not on its parts, with modulation of behavior as the test of success. Therefore, as researchers unravel the components and test the modulators one at a time, the results of experiments are intriguing but baffling. It is unlikely that we will understand the neural basis for learning until a solid theory of intentionality has been derived, by which to assemble the components into a system and to orchestrate application of neuromodulators to isolated slabs.

The neuromodulators go beyond learning. They are responsible for maintaining the global state of the forebrain (Section 4.7), which is expressed in behaviors such as waking, four stages of sleeping, and reactivity which we subjectively experience in terms of awareness, motivation, mood, affect, disposition, and the state-dependence of reactions to stimuli (Section 5.4). These components are also cut away when a ganglion or piece of cortex is removed from the brain and put *in vitro*. A large part of current psychiatric research and clinical practice is devoted to discovering the actions of these chemicals, and learning ways to enhance or diminish their actions in mentally disturbed individuals. Amateur psychopharmacologists have also thrown themselves into frenzied search for amino acids, plant extracts, neurotransmitter homologues, and dietary adjuvants to enhance their IQs, prolong their attention spans, and raise their learning skills. Wild claims are being posted on e-mail bulletin boards, but so far nothing has been found to work better than caffeine, theophylline, and theobromine (coffee, tea, and chocolate).

The neuromodulators are grouped by their chemical structures into two main classes: the neuroamines (Kandel, Schwartz and Jessup 1993) and the neuropeptides (Gorman 1989). The lists are long and still growing, and the lesser classes such as amino acids and diffusible gases (for example, nitric oxide and carbon monoxide) clamor for attention. Some better known neuromodulators and the foci of the behavioral contexts of their actions are listed in Table 6.1. Each interacts in complex patterns with other modulators and transmitters in different contexts, so this list is offered in the spirit that a sketch of unknown territory is better than no map at all. The virtue of reductionists is that they are the advance explorers opening new terrain for soldiers, missionaries, traders, and anthropologists.

Table 6.1

The phrenology of neuromodulators:
Simplistically, one gene, one hormone, one emotion

acetylcholine	memory
dopamine	hedonism
endorphins	pain relief
histamine	arousal
melatonin	alarm clock
norepinephrine	imprinting
oxytocin	orgasm
serotonin	relaxation
vasopressin	aggression

In associative learning by classical conditioning the unconditioned stimulus activates a nucleus in the brain stem, which releases norepinephrine throughout the forebrain. Blocking the action of norepinephrine prevents the olfactory bulb from forming new EEG patterns and prevents the animal from learning a CR to an odor CS (Gray, Freeman and Skinner 1986). Acetylcholine is thought to be involved in memory formation and retrieval, because the memory loss in Alzheimer's disease is associated with disappearance of the cholinergic system in the forebrain. It is suspected that dopamine and some endorphins are also involved in associative learning, but it is not known in what ways. Clearly each learning experience involves changes in many parts of the forebrain, and, owing to the broadcast of the modulators, it is likely that synapses in all parts are involved at all times. The global actions of the neuromodulators give good reason to propose that the neuropil of each hemisphere is the material basis of the unity of its intentional structure, so that our EEG recordings may manifest the global actualization of that structure in transient thoughts.

6.5 Isolation, unlearning, and pair bonding

The synaptic changes incurred during a single trial in a learning experience are widely dispersed and weak in comparison to the whole, but they constitute a finite step along a trajectory of the whole, particularly for eidetic images, which are stock in trade for scholarly research. From its beginning in and from the womb the path of an intentional structure is unique, growing from the genetically determined groundwork by the grasping for available sensory input from within and outside its own body. The same steps are not replicated in any other brain, and the structure that evolves is self-organized, with its own frames of reference and its unique patterns. We see this reflected in the EEG patterns that lack any recognizable geometry or relations between animals and are meaningless to us, except in the context of observing the behavior of the individual. It is in this sense that each brain is epistemologically solipsistic. Its knowledge comes from its cumulative constructions induced by the sensory milieu, which is also unique for each individual in the common environment, due to individual differences in physical and emotional perspective and expectancy.

The question arises: How can any two intentional structures change and converge so as to support cooperative behavior? The requirement is for a mechanism to bring about an extensive but selective and properly directed modification in both of the participating structures. The most pressing need arises during the process of reproduction by those species in which the altricial infants require prolonged care by their parents, particularly the mother. The requirement is for a mechanism in mammals (birds have different hormones) that depends on the release into brains of neuromodulators, which can selectively dissolve an intentional structure and open the way for new construction to meet environmental and developmental crises. The dissolution of an intentional structure is *unlearning*, the opposite of imprinting, which is the irreversible laying down of structure in the young. Dissolution opens the way for new learning, which imprinting does not allow.

The most promising candidate for this mechanism is the peptide oxytocin, which is released in mammals during parturition and lactation. The peripheral role of oxytocin (known clinically as *pitocin*) in promoting uterine contractions and the production of milk is well known. The behavioral effects have only recently come under intensive study (Pedersen et al. 1992). At the onset of lactation oxytocin floods through the hypothalamus in rats and modulates in complex ways the neural actions of a broad array of neurotransmitters and other neuromodulators (Arletti et al. 1992; Caldwell 1992). It is also released in the olfactory bulbs of sheep, particularly after the first litter (Kendrick et al. 1992), suggesting that the imprinting in the dam onto each new litter requires that prior imprints be dissolved, and not merely be written over, as the basis for reliable perceptual recognition, and that intentional changes take place in cortex, striatum and hypothalamus, such that the mother can recognize and nurse her young rather than attack and eat them. Changes in the functional connectivity of neurons in the breast area of the somatosensory cortex have been found with the onset and termination of lactation (Xerri et al. 1994), indicating that the perceptual systems of neocortex are also modified, perhaps most easily observed in cortical areas receiving sensory inputs from the soft tissues that surround the nipples, but probably taking place also in areas serving hearing and vision and, by hypothesis, throughout the forebrain.

Since the infant at birth has an unformed and nonfunctioning cortex (Section 2.2) the bonding of mother and child can begin unilaterally. Formation of a bond between parents is more complex. Owing to their shared genetic and experiential determinants, the intentional structures of littermates are the most similar to each other, but the genetic advantages of outbreeding require that young adults mate with individuals other than siblings. Thereby they incur the task of adapting the structures of their behaviors (minds), so as to succeed in attempts at cooperation with those with whom they choose to mate. Experimental evidence is accruing that the same neurohumoral mechanism for unlearning may have been adapted for this role through evolution. Elevated levels of oxytocin have been found in the hypothalamus of male rats (Argiolas 1992) and in the circulation of human males at the time of ejaculation during sexual intercourse, presumably related to orgasm.

A comparable release of the neurohormone in females has been documented (Carmichael et al. 1994) including contractions of muscles in the pelvic floor which accompany orgasm, which is not so easily observed as in males. The neurodynamics that determine intervals between orgasms in multiorgasmic women is no better known than that of the contractions at parturition. Apart from autonomic changes, which do not differ from those of other types of arousal, and a decrease in sensitivity to pain that suggests the release of endorphins (Section 6.6), almost nothing is known of the physiology of orgasm. Whipple, Ogden and Komisaruk (1992) found that genital stimulation is not essential. Some women can reach orgasm solely by erotic fantasy. In other studies, women who have spinal injury with paralysis and anesthesia below the level of transection develop sexual hypersensitivity of the skin of the chest at or above the level, such that gentle stimulation brings them to orgasm. The requisite plasticity of the somatosensory cortex has been well shown by work in the Merzenich laboratory (Xerri et al. 1994).

I speculate that release of oxytocin is part of an orchestration of neuromodulators upon sexual arousal prior to and during intercourse, and that it may be responsible for the profound changes that take place in behavior and belief structures, when children after puberty become parents and take responsibility for the next generation (Moore 1992; Insel 1992). Their systems of values and priorities must change abruptly. New behaviors are not instilled by neuropeptides. When the old behaviors are momentarily dissolved, the new behaviors must be learned by cooperative interaction expressed through complementary, goal-directed movements of persons having a shared environment and a common aim. Dancing is a good metaphor. A pair bond cannot form without the opportunity for extended interplay, because without re-education after dissolution, an intentional structure lapses by default to the old way. The male or female who solipsistically departs the morning after remains untouched by the night before. The deepest meaning of sexual experience lies not in pleasure, or even in reproduction, but in the opportunity it affords to surmount the solipsistic gulf, opening the door, so to speak, whether or not one undertakes the work to go through. It is the afterplay, not the foreplay, that counts in building trust.

The subject at issue is not the hedonics of sex or the awareness of unlearning (Section 7.5). I am not concerned with what feelings the administration of oxytocin might induce. In a strict behaviorist's view the positive reinforcement provided by sex conditions the performer to seek more of the same, where by trial and error one partner learns to cook and the other to make money. My concern is with the profound isolation of intentional structures imposed by the dynamics used by individual brains to make sense of an infinitely complex world, with the necessity for understanding between intentional structures imposed by the social requirements of reproduction, and with neurohumoral mechanisms that may dissolve intentional structures globally for an invaluable fresh start. Computers "re-learn" by having new programs read in. Brains need sex.

6.6 Conversion and social bonding

Mammalian pair bonds between human parents are powerful but short-term, typically lasting only long enough to get the human infant firmly onto its feet, about 2 to 4 years according to the divorce statistics in Finland and the United States compiled by Helen Fisher (1992). Goldbart and Wallin (1994) describe the intentional structure as "an internal map" in each person. Prolonged learning is required for the "deep mapping" between mental structures formed in infancy and childhood, by which early attraction ripens to lasting attachment. "When we are puzzled about a current interaction in love and where to take it, we unconsciously turn inward, where our own idiosyncratic map provides an interpretation and a sense of direction" [p. 4]. The white heat of oxytocin may precede a warm glow of endorphins, and with practice, as the internal maps converge, the solipsistic gulf may seem to disappear under habitual routine.

But this is only half the story. The formation of a new unity in a pair bond draws a boundary around the couple, which serves to classify outsiders as potential threats. The appearance of aggressive behavior toward sexual rivals is accompanied by the release of another hypothalamic neuropeptide, vasopressin.

Insel (1992) and his co-workers (Winslow et al. 1993) find that prairie voles release vasopressin when forming bonds between fathers and pups. The researchers find anatomical patterns of location of oxytocin in brains differing diametrically between an aggressive, monogamous species of voles and a polygamous species showing neither attachment nor conspecific aggression. The bonding of a pair and the attendant aggressiveness toward outsiders appear to be elaborated by differing neurochemicals.

Moreover, the boundaries of each paired self never disappear (Rilke 1984) but become fractal in their indistinctness and fluid in a tug of war, like interdigitations of land and water in tidal estuaries. When the time comes to "fall out of love" or when love turns to hate, the aggression is focused not on a rival but instead onto the partner in a different kind of dance. Virtually nothing is scientifically known about chemistries of jealousy, shame, humiliation, hatred, and despair, because the experiences are too painful and too unique in each lifetime to be subject to experimental repetitions and controls. The present research climate does not even allow research on orgasm through brain imaging by PET or functional MRI, because subjects would have to lie motionless, while a research assistant masturbates them.

Pair bonds obviously cannot account for the formation of groups larger than the nuclear family, particularly same-sex groupings, except for harems maintained by alpha males at the expense of useless drones, rogues and outcasts. Groupings among humans and pack animals such as wolves and dogs may be explained by another form of dissolution of intentional structure, which takes place during various forms of socialization and religious or political conversion. Scientific study of the process began with an accident in the laboratory of Ivan Pavlov (1955), in which some of his trained dogs nearly drowned. The River Neva in St. Petersburg was flooded by an ice jam in a spring thaw, and the dogs were rescued as they swam with their noses at the tops of their cages in the cellar. Afterward, Pavlov's workers found that the dogs had completely forgotten their prior training and had to be re-trained.

Pavlov's systematic exploration of the phenomenon revealed the biological conditions sufficing to induce this unlearning. There were three stages, starting with heightened excitation by strenuous physical activity, sensory overload by continuous light or sound stimulation, and sleep deprivation. In the second stage the continuing assault on the senses produced *paradoxical inhibition*, which physiologists have observed when muscles are pushed beyond the peak of an inverted "U" input-output curve, such that stronger stimuli give weaker responses and vice versa. The third stage of *transmarginal inhibition* is marked by collapse, demoralization, and sometimes apparent coma. The process is facilitated by isolation from normal environments, chemical stresses by starvation, emetics, and purgatives, and assaults by intense emotions such as rage, shame, and fear. Pavlov was led to his approach and findings by the context of Russian neurophysiology, which had roots in 19th-century German science, but grew in isolation from the West after World War I in a distinctive direction. This may account for failure of Western physiologists to discover the phenomenon.

The breakdown by overload was mere prelude to re-education, by which new patterns of behavior were instilled. The most important step was release from the ordeal, by a change in venue, or by some small act of kindness offering surcease and hope, and a feeling of gratitude. The usefulness of this technology was easily recognized by Pavlov's grant managers for their program of perfecting model Soviet citizens. The proof of its efficacy came in astonishing reversals of belief structure by individuals in the Moscow show trials of the 1930's. The procedures and their results have been vividly described by Arthur Koestler(1950) and George Orwell (1948, "Nineteen Eighty-four"). They have been stigmatized as "brainwashing".

6.7 Function and malfunction of unlearning

A neuropsychiatrist, William Sargant (1957), developed an interest in this technology through his use of abreaction techniques and hypnosis to treat neurotic fixations and war traumata. In his monograph, "Battle for the Mind", he reviewed the biological evidence for brainwashing and described the commonality of these procedures in a broad range of societies for engendering conversions of political and religious beliefs, with some emphasis on the British and American evangelists of the past three centuries, and, with help from Robert Graves (1948), a review of religious practices in the Ancient World.

Sargant (1974) noted the similarity of the conversion process to the histories of chronic drug users and of alcoholics, who have often reported that, when they "hit bottom" by reaching some extreme in the slow process of deterioration under prolonged intoxication, they experience a sense of intense illumination by a blinding white light. This might be interpreted as a visitation by an angel or as a phosphene from a wave of electrochemical discharge sweeping through the visual cortex. Whichever, an alteration of intentional structure is revealed by the tenacity with which reformed individuals in Alcoholics Anonymous and like organizations hold strikingly to new beliefs and behaviors. Pavlov, Sargant, and others have repeatedly observed that the strongest and most stable personalities in animals and humans are the most difficult to break down, though ultimately all fail, and the most intractable are found after conversion to hold most zealously to a new system of belief without backsliding.

The dramatic historical examples given by Sargant of the conversions that have been forced onto unwilling individuals by harsh regimes may obscure the ubiquity of the biological process of unlearning, and the crucial role it may play in many forms of social organization. In milder forms the same techniques appear in "hazing" (humiliation) of college freshmen by upperclassmen, leading to life-long love affairs with "Alma Mater"; indignities poured onto pledges to prepare them for joining a sorority or fraternity; rugged training exercises in sports to bring "team spirit" into play; indoctrination in boot camps to induce lock-step conformance to a military hierarchy of command; and corporate training sessions to establish commitment to "the firm". In more blatant forms they are found in militant religious and political groups, and especially in gangs of urban teenagers, who have the most to gain in finding their identities in close affiliations with their own kind.

These powerful techniques can internalize allegiance for a lifetime. Westerners with strong traditions of individuality and freedom of action find group discipline to be onerous, and they are repelled by overt forms of thought control and chastisement by committee. Yet intense feelings of loyalty to family, friends, church and nation are also strongly admired. More to the point, they are essential in order to provide the feelings of trust and respect that are the basis for orderly transactions at all levels of society. What has not yet been accepted is the biological mechanism of socialization by which these feelings are created. On the one hand, we decry the decay of family cohesion, the weakening of discipline in schools, and the decline of neighborhood and community spirit, and on the other hand, we avoid and in many instances bar by administrative rules the use of the behavioral techniques (*e.g.*, corporal punishment, hazing, brainwashing, manipulation), without which these social virtues cannot be instilled. This is another legacy of a perspective that fails to give due weight to the biology of brains as components in social systems. In its general aspect *conversion* is not an evil manipulation. It is a social necessity. Perhaps the same chemistry provides the mechanisms for effective transference and countertransference during psychoanalytic interactions (Menninger 1938) and other forms of psychotherapy.

We need to know much more about it. I postulate that the biological process is an abrupt dissolution of an intentional structure by an electrochemical discharge in a brain, which is preceded by various forms of physiological and behavioral stress, triggered by the release of mediating neurohormones, and followed by a state of malleability that opens the way for construction of a new belief structure to facilitate social behavior. Young people who are in process of separating from parents, and are themselves eligible to become parents, are the most vulnerable, but no normal persons are immune.

Since declarative and procedural memories are part of an intentional structure, it is problematic how they are protected or recovered. In more extreme forms of transmarginal inhibition subjects lose motor coordination, clarity of speech, and recollection of events. Some suffer complete collapse and apparent loss of consciousness. Others exhibit catatonic trances, epileptiform motor discharges, glossolalia, and incoherent shrieking. However, there is a remarkable resiliency of intentional structure, in that, if the subjects return to their normal environments, within a few hours or days their pre-existing behaviors and recollections recur. Perhaps the process is an exaggerated form of sleep with dreaming, which has its own mechanisms enabling an intentional structure each night to re-assert its unity, as it sorts through and digests new material it has incorporated during the preceding day (Hobson 1994). If so, release of a master neuropeptide, oxytocin, may accompany somatostatin in sleep. Instead of being known as the hormone of orgasm, it should be called the hormone of "satisfaction" (Pedersen at al. 1992) or "gratitude". Its central role may give new substance to the concept of gratitude in philosophy.

We should also consider what type of behavior to expect in humans if the proposed mechanism were to fail, because the best evidence for the existence and properties of a biological control system comes from the study of its disorders. The most obvious syndrome is that of the social psychopath, about whom Cleckley (1955) wrote:

> One is confronted with a convincing mask of sanity. ... One never sees the chaos sometimes found on searching beneath the outer surface of a paranoid schizophrenic. ... Only very slowly ... does the conviction come upon us that ... we are dealing here not with a complete man at all, but with something that suggests a subtly constructed reflex machine which can mimic the human personality perfectly. ... And yet one knows or feels he knows that reality, in the sense of full, healthy experiencing of life, is not here. ... The psychopath's disorder or his difference from the whole or normal or integrated personality consists of an unawareness, or a persistent lack of ability to become aware, of what the most important experiences of life mean to others. ... Let us say that, despite his otherwise perfect function, the major emotional accompaniments are absent or so attenuated as to count for little. Of course he is unaware of this as everyone is bound, except theoretically, to be unaware of that which is out of his scale, or order, or mode of experience. If we grant the existence of a far-reaching and persistent blocking, absence, or dissociation of this sort, we have all that is needed, at the present level of our inquiry, to account for the psychopath. [pp. 397-399]

Readers who are not familiar with the syndrome can find a good example of a junior psychopath in Bill Watterston's cartoon strip, "Calvin and Hobbes". Cleckley's description leaves unanswered the question of whether psychopaths experience no emotions or abnormal emotions. Due to the characteristic inconsistencies between their words and actions psychiatrists cannot know what psychopaths feel, but it appears that they are untouched by either love or hate. Other writers have taken mechanistic approaches. Menninger (1938) attributed the antisocial behavior to an unconscious and indirect search for punishment, a veiled but essentially self-destructive activity related to Freud's hypothesis of an active "death instinct". Mealey (in press) has explored game-theoretic models in the context of sociobiology, using genetics, child development, personality theory, and demographic data on the incidence of antisocial behavior as a coping strategy.

A biologically based hypothesis for psychopathia may be as incomplete as comparable explanations currently are for panic disorders, obsessive-compulsive neuroses, Tourette's syndrome, the affective disorders, and the schizophrenias, but even in the absence of a comprehensive biological theory of personality, the neurally active drugs coming from empirical research in biology give substantial benefits to individuals and to society. Search for a genetic, developmental, or regulatory failure in a neurochemical mechanism, which is postulated to dissolve intentional structure by unlearning, might help us to understand and treat this baffling psychosocial disorder. Studies of pair bonding (Insel 1992) might provide us with an animal model for psychopathia, and give a new approach to autism in children, seen as a severe form of developmentally disordered, solipsistic behavior. We should search for a complementary syndrome due to excess activity in the same mechanism, the nature of which we don't know. A good theory might also provide new techniques for the treatment of drug addiction through unlearning - fighting drugs with psychedelics in clinics, not with bullets in barrios.

6.8 Dance as the biotechnology of group formation

Anthropologists and ethnopsychiatrists have documented the prevalence in preliterate tribes of singing and dancing to the point of physical and psychological collapse during religious and social ceremonies. Typically the members of a community gather at a central place surrounded by the musicians and their instruments, the priests and shamans as masters of ceremony (Price 1982), a central altar, and icons that symbolize the tribal totems and deities. Rhythmic drumming, chanting, clapping, marching in step, and pirouetting around bonfires last for hours, through the night into the dawn, as one by one the participants drop from exhaustion. This is the moment of change. Emile Durkheim (1915) described the socializing process as the use of "... totemic emblems by clans to express and communicate collective representations", which begins where the individual feels he *is* the totem and evolves to beliefs that he will become the totem or that his ancestors are in the totem. The religious rites and ceremonies lead to "collective mental states of extreme emotional intensity, in which representation is still undifferentiated from the movements and actions which make the communion towards which it tends a reality to the group. Their participation in it is *so effectively lived* that it is not yet properly imagined." [pp. 465-472]

Verger (1954) has recorded in photographs the ceremony of ritual death and rebirth, in which participants who have collapsed into the deep unawareness of transmarginal inhibition are sewn into shrouds, are carried by tribesmen to the local cemetery, and are returned thereafter to the tribeswomen for re-birth by unsewing, revival and succor as new persons. The choice of fertility symbols and the behaviors of the participants indicate the powerful basis in sexuality of the ceremonies, which commonly become orgiastic in reaching climax.

There is no reason to doubt that these activities give great pleasure and catharsis to those caught up in the communal spirit of the events, and that immersion in the dance is followed by a refreshed sense of belonging to the tribe. What is at issue is the extent to which feelings of bonding and the formation of a neural basis for social cooperation might be engendered by the same neurochemical mechanisms that evolved to support sexual reproduction in altricial species like ourselves, and that might mediate religious and political conversions. Sargant (1957, 1974) has documented the striking similarities between the techniques used to arouse the fervor of dancers in preliterate tribes and the practices by evangelistic churches in their congregations from the 17th century to the present, in which the avowed goal has been religious conversion in the name of saving souls. Sargant also described how people who had been severely traumatized by their experiences in the First and Second World Wars found that they could relieve their neurotic tensions by means of therapeutic abreactions achieved through wild dancing in the 1920's and again in the 1950's. As he drily commented, jazz was the proper medium; waltz did not suffice.

Music as sound appeals to the ear, but the making and appreciation of music involve the entire body through the somatosensory and motor systems of the performer and the active audience (Clynes 1982). Dance on a stage appeals to the eye, but its real charm is found by the participants who shape their movements into a living and evolving unity. The strongest basis for the cooperation lies in rhythmically repeated motions, because they are predictable by others, and others can thereby anticipate and move in accord with their expectations. Music gives the background beat.

Here in its purest form is a human technology for crossing the solipsistic gulf. It is wordless, illogical, deeply emotional, and selfless in its actualization of transient and then lasting harmony between intentional structures (Wilson 1992). It works in the action-reafference-perception cycle that provides for all human understanding, and it constructs the sense of trust and predictability in each member of the community on which social interactions are based (Note 6.1). Dance alone does not suffice, but it is exemplary of the nature of wordless give-and-take by which are constructed the channels for verbal communication. Roederer (1984) proposed the utility of music for training in language skills, for understanding the musical aspects of speech, and for signalling emotional states. A more significant discovery by our remote ancestors, and even the apes before that (Williams 1967), may have been the use of music and dance for bonding in groups larger than nuclear families.

But the role of music in superstitious or sexual rites, religion, ideological proselytism, and military arousal clearly demonstrates the value of music as a means of establishing behavioral coherency in masses of people. In the distant past this would indeed have had an important survival value, as an increasingly complex human environment demanded coherent, collective actions on the part of groups of human society. [Roederer 1984 p. 356]

That accomplishment may have accompanied or even preceded the invention of fire, tools and shelter, because the maintenance, development, and transmission across generations of information about the techniques for working matter into useful forms must have required the prior existence of channels for communication to support the social interactions. These channels are intentional and not logical in nature.

The formation of a social group, such as a tribe, has its dark sides, one of which is the formation of a boundary, with the exclusion of nonself from the self that constitutes the unity. Those who do not "belong" become the enemy, which is to be walled off, expelled, and possibly destroyed, if it is perceived as menacing the welfare of the group. The process is similar to sexual jealousy, which manifests the exclusionary nature of the pair bond. Internecine tribal warfare that is fueled by the unknown chemistry of hatred is just as illogical and selfless as the bonding within a community. Outsiders are seen as objects or animals and are treated as tools or slaves. The closest living relatives of the human race, the chimpanzee, orang-utan and gorilla, all live in dense jungles inaccessible to man. A large gap separates apes and humans compared with the smaller steps that separate them from the lesser apes and monkeys. A likely explanation is that our ancestors systematically killed off the groups they could reach, that were closest to themselves but beyond the range of bonding. Comparable processes of mutual detestation and attempted extermination presently preoccupy much of the world's population at enormous cost, and nothing neurobiological is done about it, because the neurobiology of hatred is so inaccessible to scientific exploration.

Biologists refer to the phenomenon in terms of *nearest neighbor competitive inhibition, winner-take-all* networks, and *survival of the fittest.* It may well be that wholesale extermination was the necessary price for the exceedingly rapid pace of human evolution over the past half million years. Fortunately our more recent ancestors discovered civilized alternatives to death-dealing, unrestricted warfare. Music and dance have close relatives in team sports, which are forms of ritualized combat, actions and reactions that are carefully choreographed toward symbolic goals, and which instill powerful feelings of identity not only in the players as "team spirit" but in the spectators who root for the teams. Tom Wolfe (1979), in "The Right Stuff", described the process extended into space rivalry, by which Soviet and American astronauts supported by ground-based teams played the roles of archetypal heroes battling for the dominance and honor of their tribes.

Another dark side is the use of drugs (Fort 1969) such as wine, opium, and hallucinogenic mushrooms to induce the pleasurable subjective correlates of neurochemical bonding, as discussed further in Section 7.5. Repeated dissolutive trances can result in derelicts like hermits, alcoholics, addicts, dropouts, zombies, and other marginalia of society. The prehistorical records compiled by Frazer (1890) in "The Golden Bough" and Graves (1948) in "The White Goddess" show how the religious rites of the ancient world were imbued with neuroactive substances, particularly *quintessence* embodied in alcohol, which may have facilitated destructive practices such as self-castration and suicide. The emergence of savage and asocial behavior, then as now at Altamont Pass and in "the Summer of Love", appears to have led to the development of larger social structures, governments, academies and universities, by means of which to channel and control the destructive side effects of orgiastic bonding. Shamans, priests and church bureaucracies regulated the time, place and manner of ceremonies with respect to stars and seasons. Chiefs, kings and armies imposed constraints on tribes for the sake of peace and the general welfare.

With emergence of city states run by bureaucrats and academic intelligentsia, the Greeks relegated the Dionysian orgies to the lower classes. Plato banned music from his Academy in recognition of its power to degrade rational minds and subvert social order. The Catholic Church in the Middle Ages labeled the rituals "pagan" and suppressed them to maintain political control, opening the way for Apollonian music (Nietzsche 1872), such as Gregorian chants. Close harmony provided for bonding of a different kind among intellectuals, stripped of its sexual overtones. Syncopation was forbidden. The "Devil's Interval" was allegedly called that because God and the world could not exist between the beats. Physicians also used the medical term *syncope* to signify cessation of function in a transient loss of consciousness. The dialectic between Apollo and Dionysus re-emerged in the Baroque, and it continues to infuse fresh energy into music through syncopation and atonality in jazz, blues, and rock-and-roll (Note 6.1), which through radio and MTV are bonding young people in nations everywhere. They stand opposed to older generations; intentional bonding is always exclusionary.

I have considered music and dance only in regard to their roles in facilitating formation of social groups by cooperative action, putatively by releasing neurochemical mechanisms of unlearning in near-trance states with attenuation of the sense of self. A lot has been written about the biological bases for music and dance and their possible antecedence to language (Clynes1982; Pribram 1982; Wallin 1991). Even in primitive forms, such as the kölning of cattle herders in northern Sweden and the songlines in dreamtime of the Australian aborigines, the cognitive complexities of music exceed the scope of any extant analyses of neocortical dynamics. It is reasonable to suppose that musical skills played a major role early in the evolution of human intellect. Understanding of the neurodynamics of the cerebrum in language might well be advanced through studies of EEG correlates of musical performance and appreciation (Birbaumer et al. in press). That is a worthwhile task for the oncoming generation of neuroscientists in the next century.

6.9 Summary

The stretching forth of intentionality requires modification of an intentional structure by learning. The cellular basis for the process has been identified with modification of the strengths of synaptic connections in accordance with behaviorist rules for conditioning, with specific cellular changes found in long-term potentiation (LTP), with the read-out of information from the genome in the formation or dissolution of connections, with the theory of information processing by artificial neural networks, and with the complex roles of neuromodulatory chemical mechanisms exercised by chains of brain stem neurons in arousal, motivation, and reinforcement.

The socialization of an intentional structure requires repeated unlearning. Social cooperation for nurture of altricial young in mammals is done by a process of unlearning during reproductive actions, which may be mediated by oxytocin and the endorphins. The side effects of pair bonding are jealousy and conflict, in part mediated by other neuropeptides such as vasopressin. In social mammals, similar neuromodulatory mechanisms may support bonding in groups larger than the nuclear family, having been adapted by evolution from neurosocial mechanisms for mammalian reproduction. Among humans the technologies for control of the processes of conversion and the emergence of group identities are music, dance, marching, and organized sports, through which channels for verbal communication and bureaucratic control are created. Evidence should be sought for pathologies in these neurochemical mechanisms for unlearning that may underlie psychopathia, autism, and drug addiction.

Chapter 7

Self and Society

Listening is a magnetic and strange thing, a creative
force. The friends who listen to us are the ones we move
toward, and we want to sit in their radius. When we are
listened to, it creates us, makes us unfold and expand.
Attributed to Karl A. Menninger

The major technological revolutions in cultural evolution are
commonly listed as tool making, agriculture, and manufacturing,
each entailing a geometric spurt in population growth. Before
them all, perhaps, emerged the technology for bonding in groups,
since making tools, fires and shelters required cooperation
among brains. From the examples we now have of infants
crooning and playing pat-a-cake, it is plausible to assume that
our ancestors half a million years ago were already chanting and
stomping in unison around ceremonial fires, hands drumming on
chests and thighs. Our adolescents still do this in new ways, as
techniques evolve for release of the neuromodulators that may
mediate the dissolution of intentional structure in unlearning.
These capacities and their neural mechanisms must have
evolved along with striatum and cortex (Spatz 1967),
particularly with growth of the temporal lobes having the
engine of intentionality and frontal lobes having the machinery
of foresight and insight. Now we consider properties that each
brain attributes to other brains by speculation on the private
awareness that lies beyond the solipsistic gulf. It is as if we
had found intelligent life in another galaxy and could
communicate only by reciprocal transmissions of light in Morse
code. We would imagine it to have the life that each of us has
within, and try understand that inner life from our perspective.

7.1 Consciousness

Thought is a process by which Neuroactivity creates meaning,
modifies intentional structure, and constructs representations
of meaning (Section 5.7). It is a transitory actualization of
intentional structure, which has a focus in the structure, but
which allows participation of the entire structure at each step
of the flow. A meaning is the location of the focus. A state of

consciousness is a stepwise sequence of thoughts in a segment of the trajectory of the itinerant focus traced by chaotic dynamics in brain state space, including a "penumbra" in the metaphor of James (1890), but having most of the actualization in the shadow of the still participatory unconscious.

This description omits a crucial property of consciousness: awareness, a *quale* (rhymes with "collie") that provides for "a property as it is experienced as distinct from any source it might have in a physical object; a property (as redness) considered apart from things having the property" (Webster 1949). Pursuit of qualia lead us to speculate on awareness and experience. I am willing to believe that rabbits are conscious, and that every animal possessing laminated neuropil (Section 3.3) has some consciousness, though I do not extend the attribute to lesser brains or to other forms of matter (Note 7.1). Phylogenetic trees of brains in Molluscs (octopuses), Arthropods (spiders) and Vertebrates (possums) show a series of increasing complexity. I think there is an equivalent tree of conscious beings ranked in order of capacity, so that at least three times in Earth's history, evolution has independently produced consciousness based in laminated neuropil. From my analysis of EEG patterns, I speculate that consciousness reflects operations by which the entire knowledge store in an intentional structure is brought instantly into play each moment of the waking life of an animal, putting into immediate service all that an animal has learned in order to solve its problems, without the need for look-up tables and random access memory systems.

What I cannot do is to use my biological data to determine whether a subject is *aware* of what is happening in its body and its surround, or *experience* what it is thinking and feeling. The properties of consciousness that most interest philosophers, physicists and lovers, its qualia, are inaccessible to experts in neurobiology and medicine. A case in point is that of anesthesiologists, whose expertise is to remove and restore consciousness by means of drugs at the behest of surgeons. They have two methods for estimating whether they have been successful at suppressing awareness in order to minimize pain and anxiety. One is to measure some autonomic variables, such as heart rate, blood pressure and respiration, in order to detect responses to pain. The other method is to ask after recovery, "Do you remember anything of what happened during the surgery?" Patients who had marked autonomic responses to surgery commonly have no recollection. This does not prove that they were unaware at the time, since some drugs can block the construction of intentionality. This is particularly likely to occur with ketamine, which allows conversation between patient and surgeon, but which impairs recall by the patient.

Some patients who had no autonomic fluctuations report in harrowing detail, clearly not imagined, the excruciating experience of being operated on as though without anesthesia. The tendency to paralysis of motor and autonomic activity is enhanced by use of muscle relaxants such as curare to ease the task of surgeons. Volunteers who have been totally paralyzed with curare, including loss of the ability to breathe for themselves, report no loss of awareness, but on the contrary a deep sense of distress. Sometimes after head injury a state of suspended animation occurs, in which a patient by all signs is comatose and unresponsive, yet some minutes, hours, or even weeks later returns to activity and reports symptoms of continuous awareness interspersed with periods of sleep, but with a terrifying inability to communicate owing to total paralysis. The conclusion is inevitable that even the most experienced physicians cannot know whether a fellow human being is or is not aware, but can only make inferences whether the body under observation has an unfolding inner experience comparable to their own. If we cannot tell when awareness is present, *a fortiori* we can not know anything beyond what we feel, and what others are able to share with us. If stereotypic gestures, emotional expressions, and descriptive words are seen as forms of representation, then the content of conscious minds is ultimately private, not to be fully known by anyone else.

The existence and properties of consciousness are studied in social contexts. One is epistemological, in which observers want to know which other objects have the capacity for inner experience, be they animal, machine, or extraterrestrial being, and "what it is like to be a bat" (Nagel 1974). The test for intelligence proposed by Alan Turing (1950), by which an observer using a keyboard communicates with a computer to explore its performance (Note 7.1), can serve to evaluate the flexibility, adaptiveness and even creativity of a machine, and it can show whether an inventor has succeeded in constructing a device having the properties of intentionality, but it cannot

prove that the machine is aware (Herbert 1993). Another
context is ethical, in which the restriction is adhered to that
painful or lethal stimuli are not to be given unnecessarily to
objects that might be subjects, such as comatose patients,
anencephalic humans, animals, and the members of races other
than one's own. Thus the issue of consciousness is social, legal,
philosophical, and ethical, but not scientific.

We assert that there is a material substrate for intention with
its quale of awareness. We can conceive of a space having no
edges like the surface of a sphere, only expanded to some higher
dimension, beginning with a four-dimensional sphere (Note 7.2),
for which a *surface* is an ordinary sphere, and moving on to six
or more dimensions (Smythies 1994), and an evolution in time
perhaps not in one dimension as we experience it but in two
dimensions. Engineers commonly use two dimensions in time to
express frequency and phase in the complex plane, though they
have not adequately explored the implications of time as a
surface in brain dynamics. Whatever its dimensions, whether
infinite, finite or fractal, an intentional structure provides a
space of latent Neuroactivity patterns that are implicit in the
existing synaptic, chemical states of an evolving forebrain. A
sought-for stimulus at each waking moment actualizes a
dissipative structure of Neuroactivity throughout the space,
allowing all parts to contribute some influence to the
construction. Patterns have conscious and unconscious content.

Referring to the conscious part, psychologists have analyzed the
content of thoughts by subjects in normal settings and, from
analysis of their reports, have estimated that about two thirds
of the content reflect the current activities and settings of the
subjects (Birchmeier-Nussbaumer 1974; Klinger 1978). The
remaining third reflects endogenous components (Note 4.3),
some of which are clearly identified as fantasies (Sutton et al.
1994). The current content may reflect the dominance of a
cortical site of nucleation for the most recent state transition
of the whole. The focus of self-organization can be considered
as Haken's "order parameter" that "enslaves" other parts of the
brain by engaging them into the cooperative action of the entire
forebrain. The unity of intentionality might be manifested
outside the brain in the scalp EEG from waking humans (Barlow
1993; Bressler et al. 1993; Gevins et al. 1989; Lehmann and
Michel 1990). If the actualization includes overt action and

making representations, not merely maintaining silent thought, antigravity posture, or expectancy, then the site of nucleation will mainly show up in the content of action, just as sensory stimuli appear in the momentary dissipative structure. The fact that content mainly relates to the present environment (Note 4.3) may account for the utility of the stimulus-response method and the reflex, which ignore consciousness.

Why is the remaining third so important to us? Considering that the prime function of brains is to make predictions as the basis of successful adaptation, when we encounter a new object it is important that we learn whether the movements of that object manifest intentionality, in that the motions of animate and inanimate objects entail very different predictions. A curved cylinder dropping onto a walkway may be a falling branch of a tree, but it may be a live snake. Even a young child can instantly recognize intentionality in the snake ("It's alive!") and avoid it or capture it as a pet, but further attribution that it is conscious invokes codes of ethical conduct in respect to another sentient being, whether friend or foe ("Don't hurt it!" or "Step on it!"). The concept of consciousness comes into play only with the incipient formation of intentional relations among brains.

The distinction can be illustrated by the following scenario about which I have written before (Freeman 1990a). When engineers have succeeded in emulating the dynamics of brains sufficiently well, they will explore the usefulness for humans of objects that have the adaptive and unitary knowledge base provide d by an intentional structure, and they will attempt to put these objects into service. Ethicists will ask whether these objects are conscious, and having no universally accepted answer, as is presently the case with animals, will assert that ethically we will be required to treat them as though they are. Engineers may resist being morally constrained in their use of devices that they conceive as mere glorified computers. Activist groups, such as People for the Ethical Treatment of Animals and the Animal Liberation Front, will draw on their experience to deal with Machine Intelligence and the cavalier attitudes of its creators, form the PETM and MLF, and lobby for legislation to protect the perceived rights of subjects endowed not merely with intentionality but with consciousness. Courts will be formed to decide cases of alleged violations of machine rights, and the juries may then by law be half human and half humanoid. Trial by a judge or a jury of peers is our current technology for deciding questions of prior awareness, responsibility, and intent. The expert testimonies of biologists, philosophers and psychiatrists do not suffice.

7.2 The self-organizing self

Universal determinism grew like a pall of industrial smog over 17th-century Europe, and, like acid rain, it continues to erode our sense of individual responsibility. Leibniz (1670) appealed to "the pre-established harmony between all substances, since they are all representations of one and the same universe" (p. 268). Spinoza (1674) concurred. A man differed from a rolling stone only in having the illusion of choosing to go downhill:

> Further conceive, I beg, that a stone, while continuing in motion, should be capable of thinking and knowing, that it is endeavouring, as far as it can, to continue to move. Such a stone, being conscious merely of its own endeavour and not at all indifferent, would believe itself to be completely free, and would think that it continued in motion solely because of its own wish. This is that human freedom, which all boast that they possess, and which consists solely in the fact, that men are conscious of their own desire, but are ignorant of the causes whereby that desire has been determined. [p. 390]

No freedom? From a premiss similar to the panexperientialism (Section 2.6) of Whitehead, he led scientists and the public into environmental determinism, seeing no power in self-organizing dynamics of solipsistic brains, which can take chaotic initial conditions and transform them into wonders. The Cartesian dogma, *"je suis ... une chose qui pense"* (1637 p. 73, "I am a thing that thinks"), was changed by existentialists (Grene 1948) to: "I act, thereby I exist". In my view the saying is again changed: "My self acts, and I perceive", since the only way the self can know anything is to stretch forth (Sections 1.4, 4.6) and stir the pot to taste the soup. This is Existentialism without the Angst or Ego. The "I" is late awareness of a self, not the mover. The self is the intentional structure as it is actualized in its totality by thought and judged by its thoughts about itself. Its intentionality can be explored by stimulus-response dialectics but, as with any object, cannot be grasped in its entirety, not even by awareness of itself or by its representations to itself.

WJF's cogito [handwritten annotation in left margin]

and, since thought is brain function for WJF, self is a brain function so WJF conceives of perception as a brain function albeit undetectable [handwritten annotation at bottom]

A specific act begins with emergence of a dynamic state, with its site of nucleation somewhere in the limbic system. An actualized pattern is transmitted as commands to the motor systems and as efference copies to the sensory systems to prime them for the consequences of the intended muscular activity. The act is completed upon reception of new stimuli, construction of patterns of Neuroactivity by state transitions in the sensory cortical dynamics, transmission of the constructs by stages into the limbic system for multimodal convergence, and incorporation in the intentional structure by synaptic modification in updating the cognitive map, thereby setting the initial conditions for the state transition into the next act.

The triad of sense of self, causality, and free will are qualia of this process. The sense of self is an awareness of unity and boundary. Cause is an awareness of the self stretching forth and acting into the world. Free will is an awareness of the wholeness, by which the self actualizes the potential it begins with in its genes and adds to with its experience. It is not a capricious change in direction, which is seen in the Brownian motion of particles, but the self-realization that is exemplified by Martin Luther's description of his voluntary action: "Here I stand. I cannot do otherwise." In modern terms, freedom is going to your room and doing your homework.

The facilitated state transition in a macroscopic dynamical system, which is triggered by microscopic fluctuations and which leads to a prepared basin of attraction, is an archetype of self-organization. It breaks the chain of cause with the past of the system, because the outcome of the transition is never fully predictable, and "chance" is not a "cause" (Barfield 1965). Chains of state transitions can be extremely regular, as in embryological development and the exercise of habits in behavior, but in each transition of every chain there is the possibility of a new direction emerging, which can then diverge exponentially from what might have been expected as the regular path. Statistical regularity is found in large collections of people and particles. Physicists could feel comfortable about causal relations among atoms as long as they were thought to be like billiard balls, but radioactive decay should have alerted them to the individuality of atoms. An atom does not have the intentional structure with which to choose when to split and cease to exist as a unit, and no one knows when or by what agency it will happen, but the intentional self exercises choice at each moment of its unfolding life trajectory, without prior awareness until the new path emerges, thereby transcending not the fixed past but the illusion of causal constraints on its future growth to wholeness. By foresight and reason the self can pre-arrange a time and path at selected branch points.

Onset of awareness of a decision by the sense of self, coming after the self has reached its decision and begun to act, may have the same half-second delay as the awareness of stimuli, which comes after the arrival of the stimulus-evoked pulses in sensory cortex (Sections 4.5, 5.4). Thus awareness is not a cause of action but the emergence of an update of intentionality, accompanying activation of thought to sort through antecedents and consequences of an act initiated by the self. It is common, for example, for the self to hear its words as they are being spoken, already to regret saying them. Complicated actions into the world that are familiar from long practice, such as driving an automobile, are commonly done with little or no awareness.

The concept of universal determinism, by which all actions are attributed to environments, genes (Herrnstein and Murray 1994) or experiences, is a myth drawn from unfounded extrapolation, which robs the self of an awareness of its own power and enslaves it to constraints imposed by others in the names of science and societal power. Undeniably each act emerges from a past that cannot be changed, including the given cultural milieu of Heidegger's "thrownness", but each moment has the initial conditions for the next state transition, and the new direction of change is not ordained. Habit and strict regularity are hard enough to overcome; the label *cause* says: "Don't bother to try". The basis of the sense of cause is a quale of human perspective, like the flatness of earth and the motion of the sun across the sky. The proper role for causality is to justify self-reliance, not to fix the blame somewhere else. Who knows what we may do or discover, when we free ourselves from this succubus?

Further insight into the nature of self comes from obsessive-compulsive disorder and its colorful variant Gilles de la Tourette's syndrome. Most people commonly experience the need to wash their hands again before going to bed or to check the lock on the door and the light in the living room an extra time, but when twenty or thirty times more fail to assuage a gnawing anxiety, the malady becomes disabling. Those suffering Tourette's have involuntary tics, twitches, spitting, and temper tantrums, as well as compulsively repetitious actions. About a third of them yield to outbursts of obscene language. The feeling is described as "having poison ivy all over your body for 20 years and being told not to scratch" (Seligman and Hilkevich 1991). The symptoms change with time and have the quality of a mad desire to violate social conventions. Once thought to be an obscure psychiatric malady, Tourette's is now known to be the most common genetically transmitted neurobehavioral disorder, and it has entered into pop culture. In a recent movie, "Burglar", actress Whoopi Goldberg hurled street epithets at a police sergeant, and her lawyer said to him: "Tourette's, you know!" The two nodded sagely, and she walked free.

Geneticists say a bad gene causes the disorder, but the label is gratuitous and adds nothing to a search for regularities. If the search leads to a treatment by replacing a bad gene, an ethical act is envisioned, and cause enters by the process of persuading the ethical review committees and the patients that the procedure is justified. Otherwise the victims have a choice of what to make of their lot. For example, as with obsessive-compulsive disorder the symptoms of Tourette's can be relieved by treatment with drugs, but the side effects of dulled perception, blunted affect, and loss of creativity lead many victims to stop the treatment, accept the social opprobrium, and get on with constructive living. Another example is sexual preference, which appears to be set in early development (Hamer and Copeland 1994), but gives a choice of what to do about it.

7.3 Self, reafference, and causality   *by what ?*

The *sense of self* is distinct from the self as an awareness of meaning within the intentional structure. Awareness need not accompany action, but if it does, from introspection we may infer that an emergent limbic state is experienced as an intent, the motor command as a sense of effort, the efference copies as a sense of expectancy of the sensory input that is to follow the movement expressing the act, the focus as attention, and the construction and combining of patterns as perception. The expectancy is based in the actualization of the intentional structure in the Neuroactivity of the sensory cortices by

reafference prior to perception.   If the thought process includes
the quale of an awareness of self in action, and if awareness
includes a capacity for generalization and abstraction over many
acts, then the sense of self includes "I cause this act" with
motion, and "I perceive this effect" with an emergent construct.

If understanding of the world is constructed entirely by an
arcuate process of stretching forth, taking in, and modifying
synapses, human knowledge is strongly colored by these qualia,
and *cause* is the self's ultimate metaphor in epistemology. Our
ancestors extrapolated the concepts of consciousness and
awareness as spirits inhabiting various objects in their world,
and we still extrapolate cause and effect to objects and events
in our world, no longer in terms of their having purpose, for we
are not that naive, but in terms of an unknowable directive
agency.   Philosophers from Aristotle with his "four causes"
(material, formal, efficient, and final - "that for the sake of
which something is done") to modern times have re-shaped the
metaphor of causality almost beyond recognition, first into
religious predestination and lately into scientific determinism.
Neither is consistent with the equations forming the articulated
skeleton of physics, which work equally well forward and
backward in time.   Physicists can't use them to explain why we
can't unscramble an egg, and they puzzle over the "paradox" of
"Time's Arrow".   Considering that a standard philosophical
method is *reductio ad absurdum*, it is astonishing that the
skepticism of David Hume (1739) regarding causality is not
more widely shared.   Putnam (1990) made a bold start:

Hume's account of causation ... is anathema to most present-
day philosophers. Nothing could be more contrary to the spirit
of recent philosophical writing than the idea that there is
nothing more to causality than regularity or the idea that, if
there is something more, that that something more is largely
subjective. [p.81]

He came closest to my position in his question:

If we cannot give a single example of an ordinary observation
report which does not, directly or indirectly, presuppose
causal judgements, then the empirical distinction between the
"regularities" we "observe" and the "causality" we "project
onto" the objects and events involved in the regularities

collapses. Perhaps the notion of causality is so primitive that the very notion of observation presupposes it? [p. 75]

In the end, he opted for Searle's aspectual dualism (Section 2.7):

The causal structure of the world is not physical in the sense of being built into what we conceive of as physical reality. But that doesn't mean that it is pasted onto physical reality by the mind. It means, rather, that "physical reality" *and* "mind" are both abstractions from a world in which things having dispositions, causing one another, having modal properties, are simply matters of course. [p. 95]

7.4 The social utility of self and cause

In my view the feelings of cause and effect are useful in several ways. They help us to assign priority to one or a few inputs by controls within collections of contiguous inputs that we give to an experimental system. They help us to construct convincing narratives of events in time and space. They enable us to predict with confidence the outcomes of our actions. No one would perform an experiment or run for election without some basis for expecting an effort to make a difference in the future. Societies would not go to the trouble of banning lead in gasoline or smoking tobacco, if their statistical relations to ill health were not labelled with the red flag of causation. Therefore, these qualia of understanding are necessary attributes of human explanations that precede social actions, but they are properties of minds attributed to events and objects in the world by observation, which is intentional structure in action.

The pernicious aspect of causality becomes apparent when the complexity of events exceeds the scale of personal action. This happens when the scope of description and comprehension involves numerous quasi-independent elements that are in feedback with each other diffusely, continually, and nonlinearly. We quickly lose the thread of causality and are left only with relationships. Chaoticists like to say that the flapping wings of a butterfly in Brazil can cause a hurricane in the Atlantic Ocean, in order to illustrate sensitivity to initial conditions, but this is absurd (Note 3.9). Which butterfly, and by what causal chain? The greatest advances in science of the past three centuries - Newton's theory of gravity, the cell doctrine of Virchow, the

Darwinian concept of evolution, the field concepts of Maxwell and Faraday with "action at a distance", their extensions by Einstein into relativity, and the formalisms of quantum mechanics - have cores of noncausal relationships, onto which have been grafted explanatory causes. Many have been mistakes, like "ether" to carry light waves, "hidden variables" to explain nonlocal quantum effects, the circular argument of "survival of the fittest" to explain natural selection, and the germ theory of disease, which worked in surgery but not in psychiatry. It is in social applications of science where the label of "cause" is properly used. Assignment of cause of death, for example, is a legal responsibility of physicians for purposes of public health. Pathologist can only describe the condition of a body post mortem, stating that a patient "died with" a lesion ("How"). Coroners and epidemiologists write "died of" a disease ("Why").

The development of a scientific theory, particularly if it is expressed in time-reversible differential equations, is best accomplished without use of concepts of cause and effect, as I have undertaken in this book. Good science requires the use of controlled experiments to weed out extraneous associations, and it depends on construction of tight matrices of relations. Reliance on a sense of cause is particularly treacherous in thinking about relations between microscopic and macroscopic properties of a population. Reductionists may ask, for example: "How does a stimulus cause neurons in cortex to enter the right basin?", which is like asking, "How · does water cause its molecules to flow in convection cells, when they prefer to go in a vortex?" Despite its appeal, we can say about causality what Laplace is wrongly alleged to have said, when asked about the place of God in science: *"Je n'ai pas besoin de cette hypothèse"* (I have no need of that hypothesis.) Only after the theory and the design of experiments are in place should causality come into play, when action begins, not with "What do I know now?", but with "What do I do next?", like an architect who assumes, for his purposes of design, that his part of the world is flat.

The senses of self, freedom of action, and causation are powerful tools that brains use to bridge solipsistic gulfs and achieve emergent goals of human societies. They reflect the mechanisms for inducing feelings of guilt, shame, regret, and responsibility, which are indispensable in the hands of parents, teachers, shamans, priests, and politicians for educating youth and curbing the appetites of sinners, without resorting to pain, jail, damnation and capital punishment. Though often called an "illusion" (Brown 1977; Fischer 1990) the sense of self makes possible a satisfying life in family and community (Brothers 1990), because the main work of the "I" is to rationalize what the self has already done or decided to do unconsciously. Freedom of action in self-organizing limbic dynamics is not the same as self control, and taking responsibility for one's self is more like trying to control one's teenager than one's automobile.

Among the tasks of neuroscience are those of understanding the neurodynamics and the neurochemistry of these feelings in education, which should be explored in the context of a social process of interaction among peers and leaders, not as an assembly line for conditioning behavior and using diet and drugs to raise IQ's, ameliorate attention deficits, and reduce the hyperactivity in exceptional individuals.   It is the biological evolution of social brains that has been sadly neglected, owing to an inadequate conceptualization of the solipsistic gulf, a neglect deriving from the engineering viewpoint of "the brain" as an adaptive filter, information processor, and symbol manipulator having keyboards, microphones, and scanners for input channels.   Children deserve better.   The work of Piaget (Note 4.7) has been outstanding, but it needs biological support to help it withstand the reductivist erosion from computational neuroscience and deterministic neurochemistry and genetics.

The self arises in the indivisible intentional structure of an intact brain.   Sperry (1982) showed that a permanent division of an intentional structure can be made by cutting the corpus callosum connecting the cerebral hemispheres, the "split brain". In contrast, the awareness of self by the actualization of thought is more easily subject to fractionation.   This is to be expected in a dynamic system that jumps by state changes from one domain of function to another, and it serves one's itinerant daily changes in roles as parent, worker, teacher, student, and so on.   A transient split can be induced by hypnotism, which is an exaggerated form of attentiveness and concentration, and pathological dissociations are observed in neurological diseases involving temporal lobe epilepsy with attendant fugue states.

In multiple personality disorder (MPD), now known as dissociative identity disorder (DID in DSM-IV), the sufferer has an intentional structure that actualizes in fragments like a fertilized egg that has split into twins, triplets, and more. Each actualization develops a fabric of memories, moods, desires, behavioral traits, and even diseases such as asthma *versus* psoriasis *versus* shingles. The switch from one actualization to another is abrupt, unpredictable and often total. In untreated patients the awareness by each actualization of the existence of the others may come only through experiencing the social consequences of the prior behaviors of other minds. This illness lies beyond comprehension and treatment through neurodynamics at its present level of development, but the similarity of the syndrome to the behavior of other unstable dynamic systems of simpler kinds gives reason for hope that the theory will some day match the complexity of helping these victims to socialize and knit together their scattered senses of self, especially when one form threatens suicide, which would be the murder of those others actualized from the same intentional structure.

7.5 The qualia of learning and unlearning

Solipsistic brains have evolved in physical and social environments that put high survival value on capacities of brains to overcome their isolation, so it is not surprising that the dynamics and chemistries of brains serve to shape their intentional structures by learning in the continuing update of adaptive social behaviors. A compelling quale accompanies learning when an insight is hugely successful. This is the "Eureka!" experience, the converse of unlearning, which brings a sense of closure, order, insight, connection, truth, and beauty, which conceivably may have the form of a global state of coherence in brain activity, and which may involve a flood of diverse neurohormones such as dopamine through the intentional structure. To some extent the feeling has been identified with specific neurochemicals by experiments in humans who have reported their experiences after taking neurotransmitters or their homologues by mouth or injection. Although vasopressin is associated with aggression, it seems nothing is known about the neurochemistry of hate. Hedonic hormones are best understood, for the obvious reason that few volunteers take twice a drug that induces bad feelings. Dopamine is associated with hedonic feelings (Schneider 1989) and reward, whereas norepinephrine gives feelings of fear and trepidation. Whether they act in competition or cooperation is unclear, but the balance may make the difference between a "good trip" and a "bad" one, an example of the *state-dependence* (Sections 4.7, 5.4) of behavioral reactions to brain inputs. Amphetamine and cocaine are both chemically related to dopamine and norepinephrine. Each engenders the feelings of omniscience and omnipotence, which normally follow efforts that culminate in passing an exam, breaking a sports record, or winning an election. The pleasure of victory in a bottle explains why the drugs are so addictive to those persons without other access to the desired qualia.

Scientists may also become addicted to the thrill of discovery and thereby suffer impairment of their critical judgement. The strength of conviction with which a belief is held is more closely related to the concentrations of the neuromodulators by which it is mediated than to the degree of truth involved. While researchers are duty-bound to maintain skepticism in the face of feelings of elation and wait to replicate before publishing, most of us most of the time rely on untested convictions and the appeal of euphoria to get through the day. Intense experiences provided by endogenous brain chemicals can support the strength and stability of vision in an outstanding religious, political or scientific leader, who can maintain a sense of direction in times of social chaos and rapid, unpredictable social change. It can also support shared, rigid convictions that masquerade as common sense in racial bigots, religious zealots, political fanatics, and scientific cranks. Yeats (1921) wrote, "The best lack all conviction, while the worst are full of passionate intensity." Humanists, skeptics and agnostics have traditionally formed a loose constituency, characterized by pluralism, tolerance, and flexibility, but liberals are poor visionary leaders in times of evolutionary crisis and chaos. We need a better understanding of the neurodynamics of intentional structures, particularly of the mechanisms by which some are flexible and others are rigid, and how, in accordance with complexity theory (Section 5.4), we might comprehend and take advantage of the extremes of character. Both traits have value in societies.

While oxytocin (Section 6.5) may mediate feelings during sexual climax, it may also be involved in the onset of transmarginal inhibition and states of spiritual ecstasy. A first full-blown sexual experience in adolescence can have the neural impact of a concussive blow on the head. The process of unlearning and the dissolution of intentional structure may be experienced as a loss of identity and boundary, the fusion of one's self with another self, a failure of control of volition and direction, and a frightening sense of strangeness in familiar surroundings. Less well understood is the malleability in the belief structures of the participant individuals that follows orgasm, especially in those adolescents on the threshold of breaking away from family and undertaking child rearing, but also in middle age on the threshold of second childhood, or in old age near dying.

This mechanism may mediate falling in love (May 1969). Bourgeois societies traditionally see the importance of first sexual experience for imprinting character, and under the ideals of chastity, purity, and protection of property have shielded their nubile daughters from contacts with males not of acceptable social class or race. Pluralistic societies in modern industrial nations relax their behavioral controls by tolerating "free sex" and random matings across cultural and racial lines, thus gaining more cohesiveness in the nation state, but at the cost of diminished familial allegiances manifested in higher rates of divorce and single parenthood. A failure to understand the biology of sexual initiation rites as techniques to weaken existing belief structures, preparatory to replacing them with new ones, has also led to efforts to stamp out teenage gangs, instead of comprehending and using this natural process for constructive social action (Note 7.3). The intense need for love (eros, not to be confused with its mammalian underpinning, sex) expresses the endless search for close contact with others.

The release of neuropeptides in the class of endorphins into brain and spinal cord is accompanied by relief from pain. Athletes and joggers who are engaged in strenuous exercise to the point of pain may conscientiously persevere in order to "break the pain barrier", and by succeeding in triggering the release of endorphins, experience the "runner's high", pound into pieces the cartileges in their hips, knees, and ankles, and support the "orthopedist's high". Endorphins may serve more than pain control by supporting feelings of bliss and tranquillity, for which the desired archetype is a happy family. A strong sense of well being may be an important quale during the period of recovery from transmarginal inhibition, by which the positive value of the social environment of family or tribe is imprinted after unlearning. This action is simulated by morphine and heroin in bringing dream-like states of wonder and lethargy, with lessened pain, anxiety, and boredom. Learning after unlearning is more likely to be painful, as it is mediated, probably, by norepinephrine and acetylcholine (Table 6.1).

Histamine is associated with arousal (Sections 4.7, 6.4), the motivation of brains for the undertaking of learning experiences. Blocking of its actions by antihistamine drugs is accompanied by drowsiness and blunting of thought and affect, which are dreaded side effects in persons with hay fever, and are desired goals of persons with anxiety who take Valium, a tranquilizing antihistamine (Freeman 1993). Serotonin is associated with feelings of well-being, equanimity, and relief from depression. Mimicking of its actions by LSD (Aghajanian 1994) and related hallucinogens (Fischer 1971) is accompanied by distortions of perception of time, space, body, and the visual surround. Brains normally locate objects outside their bodies (Section 4.5) but under LSD may also locate themselves outside and see their bodies from unusual points of view in space and time. These screwball out-of-body experiences are traditionally induced by religious psychedelics, but they are comparable to those of the 19th century that were induced by nitrous oxide ("laughing gas") and chloral hydrate. It was apparent then as now that many chemicals, such as gasoline, paint thinner and glue, can induce the qualia of learning and unlearning, giving rise to a powerful conviction that one has at last found the secret of the universe, or the source of all knowledge and power (Eco 1992), which fades like a mirage as a brain rids itself of a chemical intruder.

7.6 Spiritual leaders and psychedelic tourists

Some people turn to chemicals as a way to deepen the privacy within solipsistic chasms, and in order to retreat from social stress into inner space. A few have induced these states so as to peer through the solipsistic bars and dirty windows in order to see what is "really there", although, as minds disintegrate, what comes are swirls and tinglings, and ultimately the points of receptor inputs like stars, flies or grains of sand. Huxley (1954) demonstrated how far an experienced writer can go into chemically induced abnormalities of perceptual neurodynamics and return with coherent descriptions. Most people merely seek pleasure and escape from pain, anxiety, and boredom in altered states referred to as "turning on", or getting "aglow", "high", "loaded", "stoned", or "spaced". Researchers who pursue scientific studies of awareness have their work cut out for them, to replicate and measure under controlled laboratory and field conditions the qualia of these pharmacological pleasures, fantasies, escapes, chaotic illusions, and breakdowns.

Solipsistic brains also seek union with spirits larger than those of other minds and societies. Once embarked in this direction minds encounter no logical barriers to finding spirits in animals, rocks and plants, in the least particles of physics, in Gaia, or in the entire universe. The safest course for a brain may be to act as if there were others "out there", in what mathematicians call "Pascal's wager". If it is mistaken, it suffers mere loneliness, but if it is correct, it gains early warning of opportunities and dangers. The same scenario is played for the same reason on a world-wide scale by cosmologists like Carl Sagan in search of extraterrestrial intelligence. The tenacity with which humans hold to the belief that something out there cares, despite what Stanislav Lem (1983) called the "silencium universi", clearly manifests an important aspect of intentional dynamics.

A problem in the search for encounters of a spiritual kind is that brains are normally quite stable and locked into the tasks of daily living that evolution designed them for. They cannot lightly go into chemically mediated state transitions that give access to altered states of mind. A natural disposition to slip the press of social constructs and go alone on a solipsistic journey appears to be rare, even more so when it is combined in the person of an artist, poet, or preacher with the ability to write into a diary some compelling representations of the lonely visions. Brains can more easily enter into exalted states by means of starvation to alter brain chemistry, flagellation to add pain, meditation to induce sensory isolation, and infection to bring fever and hallucination. These techniques have been the stock in trade of hermits and mystics. The reports of these spiritual voyagers clearly have value for stay-at-homes, in much the way that geographic travelers to foreign lands are eagerly sought out for the tales they can tell.

Societies usually have sufficient wealth to support and even encourage idealists, as long as there are not too many of them. Few individuals have the stamina and perseverance that are required to achieve visions by self-discipline alone. Where trouble comes is in the use of exogenous drugs to induce altered states that have qualia comparable to those more honestly achieved, but that lack the depth and richness of intentional structures characterizing disciplined visionaries such as Hieronymous Bosch, William Blake, and the prophets of old. Psychedelics make it easy to get high and experience fluctuating colors and distortions of body image, but the residue is more likely to be a hangover than an increase in competence to stretch forth, encompass a new world, and objectify it in representations such as paintings, posters, poems, movies, and novels for the benefit of others.

The ease with which drugs can be acquired and ingested has opened the gates to increasing numbers of transients whom Roland Fischer (1990, 1994) sees as "drug tourists", who seek pleasure and not self-knowledge.   He has described the use of psychedelics and related psychoactive compounds to induce altered states of consciousness that form a spectrum, ranging in one direction from "normal" awareness to deep meditation and in the other to ecstasy.   At either extreme the individual may experience transcendence of the isolating gulf and sense a union with another consciousness and loss of the sense of self.   That union is not accessible by witnesses of behavior during religious transports.   People who are stoned, anesthetized, or in ecstasy must recover to speak or write about their experiences, in order that they be socially validated and made the basis for cooperative behaviors.   Fischer (1994) noted that the sense of self is lost in psychosis, as well as in mystical rapture:

But while the mystic has a good trip without a self, the psychotic loses control.   The mystic, of course, can rely on the support of the social mind of his/her era (particularly during the 16th and 17th centuries) whereas the psychotic is left alone with the loss of an important illusion that is necessary (from the 18th century onward) for mental health. [p. 20]

The inward turning of the drug user contrasts with the outward turning of the dancer.   To dance is to engage in rhythmic movements that invite corresponding movements by others.   The reciprocity fosters transcendence over the boundaries of self in physical and emotional communion.   Music and dance integrate people into societies (Note 6.1); recreational drugs isolate them.

It is not surprising that societies "make war on drugs" to minimize their use and the resultant tendency to disintegration.

After explanations by neurobiologists are done, philosophers, physicists, and the book-buying public may still hunger to know: What is the essence of awareness in consciousness? If they choose a causal approach, they are stuck with Aristotle's four causes: How is it made? How is it attached to neurons, microtubules, atoms, or quanta? What are its laws? What is it for? But if causality is seen as a quale attaching to the process of observing regularity, then the question is religious. For theists like Aquinas awareness is God's gift that we may know Him/Her. For atheists like Nietzsche (1885) it is the curse of insomnia. For poets and mystics it is Critchley's (1979) "Divine Banquet". For agnostics like Mencken (1946) and Shaw (Chapter 4) it is something to have fun with. What more can one ask?

7.7 Summary

Minds are collections of thoughts and bodies beliefs, which are the actualization of intentional structures in brains. Consciousness is an attribution by each brain to other brains in recognition of the existence of others besides the self, serving to distinguish intentional from non-intentional acts. Awareness is subjective experience of consciousness in feeling and thought. It includes the sense of self corresponding to its unity, the sense of hope to its wholeness, and the sense of cause to its stretching forth through reafference. Awareness of self is not in control but continually runs to catch up with the self, half a second late but backdated. Causality is properly used to describe intentional actions and their consequences. It is a property of the act of observing that attaches a quale to an observed object or event. Extrapolation of causality into the world is equivalent to attribution of spirits to objects, and it leads to the doctrine of universal causality and its religious form, predestination. The neurochemicals that operate on intentional structures give rise, singly and in combination, to differing states of awareness, many of which can be induced by ingesting exotic drugs that are related to the neuromodulators. Compared with dancing and sport, which invite and sustain social cooperation, intoxication with drugs is divisive and debilitating, which explains the adverse reaction of society to their widespread use.

Epilogue

Penetrating so many secrets, we cease to
believe in the unknowable. But there it sits
nevertheless, calmly licking its chops.
H. L. Mencken [1956 p. 241]

Nietzsche (1885) alluded to his conversion experience with the
collapse of belief structure in "The Grave Song" of Zarathustra,
where his theme recurs about understanding through dance:

"All days shall be holy to me" - so spake once the wisdom
of my youth: verily, the language of a joyous wisdom.
But then did [death] steal my nights, and sold them to
sleepless torture. ...
And once did I want to dance as I had never yet danced:
beyond all heavens did I want to dance. Then did ye
seduce my favorite minstrel. ...
Only in the dance do I know how to speak the parables of
the highest things: - and now hath my greatest parable
remained unspoken in my limbs. [p. 369]

A poet is one self, but has the sense of many selves: the scribe
who takes dictation from the self, the critic who revises and
chills the spirit, and the itinerant visionary in self control.
Sometimes they come into conflict, and a mind disintegrates.
An uncommon but not rare form is an awareness of the *presence*
of "another" or a "visitor", which may persist for hours or days.
T. S. Eliot (1922) noted [p. 73] that he was influenced in writing
"The Waste Land" by one of Shackleton's Antarctic expeditions:

Who is the third who walks always beside you?
When I count there are only you and I together
But when I look ahead up the white road
There is always another one walking beside you,
Gliding, wrapt in a brown mantle, hooded
I do not know whether a man or a woman
- But who is that on the other side of you? [p.65]

The experience accompanies some forms of postencephalitic
psychosis and epilepsy. When it is reported by healthy people, it
usually comes under conditions of physical stress and isolation,

such as mountaineers suffering lack of oxygen, shipwrecked
sailors lost at sea in open boats, and inmates of concentration
camps. Charles Lindbergh felt this in the night of his 32 hour
flight across the Atlantic. The presence is usually vague and
unseen, what James (1890) called a weak hallucination, but
carrying an emotional portent of threat or protection from harm
that manifests the eternal concern of brains for what is about
to happen. When the presence takes the attributes of the self, it
is experienced as an alter ego or, in German literature, as the
Doppelgänger, brooding in condemnation of the dilettante. In
former times the visitor was experienced as a personification
of a local deity, guardian or satanic angel, God or Devil, while
today it may be felt convincingly as an extraterrestrial being.

Considering the possibilities for disruption and disintegration
of the sense of self, its normal stability is amazing. In times of
extreme environmental change, the old ways of coping may no
longer suffice. An onset of instability in the sense of self may
be non-itinerant, chaotic search for a viable alternative, like a
random walk or a cast of the I Ching. A cohesive personality has
survival value when the environment is predictable, which
justifies the appeal of the biological mechanisms of unity in
intentional structures, but other strengths may appear in human
adaptations to unimaginable conditions coming from unknowable
futures. An appropriate response to overwhelming complexity
and impossible odds is a flight into chaos, like a moth, which
veers predictably away from the sonar signal of a distant bat
but tumbles unpredictably in a chaotic trajectory when the bat
is too close for evasion by normal flight maneuvers. Another
response is to create a protector in order to walk the dark alley.

The sense of "another" seems closely allied to extrasensory
perception (ESP), when a "presence" is hypothesized to be a
"transmitting" brain elsewhere in "space-time" sending "signals"
to a "receiving" brain by channels unknown to science. I respect
the ingenuity in experimental design and statistical analyses of
data in some tests of the hypothesis (Schlitz and Honorton
1992; Herbert 1993; Bem and Honorton 1994; Hyman 1994), but
remain skeptical, owing to the solipsistic barrier, which is not
merely scalp and skull, but structure. Each brain has its unique,
self-organized pattern, built from infancy. To me, the ESP data
are coincidences that are not at all improbable, given the
millions of events in a waking lifetime. The likelihood of the

outcome of any one test may seem well below chance levels, but this is deceptive. The numerical probability of an event is calculated over a distribution of like events. The tests may include circumstances that are common, when properly seen in the context of their kind, else the phenomena would not have been experienced by well over half the world's population. Some of the factors at play are the capacity of a solipsistic brain for constructing patterns where none exist, its suggestibility, its sense of causal influence externalized to objects and events in its surround, and its need and ability to find purpose in external events, in order to give them meaning, which is to knit them into its intentional structure. The sense of conviction and certainty attaching to paranormal experiences is highest when they occur in or just preceding emotional episodes, particularly those involving threatened or actual death of someone close, but the neurochemicals accompanying strong arousal and a sense of closure are not conditional on the truth of the circumstances, in which their release and neural actions take place (Section 7.5).

Validation of ESP would also require radical changes in how we conceive causality, space, and time, but this is not a counter-argument. Repeated changes have occurred in all three during recorded history, particularly in the past four centuries. The scientific conception of cause was drastically changed by Newtonian dynamics, when the idea of "action at a distance" was accepted by scientists, despite its association with psychic spells cast by witches and astrological influences of planets on personalities. Its presently accepted form is untenable, I think, in view of the neurodynamics of reafference (Sections 4.6, 7.3).

In ancient and medieval worlds "time" was circular, measured in days, years, and generations; space was bounded by the spheres. In Newtonian dynamics the equations required that time be expressed by a straight line with units in equal measure running in both directions to infinity. Cartesian coordinates required that space have three linear dimensions without end, though the flat earth was ensphered. In the past century time has been terminated in the Big Bang and the Big Crunch, with the possibility that it runs in a circle after all, if the universe repeats in Bangs and Busts. It may even be wrinkled. Space has been curved onto itself into something like a doughnut, or maybe two of them, back to back, with "black holes" in one matching "white holes" in the other. Each model subsumes those preceding as an approximation by changes in scale to include the very small, the very large, and the fractal, all increasingly far from experimental testing (Lindley 1993). Possibly, time might better be expressed in two dimensions as a complex number. Space has for a century been conceived in dimensions exceeding three (Smythies 1994). Poincaré (1913) asked why we see in three dimensions, and his answer was that we move in three dimensions. Humans experience the world in 3-D, but cannot *experience* space in more dimensions, because we cannot move in higher dimensions, though virtual reality may make this *seem* possible (Note 7.2).

These historical precedents show that prevailing concepts of time, space, and cause have repeatedly been changed by new data. Views founded in relativity and quantum mechanics are no more inviolate than the Newtonian view. At present the search for radically new theory is largely by physicists, because their field gave the previous changes (Smythies 1994). Current hypotheses, to the effect that quantum wormholes, mini-black holes, gravitons, magnetic monopoles, and distortions of local space-time by quantum gravity wells in synapses may offer channels for nonlocal communication of psychons and engrams between human brains, tend to suggest that some physicists are underemployed since the SSC (superconducting supercollider) was abandoned.

Biologists mistrust theory, because their subject is so diverse, and technology has filled their plates for the moment. New theory will come from neurobiology, since brains construct our senses of time, space, and cause. We now have the necessary techniques to observe the neural activity in awake animals and model the Neuroactivity of the populations. Our present models expressed in features, clocks and cognitive maps are misleading and preempt more creative thinking. We need to measure activity patterns of the several limbic populations, while our experimental animals are solving problems in their own space and time, and use the data to construct heuristic models of the Neuroactivity of cause, space and time based in neurobiology. This has been the scientific method for 300 years. It is hard work, but not mystical, and nowhere near the paradox of "the mind" trying to explain itself. Surely in the next millennium our descendents will know much more about these matters.

Notes

2.1 Information theory applied to arrays of neurons

The process of sensation consists of expressing a momentary field of energy in a set of point values conveyed by the pulses of selected receptor cells. We can represent them with binary digits. Numerous variants of information theory have been devised to explain what brains might do with these pulses, seen by statisticians (Brillinger 1981) as *point processes*. One variant views neurons as feature detectors by virtue of their synaptic connections, which are adaptively shaped by learning during growth (Section 6.2). Neural networks (Section 6.3), sees neurons as binary switches in nets performing symbolic computations (McCulloch 1969). They are modeled with matrices (Amari 1977) or tensors (Pellionisz and Llinàs 1985). An example is their neural network for learning coordinated movements of limbs, which was simplified by Churchland (1986) to describe visual guidance of crab claw motion (Section 5.5).

2.2. Ecological maps of affordance and effectivity

According to Shaw et al. (1990), "Gibson, like Tolman, would disagree with Skinner ... that the organism is merely a 'through-put system'. For Tolman, cognition can embellish the stimulus, while for Gibson [1979], stimulus must be informative about the environment in ways that a stimulus, as a physiological 'goad' or a reflexive 'force', could never be. They both endow [the organism] with a complex interior - which Tolman cites as the residence of cognitive functions and Gibson as the seat of a tunable (not necessarily linear) information detection operator which resonates to qualitative environmental properties (*i.e.* affordances). For Gibson, the environment that surrounds an organism is real and objective for each organism" [p. 586]. They resolve a paradox they see, in combining past experiences and future goals, by proposing a dual Minkowski space with the two cones of past and future melded at the apex of the present, and:

... an environment of information which dynamically links a socially invariant exterior with both a biologically invariant interior frame, on the one hand, and with a still more exterior physically invariant frame on the other. That psychological inverse dynamics must couple energy with information across a frame exterior (observable) to one and interior (controllable) to the other, and vice-versa, defines what is meant by an ecological map. [p. 587]

Their theory has great promise, though my data do not support their "invariant interior frame" (Section 3.7), nor the attribution of information to objects in the environment (Section 4.2).

2.3. The "quality of understanding" in Roger Penrose Penrose (1994) emphasizes that physicists have encountered consciousness in the attempt to solve the measurement problem in quantum mechanics, whereby an observation by a conscious observer collapses a wave function. He bases his "search for the missing science of consciousness" on putative nonlocal states of quantum coherence in neural microtubules.

The computer-like classically interconnected system of neurons would be continually influenced by this cytoskeletal activity, as the manifestation of whatever it is that we refer to as "free will". The role of neurons ... is ... like a *magnifying device* in which the smaller-scale cytoskeletal action is transferred to something which can influence other organs of the body - such as muscles. Accordingly, the neuron level of description that provides the currently fashionable picture of the brain and mind is a mere *shadow* of the deeper level of cytoskeletal action - and it is at this deeper level we must seek the physical basis of mind! [p. 376]

Neurobiologists say his model is a throwback to the Golgi reticular hypothesis, disproven by Sherrington (1906) and Ramón y Cajal (1911), and unsupported by an appeal for "new laws of physics". They say an action potential cannot amplify quantum states, because it is a thermal shock that disrupts coherence. An axon does briefly cool during a pulse (Abbott 1960), due to the refrigerant expansion of sodium ions into the cytoplasm, but the drop in temperature is quickly overtaken by heat from oxidative metabolism to move the sodium out again. Dendrites produce 95% of the waste heat of brains, forming a heat bath for axons (Bulsara and Maren 1993). Physicists say brains are too large, warm, and weak for quantum coherence. Penrose says superconductivity is macroscopic coherence that has been achieved at temperatures approaching Siberian winter nights, and that it may be found at normal brain temperature owing to "ordered water" in the microtubules. Philosophers say assigning "understanding" to quantum states is a category mistake.

2.4 Neural activity *versus* Neuroactivity
This distinction is the difference between what neurons do and the noises they make. An action potential is *all-or-none*, so that biologists count the pulses/second to measure activity in a nerve. However, the amplitude of action potentials varies, and their effects at synapses are subject to many variables. Their electric fields are often unobservable, so their only sign is their effect on other neurons. Ultimately, the only way to know what a neuron does, which is to assign meaning to its "noise", is to represent its Neuroactivity by a state variable, Q, called an *activity density function* (Freeman 1975) in equations, in which parameters represent the physical and chemical properties of neurons, and yet other state variables represent behavior.

3.1 The theory of measurement in neurobiology
To express something in a finite set of numbers we choose a small piece of whatever we want to measure, such as a length, duration, mass, etc., and add the pieces until the two quantities are as close as we can get them. We repeat the process to get a collection of numbers, find the mean, and calculate the variation to get a *standard error*, which expresses the messy aspects of getting the sum together and having to *round-off*, when the last piece is too big or small. Each kind of selected piece defines a coordinate axis, such as time, mass, or energy. To measure the signs of Neuroactivity, which take the forms of time-varying quantities, such as action potentials and dendritic waves, we require pieces of wave forms, such as a pulse, step, and damped sine wave. These are called *basis functions*. They are defined by equations with *parameters* (Section 2.1). Each parameter, α, specifies an independent coordinate axis and a dimension in the measurement space. To measure brain waves we choose a set of basis functions and fix a standard amplitude for each, then add them until the pile matches the observed activity. We then say we have *decomposed* a wave into its basis functions. A powerful method to define and measure basis functions for the EEG is autoregression (Wright, Kidd and Sergejew 1990).

Measuring chaos is really difficult. There are no good basis functions, only digitizing pulses and Fourier components. We don't know how many dimensions there are. The dimensions aren't even integers (Grassberger and Procaccia 1983). We can't capture the smoothness of flow with numbers, because we can't make the numbers infinitesimal. The brain processes are nonstationary, unpredictable, and unreproducible. What gives hope is that an appeal to chaos expresses belief in hidden order and the possibility of control, whereas an appeal to randomness is a resignation to complacency and ignorance (Barfield 1965).

3.2 Peripheral *versus* central neural "codes"
The term "code" is used in neurobiology with the same intent as in genetics, to express the transfer of information from the past into the future. In genetics the four bases are letters in an alphabet; in neurobiology the pulse is a binary digit, and an axon is a labeled line. A "code" is a set of symbols made by humans to measure, store and transmit information. In neurobiology it is a metaphor. The microscopic code for reception and sensory preprocessing is the pulse frequency of a selected subset of neurons in an array. The macroscopic code for perception is the pulse density distributed as an activity density function, Q, over an entire population, like an interference pattern in a hologram. No neuron is more or less important than any other (Section 5.3).

3.3 Quantitative relations between pulses and waves
Equations describe the transformations by which pulse trains are converted to dendritic current and *vice versa*. We use a symbol p to represent the pulse frequency, a symbol v to represent the dendritic wave amplitude, and Q to denote the Neuroactivity of the neuron as inferred from measurements of the recordings of p and v. The equations have the general form exemplified by $dQ/dt = \beta v - p$ (rate of change in Neuroactivity, Q, equals dendritic input, v, times a parameter β, less the present pulse frequency, p). They express numerically the rules by which each variable depends on the amplitude and rate of change of other variables. The rule states how the neuron operates on its input to give its output, so the equation describes the function of the neuron. Contrary to what Popper and Eccles (1977) say, the falsification of a rule is not easy. Failure of agreement is because the experiments were not done correctly Good experimentalists may try for years to get it right before defeat, enticed by the beauty of their hypotheses.

The next step is to evaluate the desired quantity Q from the measured observables, p and v. Two more equations are needed to relate the observables to the Neuroactivity, Q, since the observables are epiphenomenal noise that have no direct influence on the underlying activity of the neurons (Freeman 1975). Validation of an estimate for Q depends on knowing what happens in the targets of the neuronal output and, ultimately, in behavior. This description is naive, in that each of the transforms consists of a complicated chain of electrochemical events (Kandel, Schwartz and Jessel 1993). It is sophisticated, in that it abstracts the essentials, in order to go between levels of function, down to the genome and up to social behavior.

3.4 Population pulse-wave relations: *Sigmoid curve*
I found a close statistical relation between the local pulse density in a neighborhood of a population and the amplitude of its macroscopic wave (Freeman 1975) and have constructed an equation that predicts the axonal output for dendritic current input (Freeman 1979). With strong inhibitory current, the pulse output is zero. With strong excitatory current, the pulse output saturates at a maximum. In between these extremes the density of firing increases smoothly in what has come to be called since its discovery (Freeman 1967) the *sigmoid curve*. It resembles a ski-jump as seen from one side. The wave-pulse relation at trigger zones in neuron populations is intrinsically nonlinear. In this, it differs from the relation between pulse input and dendritic current at synapses, which is normally kept within a narrow linear range. This static nonlinearity gives interesting, simplifying properties to population dynamics (Freeman 1992a).

3.5 Further comments on the binding hypothesis
Criticisms of this solution to the binding problem (Tovée and Rolls 1992; Hardcastle 1994) are that too few neurons have been observed to synchronize their pulse trains; that the time required for synchrony to develop is too long; that cortical neurons fire aperiodically and not rhythmically; and that the binding hypothesis offers no mechanism by which a target of visual cortical transmission can distinguish the synchronized pulses of a network representing an object from other pulses representing the visual background. Other hypotheses posit groups of neurons that fall short of populations, in that the sum of pulse trains from a neural aggregate represents a sensory stimulus. Georgeopolis et al. (1986) have recorded in monkeys from a collection of visual cortical neurons having designated features, and have shown that the vectorial sum of features is a

better predictor of the conditioned response to a stimulus than any one cell. Miyashita (1993) has shown that the element of function is a group of neurons corresponding to a cortical column, which can be kept firing by means of interaction, can be "tuned" to objects by learning and can be prospectively activated by associational connections. Amit (1989) offers a population model for short-term memory based on "reverberatory" activity in chains. These models provide no mechanisms of read-out of the groups, since the center of gravity of observed pulse trains of neurons in a column gives a point estimate of the amplitude of one local mean field, like a pixel, but the actual cortical output is a spatial pattern of Neuroactivity over all the neurons, including columns firing and not firing (Freeman 1975).

3.6 Surgical, pharmacological analysis of olfaction
When the path from the bulb to the olfactory cortex is blocked, cortical action potentials and EEGs vanish, and bulbar EEGs show periodic oscillation on inhalation (Freeman 1975; Gray and Skinner 1988). On recovery, normal action potentials and EEGs return, showing that background activity and bursts induced by inhalations are global properties of the whole olfactory system. They are not due to a point attractor perturbed by noise. They manifest a chaotic attractor that is maintained through coupling of oscillators in the bulb, nucleus and cortex (Freeman 1987a). Bulbar Neuroactivity is transmitted to cortex by surface paths, and forebrain Neuroactivity is returned by deep paths. Cortical transmission is always bidirectional. State transitions in the bulb are shaped by sensory input, and also by Neuroactivity that comes from the parts of the forebrain the bulb transmits to, and that carries messages for reafference and control (Section 4.6).

Learning in the olfactory bulb is chemically controlled by other parts of the forebrain (Gray, Freeman and Skinner 1986). We placed electrodes in rabbits to measure EEGs and cannulas in the bulbs to inject a drug that blocked norepinephrine (Section 6.4). This is normally released in the bulb by the brain stem after punishment or reward, whereby a new spatial pattern of EEG activity appears as an animal acquires a conditioned response to the odor. When the action of norepinephrine was blocked, the EEG patterns did not change during training, nor did the rabbits acquire a conditioned response. When we gave the rabbits an odor with no reinforcement and injected norepinephrine only into the bulb, the spatial pattern changed dramatically, and behavior did not. (Such changes don't occur normally without reinforcement.) The centrifugal pathways don't have the anatomical specificity to carry centrally stored "memories" of past activity patterns that are to be "compared" with present sensory input, as has been proposed in several computational models of olfactory systems (Note 3.8). Instead, they carry global modulations constituting generic commands, such as "turn on", "turn off", "imprint", "habituate", bifurcate", "unlearn", and so on. The centrifugal connections from the forebrain into the olfactory system are essential for its operation, and they carry a variety of neuromodulators (Table 6.1, Section 6.4). Their mechanisms and roles are still largely unknown. Similar sets of coupled oscillators (populations of excitatory and inhibitory neurons) are found everywhere in the cortex. Areas of neocortex also go silent after loss of input (Burns 1958).

3.7 Macroscopic activity in multi-pulse recordings
The number of neurons that can be accessed by recording pulse trains simultaneously from multiple electrodes with present techniques is too small to give access to macroscopic patterns, for which the EEG is more suited. I estimate that the fraction of variance in the pulse train of each neuron that is covariant with the population wave form is about 1 in 1,000 (Freeman 1992b), so the present limit of about 100 neurons is 10 times too small. The EEG potentials accompany synaptic currents that flow between the neurons and sum as scalar values (Freeman 1975, 1992a). That sum is an epiphenomenon like a noise, for it does not bind the cells together. The binding is done by the innumerable synaptic interactions between the neurons to give the local mean field of the ensemble. EEGs are signs of the macroscopic Neuroactivity of populations, while the pulse densities in the populations carry the activity from one place to another. When multiple recordings of pulse trains are made simultaneously, the participation of neurons in populations are seen as covariances called "phase locking", "binding", "synfiring" and "reverberation" (Abeles M 1991; Aertsen et al. 1994; Amit 1989; Eckhorn 1991; Georgeopolis et al..1986; Krüger 1990; McNaughton 1993; Rolls et al. 1989).

3.8 Theories of olfaction: The utility of oscillation
Most computational models in olfaction (Grossberg 1987; Schild 1988; Li and Hopfield 1989; Haberly and Bower 1989; Shepherd 1991; Liljenström 1991; Granger et al. 1991; Wilson and Bower

1992; Érdi et al. 1993) emphasize the odor specificity of the single neuron responses to odorants. Recordings from the olfactory lobes of insects have recently replicated observations in vertebrates on the selectivity of single neural responses, and also revealed oscillations in the firing probabilities of single neurons comparable to the gamma oscillations in vertebrates (Laurent and Davidowitz 1994), supporting the widely held view that: "The specific subpopulations in the sequence are odor-dependent, which suggests that the spatiotemporal dynamics of neuronal firing may constitute a code ..." (Tank, Gelperin and Kleinfeld 1994), but "Freeman and his colleagues have reached a different conclusion" from EEGs, owing to "the averaging that is inherent in measurements of surface potentials." [p. 1820]

Their suggestion implies that the smoothing of pulses by the summation of dendritic potentials degrades an odor specificity that is more clearly seen by recording pulse trains from single neurons. They are correct that odorant specificity in the odor *sensory code* is best read by recording microscopic pulses. However, in the *perceptual code* a macroscopic EEG does not reflect odor but instead the inferred meaning. Owing to spatial divergence and temporal dispersion in the lateral olfactory tract, which differs from the topographic mapping of the olfactory nerve, neurons in olfactory cortex receive bulbar input only after spatial integration, which (Section 3.8) extracts the globally coherent oscillation constructed by the bulb (the percept) and smooths the outputs of sensory-activated neurons (the recept). Neurobiologists can more easily read pulses than EEGs, because they know the odor and not its meaning for the subject, but the olfactory cortex reads the percept in local mean fields carried by bulbar pulse densities, and not the sense data in individual pulses. The utility of oscillations lies in extracting "the bottom line", washing away ("laundering") sense data as having done their job. For this operation to succeed, the array of coupled local mean field generators must share a nonzero, instantaneous frequency (Section 3.8) and phase (Section 3.9, Note 3.10), whether the oscillations are periodic or chaotic (Freeman 1975, 1991a).

3.9 Chaos, randomness, noise: Digital determinism
Chaos is a way of life for some and anathema for others. Its essence came to light with the discovery that some simple differential equations that were thought to have only steady or

periodic solutions can have aperiodic solutions as well, and when they are not periodic (clock-like), they are unpredictable for just that reason. Turning the argument around, when we see irregular activity, we hope to find hidden order and underlying simplicity. An example I have used in lectures is the Tokyo train station. The seemingly random motion of passengers at rush hour is governed by the simple rule of "get to the gate expeditiously without hitting anybody". When a track change is announced, the pattern simply changes. If a bomb explodes, the rule changes to "save yourself", and the activity goes out of control. It is still not random, like the sound of a waterfall or the radioactive decay of a particle, but it exhibits what aficionados call "high dimensional chaos", because it is less orderly than before. Noisy data conform to the law of large numbers, but chaotic data do not (Kaneko 1990), owing to the interactions that reduce the internal degrees of freedom. Chaos is oxymoronically called "deterministic" as distinct from "stochastic" meaning random, because the equations have the same form as Newton's equations, and they give the same solutions for the same initial conditions. This is deceptive. The solutions hold only when the equations are solved digitally, but numerical solutions aren't real. They are *pseudotrajectories* (Hamel et al. 1987) shadowed by an underlying true trajectory.

3.10 Anomalous dispersion: A means of phase locking

An unsolved problem is how near-zero phase lag occurs between oscillations of widely separated neurons (Gray and Singer 1989; Gevins et al. 1989; Eckhorn 1991; Bressler et al. 1993). Phase gradients in the olfactory bulb show that the group velocity of a state transition exceeds wave velocity of synaptic transmission by one or two orders of magnitude, suggesting that broad band synchrony is imposed over wide cortical areas by *anomalous dispersion* (Freeman 1990b). This dissociation is comparable to hitting the end of a metal bar with a hammer and having the sound get to the other end long before the mechanical thrust. It means that synchrony of firing is a macroscopic property that "phase locks" neurons that may appear as pairs in networks. The shape of bulbar phase gradients, a cone in spherical coordinates (Freeman and Baird 1987), suggests that axonal delays impose a limiting velocity onto neuropil, making it a relativistic medium with an *event horizon* analogous to a Minkowski space (Note 2.2).

4.1. Neuropil in the forebrain of salamanders

Herrick (1948) summarized 50 years of analysis of evolution of vertebrate brains in "The Brain of the Tiger Salamander". The forebrain is so primitive, except for hippocampus, it is nearly devoid of cortical laminations and clustering of neurons into nuclei in thalamus and striatum (Roth 1987). Each hemisphere is a single mass of neuropil. Herrick identified the prototypical olfactory bulb, pyriform cortex, hippocampus, striatum, septum, and amygdaloid nucleus by the topology of connections, not by the cytoarchitectures. Some anatomists deny that amphibians have cortex, not even hippocampus (archicortex), and claim that it first appears in laminated neuropil of reptiles and birds as three-layered paleocortex. Six-layered neocortex is found only in mammals. Anatomists have found that the salamander brain is derived from an older, more complex brain by neoteny: arrest of development before maturity, such that an undifferentiated state is retained in adults, giving more flexible adaptation to changing environments. Human faces exemplify neoteny; adult humans more closely resemble infant apes than adult apes.

4.2. Maclean's Triune Brain: Reason *versus* emotion

Evolution of the human brain from its salamander-like origin has taken 400 million years. Maclean has summarized this growth in his concept of "The Triune Brain" (1969). The midbrain and basal ganglia, together with a thin shell of cortex including the hippocampus, comprise "the reptilian brain". Surrounding this core is a ring of cortex and striatum in lower mammals called "paleomammalian" and identified with the limbic system. Overarching the limbic system is the "neomammalian" brain found only in higher primates. Each brain:

> ... has its own peculiar form of subjectivity and its own intelligence, its own sense of time and space and its own memory, motor, and other functions. ... The reptilian brain is fundamental for such genetically constituted forms of behavior as selecting homesites, establishing territory, engaging in various types of display, hunting, homing, mating, breeding, imprinting, forming social hierarchies, and selecting leaders. [1972, pp 8-10]

He emphasizes the rigidity of reptilian behavior, the compulsion to repetition, and the cardinal importance of territory. His surrounding limbic system incorporates parts of all four lobes and the amygdaloid, and it provides mechanisms for the feelings that accompany the "selfish demands of feeding, fighting, and self-preservation". The neomammalian brain so dominates the human brain that the limbic system is difficult to see. It "gets most of its input from the world through the eyes and ears, and it is externally oriented toward manipulations for science, industry, and politics". Maclean says its main task is to control the emotional impulses of paleomammalian brains and the blind territorial ambitions of reptilian brains, so that conflicts might be settled by reason and compromise instead of by bloodshed.

Maclean's theory carries substantial 19th-century baggage. The hierarchical control of lower centers by inhibition from higher centers derives from Hughlings Jackson's (1884) concept of successive levels of control (Section 2.3), which is revealed by "devolution" as deterioration of cortex releases lower centers to autonomy and escape from reason. His treatment of reptiles fails to credit their incredible accomplishments in living on dry land, and deprives them of the prototypic limbic system that they share with fish and salamanders. He has reduced the limbic system in mammals to the generator of emotions instead of intentional behavior, misleading the artificial intelligentsia, who see the main work of neomammalian brains as the elaboration of ideas by intellect, from which the finished products are sent to the paleomammalian brain for attachment of appropriate emotions and values, like bumpers and coats of paint for automobiles on an assembly line. This computational view is encouraged by separating reason from emotion in the dichotomy stemming from Plato (Note 7.3). In this he goes along with the view that rational behavior is "better" than emotional behavior. But reason and its quale, emotion, rise together to heights of musical, poetic, or dramatic composition, and fall together in postconsummatory and postcopulatory torpors. Rational acts can be passionately engaged in or coldly executed with unspeakable consequences, while illogical, destructive acts can be done feverishly or with no apparent care. Both are governed by the unexplained "laws of neuropil" (Section 2.7).

4.3 Engrams, local storage, and Wilder Penfield

The hippocampus or nearby temporal pole are not sites where memory is located. That idea is based on results of electrical stimulation of temporal lobe in patients who were undergoing surgical excision of lesions that were associated with temporal lobe epilepsy. The neurosurgeon Wilder Penfield (1975) reported on 40 of 1132 patients so stimulated, who described episodes of recall like seeing clips from old movies or hearing tapes from forgotten voices and songs. The results, not replicated by other surgeons, have been explained by psychologists (Fischer 1990; Birchmeier-Nussbaumer 1974) as due to prompting of the patients, their desire to please the surgeon, and, in some cases, by induction of an aura presaging onset of an epileptic seizure for which surgery was being done (Ojemann 1986). Despite these detailed explanations of the 3.5% of patients who showed the effect and the failure to reproduce it by others, the report lives on in the popular mind as an established medical "fact". That tenacity tells us more about our need to fit data into prevailing computational models than it does about how brains operate. It is a myth that continues to fuel the endless search for the molecule, modifiable synapse, dendritic spine, nerve cell, or neural netlet in the hippocampus as an address or carrier for each bit of information in "the memory banks".

4.4 Range control in multisensory convergence
Convergence of input from the sensory cortices poses the problem for the entorhinal cortex of limiting the range of input, for which the summed amplitude cannot be predicted. If it's too high, the receiver saturates and blocks; if it's too low, the input pattern is lost in noise (Grossberg 1987). The same problem occurs at the entrance to the olfactory bulb, where the convergence ratio of input to output is 500 to 1. The problem is solved by neurons in the input layer of the bulb, the periglomerular cells (Martinez and Freeman 1984), which take the logarithm of input by a neural mechanism that looks like *presynaptic inhibition* but is not (Freeman 1975, 1993). Similar mechanisms in vision, audition, and touch are responsible for conformance of sensation to the Weber-Fechner power law expressing range compression. At the entrance to the hippocampus there is a layer of neurons, the dentate fascia, which are described as "inhibitory" by Buzsaki et al. (1994), which have synaptic connections and chemistries that are analogous to those of the periglomerular cells, and which may normalize the entorhinal input density and take its logarithm by the same mechanism. This kind of "janitorial" operation is overlooked by most neural networkers, but it becomes obvious in the perspective of neurodynamics.

4.5 Sensory neglect, body image, and phantom limb

I first encountered sensory neglect in a patient recovering from a stroke damaging her right hemisphere. Sitting up for the first time, she asked for cosmetics, then carefully brushed her hair and applied lipstick and blush to her face only on her right side. When I handed her a mirror, she took it with her right hand, looked at her reflection, and asked, "What's wrong?" For weeks, the left side of her body belonged to someone else. This "neglect" syndrome is the obverse of the "phantom limb", which is the persisting perception of a limb that has been lost. Most patients suffer paralysis of the phantom, but one of my patients took delight in waving his phantom arm through his chest and head. Related, though differing, phenomena are found following damage to the occipital and temporal lobes, showing that the operation of spatial orientation and the localization of events in personal space is not restricted to the limbic system. Limbic primacy is shown by experiments in mammals, in which the neocortex is surgically removed, leaving the paleocortex intact. Behavior is severely impaired, but it is still intentional.

4.6 Synesthesia: the complexity of cerebral cortex

Multimodal convergence as one factor in perception offers a basis for future exploration of synesthesia, in which perceptions are mixed across modes, colors being heard, odors being felt, and so on. Cytowic (1989) sees synesthetes as "cognitive fossils" manifesting primitive, undiscriminating perception that may hold for all lower mammals. "The neocortical mantle is not a higher rung on the ladder, completely suppressing everything below it, but is built as a detour in the ladder, interposed between brain stem and limbic brain" [p. 21]. "The most important type is idiopathic synesthesia, the involuntary stimulus-induced union of the senses, which is present in childhood and persists for a lifetime. The remaining types are simple synesthesia (which does not necessarily require a deafferented sensory field), epileptic synesthesia, and induced synesthesia (both electrically induced and drug induced)." (p. 325) There is a barrier to exploring synesthesia in animals. We can't tell what they feel (Section 7.1).

The refinement of perception may depend on size of the cerebral hemisphere. Studies of vertebrates suggest that the size of a "patch" of cortex capable of spatially coherent oscillation is up to 2 centimeters across. This far exceeds the hemisphere of a salamander, suggesting that its perception is synesthetic. In round numbers a brain of a rabbit might be a "mosaic" (Calvin 1994) of 10 patches, that of a dog 100 patches, and that of a human 1,000 patches, with similar increases in power of discrimination. The EEG data in this book come from patches. The dynamics of assemblies of patches is unknown, and it can be expected to require development of a higher level of macroscopic organization than KIII sets (Freeman 1975, 1992a).

4.7 "Deep structure": Chomsky *versus* Piaget

Linguists, notably Chomsky (1975), have identified homologous syntactical structures in all of the world's 3,000 languages and inferred that a neural "deep structure" is built in accordance with genetic instructions into human forebrains. Comparable syntaxes have been found in uses of channels without speech, as in American Sign Language, storytelling with body movements and dances, whistling languages in the Pyrénées and the Canary Islands, and drum-talk in central Africa based in complex rhythms and tonal patterns. Neural structures must exist within pairs of brains that have sufficient similarity to support communication, and the experimental evidence gathered by Piaget (Inhelder and Piaget 1955) shows that the similarity grows in stages during the socialization of children. The concept of "deep structure" as an innate set of logical rules that precede growth and are selected for (Section 1.4) resembles the "group selection" of synaptic networks in Edelman's (1987) treatment of "the brain" as if it were an immune system. "Deep structure" and "group selection" have not been useful concepts for neurobiologists in their studies of brain function.

5.1 Three failed approaches to building brains

These are symbol manipulation according to rules (Craik 1943; Turing 1950; Fodor 1981), neurocomputation using information theory, numbers, and neural networks (Lucky 1989; Schwartz 1990; Churchland and Sejnowski 1992; Bower and Beeman 1994), and analog systems (Ashby 1960; Walter 1963; Pellionisz and Llinàs 1985; Eisenberg et al. 1989). Since discreteness is found at both microscopic and macroscopic levels of brain function, that property does not distinguish brains from digital computers and certainly not from analog computers (Section 2.6). In fact, the threshold property of transistors is determined by equations that are very similar to the Hodgkin-Huxley equations for the nerve action potential. The microscopic all-or-none ("bi-stable") property of pulses (referring to alternation between two attractors) is the basis for the cortical state transition, because the bi-stable EEG burst is the macroscopic equivalent of the microscopic bi-stable action potential (Note 3.4). What is lacking in computers is the sequence of macroscopic state transitions mediated by microscopic pulses in populations.

5.2 Stabilizing aperiodic cortical neural activity
Brains are not stable in this way, except in Parkinson's disease (Sacks 1985), in which rigidity and tremor (fixed point and limit cycle attractors) replace physiological tremor (chaotic attractor). The lock-down of digital pseudotrajectories into limit cycles is avoided in computers by adding noise in the form of pseudorandom numbers. Perhaps the pseudorandomness of pulse trains of cortical neurons maintains robust brain chaos. Stability of chaotic orbits is further enhanced by distributions of transmission times within populations (Freeman 1975, 1992a), which act as low pass filters to reduce the noise inherent in the otherwise overwhelming preponderance of irrelevant microscopic fluctuations (Prigogine 1980).

5.3 Definitions of thought: Heidegger *versus* Piaget
... the traditional doctrine of thinking bears the curious title 'logic'. ... The answer to the question 'What is called thinking?' cannot be settled, now or ever. If we proceed to the encounter of what is here in question, the calling, the question becomes in fact only more problematical. When we are questioning within this problematic, we are thinking. Thinking itself is a way. We respond to the way only by remaining underway. ... This movement is what allows the way to come forward. That the way of thought is of this nature is part of the precursoriness of thinking, and this precursoriness in turn depends on an enigmatic solitude. ... The things which we conceive and assert to be the results of thinking are the misunderstandings to which thinking inevitably falls victim. Only they achieve publication as alleged thought, and occupy those who do not think. [p. 68]

Heidegger (1968) captures here the solitary nature of thought; its fleeting, unreproducible trajectory of Neuroactivity; its illogicality; the poverty of its outcome in the reduction of its content to words for representation; the frustration about that poverty; and the circularity of a mind thinking about its own operations without external reference points. Educational and developmental studies contrastingly offer rich introspective representations that might be related to Neuroactivity and its dynamics, as in this example from Inhelder and Piaget (1958):

> In sum, far from being a source of fully elaborated "innate ideas," the maturation of the nervous system can do no more than determine the totality of possibilities and impossibilities at a given stage. A particular social environment remains indispensable for the realization of these possibilities. It follows that their realization can be accelerated or retarded as a function of cultural and educational conditions. This is why the growth of formal thinking as well as the age at which adolescence itself occurs - *i.e.*, the age at which the individual starts to assume adult roles - remain dependent on social as much as and more than on neurological factors. [p. 337]

The additional steps in making the connection to the neurology are the systematic analysis of the dynamics of neurohormonal control systems, as they evolve from birth through childhood and adolescence to maturity, and an investigation of the basis of logic in the dynamics of neuropil. Both fields are wide open to further exploration and discovery.

6.1 An example of the value of music in society

Africans brought to the Caribbean and South America in slavery were allowed to keep their drums and songs in religious ceremonies. Verger (1954) illustrated close parallels between beliefs and practices in West Africa, Haiti and Brazil. Africans brought to North America were denied use of drums after the Stono slave rebellion in South Carolina in 1740, because the slave masters were frightened by a mode of communication and organizing that was beyond their understanding and control (Wilson 1992). The law stated: use a drum in public, lose a hand. An exception was New Orleans, where slaves were permitted to make music once a week, which some ethnomusicologists (e.g., Stearns 1958) think was decisive in the emergence of jazz there. The spiritual need for expression in rhythmic movements of communal drumming and dancing was so powerful, that some people used water barrels and cooking pots with skins stretched over the openings, easily brought out from hiding, while others developed their syncopated rhythms in gospel singing, chanting, clapping, and drumming with the feet: tap dancing. The break in continuity of cultural transmission led to marked differences between black communities in North and South America in modes of socializing, owing to suppression of a critical means for instilling cultural understanding through song and dance.

7.1 A complement to the Turing test: Play games
Complementary to the Turing (1950) test for intelligence is a test for intentionality by an ability to play games (Brown 1994). While exploring the grounds of a marine biological station in Hawaii I saw a concrete tank with iron bars enclosing its top. A tentacle with suction cups thrust upwardly, waving languidly. I touched it with my right finger and we entwined. Another tentacle emerged and connected with my left finger. In a gentle tug of war I leaned over to look through the bars into the exotic eyes of a 4-meter octopus. A jet of seawater gushed in my face, and I retreated to clean my glasses. Next morning again I enjoyed wrestling accompanied by a face wash, after removing my glasses. It is sad that machos in SCUBA gear make sport of ripping these shy animals from their Puget Sound dens.

7.2. Kinesthetics, 4-D geometry, and virtual reality
Computer graphics and virtual reality might make it possible for humans to move in four dimensions, so a new way may open to educate ourselves beyond the current limits of our perception. Otto Rössler has described moving through a four-dimensional cube as equivalent to exploring a house with eight rooms, and this is merely the simplest Euclidean form to practice with. There can be no perceived delays in computing the 2-D images as the hacker flies through 4-D structures, because the changes in visual responses with movements of the flight controls must come within the time frames humans are adapted to (Freeman 1988). It might be like flying an aircraft with a 6-D spaceball in each hand. Adequate commercial software is not yet available to support this exploration, but it will be written when enough people catch on that this new frontier waits on their PC's.

7.3 The madness of love: Shakespeare *versus* Plato
History and literature are filled with examples of the disastrous destabilization of individuals and societies by intoxication with love, none more compelling than Shakepeare's telling of the fall of Troy engendered by Paris' theft of Helen,

which he mirrored in the love affair of "Troilus and Cressida". The philosopher-king, Hector, while debating the possible return of Helen in exchange for peace (Act II, Scene ii), declaimed:

'Tis mad idolatry
To make the service greater than the god;
And the will dotes that is inclineable
To what infectiously itself affects,
Without some image of the affected merit.

He meant it was insane to sacrifice real advantage for mere honor, and to let desire lead to self-destruction with nothing gained in return. But the hothead Troilus was beyond reason, and he writhed (Act III, Scene ii) while waiting for Cressida:

I am giddy, expectation whirls me round.
The imaginary relish is so sweet
That it enchants my sense.

Plato, in "Phaedrus", would perhaps have agreed that love is a malady, "... if it were an invariable truth that madness is an evil, but in reality, the greatest blessings come by way of madness, indeed of madness that is heaven sent" [~400 BC/1961 p. 491]. The voice of Socrates goes on to describe four kinds of madness: the gift of prophecy; the gift of healing; lyric poetry; and love, which is "... a gift of the gods, fraught with the highest bliss. And our proof assuredly will prevail with the wise, though not with the learned." His proof invokes "the union of powers in a team of winged steeds and their winged charioteer", the soul who, in trying to merge divine reason and besotted wickedness, crashes and loses his wings. "Mark therefore ... the fourth sort of madness - to wit, that this is the best of all forms of divine possession; ... and when he that loves beauty is touched by such madness he is called a lover. Such a one, as soon as he beholds the beauty of this world, is reminded of true beauty, and his wings begin to grow; then is he fain to lift his wings and fly upward; yet he has not the power, but inasmuch as he gazes upward like a bird, and cares nothing for the world beneath, men charge it upon him that he is demented" [p. 496] What follows concerning divine transports of humans in love (eros, friendship) is unsurpassed in clarity and beauty. We don't understand the chaotic processes of reason, emotion, and despair in isolation, but we do have wings by which to cross the solipsistic gulf.

References

Abbot BC (1960) Heat production in nerve and electric organ. Journal of General Physiology 43: 119-127. [160]
Abeles M (1991) Corticonics: Neural Circuits of the Cerebral Cortex. Cambridge UK: Cambridge University Press. [55, 165]
Abraham FD, Abraham RH, Shaw CD & Garfinkel A (1990) A Visual Introduction to Dynamical Systems Theory for Psychology. Santa Cruz CA: Aerial Press. [25, 42, 63, 65]
Adrian ED (1950) The electrical activity of the mammalian olfactory bulb. Electroencephalography and clinical Neurophysiology 2: 377-388. [39, 58]
Adrian ED, Bremer F & Jasper HH (1954) Brain Mechanisms and Consciousness. Oxford UK: Blackwell. [13]
Aertsen A, Erb M & Palm G (1994) Dynamics of functional coupling in the cerebral cortex. Physica D 75: 103-128. [165]
Aghajanian GK (1994) Serotonin and the action of LSD in the brain. Psychiatric Annals 24: 137-141. [151]
Alkon D (1992) Memory's Voice: Deciphering the Mind-Brain Code. New York: HarperCollins. [21, 36, 113]
Amari S (1977) Neural theory of association and concept formation. Biological Cybernetics 26: 175-185. [116, 159]
Amit DJ (1989) Modeling Brain Function: The World of Attractor Neural Networks. Cambridge UK: Cambridge University Press. [64, 164-165]
Andersen P & Andersson SA (1968) Physiological Basis of the Alpha Rhythm. New York: Appleton-Century-Crofts. [88]
Anderson JA & Rosenfeld E (1988) Neurocomputing: Foundations of Research. Cambridge MA: MIT Press. [116]
Argiolas A (1992) Oxytocin stimulation of penile erection. In CA Pedersen, JD Caldwell, GF Jirikowski & TR Insel (Eds.), Oxytocin in Maternal, Sexual, and Social Behaviors. Annals of the New York Academy of Sciences, Vol. 652: 194-211. [121]
Arletti R, Benelli AA & Bertolini A (1992) Oxytocin involvement in male and female sexual behavior. In CA Pedersen, JD Caldwell, GF Jirikowski & TR Insel (Eds.), Oxytocin in Maternal, Sexual, and Social Behaviors. Annals of the New York Academy of Sciences, Vol. 652: 180-193. [121]
Ashby WR (1960) Design for a Brain: The Origin of Adaptive Behavior (2nd ed.). New York: Wiley. [116, 172]

Barfield O (1965) Saving the Appearances: A Study in Idolatry. New York: Harcourt Brace. [106, 142, 162]

Barlow HB (1972) Single units and sensation: A neuron doctrine for perceptual psychology? Perception 1: 371-394. [35]

Barlow JS (1993) The Electroencephalogram: Its Patterns and Origins. Cambridge MA: MIT Press. [22, 56]

Barrie JM, Freeman WJ & Lenhart M (1994) Cross-modality cortical processing: Spatiotemporal patterns in olfactory, visual, auditory and somatic EEGs in perception by trained rabbits. Society for Neuroscience Abstracts 414.10. [2, 95, 99]

Bartlett F (1932) Remembering: A Study in Experimental and Social Psychology. London UK: Cambridge University Press. [23]

Basar E (1980) EEG Brain Dynamics: Relation Between EEG and Brain Evoked Potentials. Amsterdam: Elsevier. [44]

Basti G & Perrone A (1993) Time and non-locality: From logical to metaphysical being. An Aristotelian-Thomistic approach. In GV Coyne & K Schmitz-Moorman (Eds.), Studies in Science and Theology: Part 1. Origins, Time and Complexity (pp. 31-74). Rome: Labor et Fides. [15]

Bem DJ & Honorton C (1994) Does psi exist? Replicable evidence for an anomalous process of information transfer. Psychological Bulletin 115: 4-18, 25-27. [156]

Bergson H (1907/1944) Creative Evolution. New York: Random House. [31, 37, 38]

Beritashvili IS (1971) Vertebrate memory (JS Barlow & WT Liberson, Trans.). New York: Plenum. [73]

Berkowitz CG & Tschirgi RD (1988) The biological foundations of space and the evolution of spatial dimension. Journal of Social and Biological Structure 11: 323-335. [69]

Birbaumer N, Lutzenberger W, Rau H, Mayer-Kress G, Choi I, Braun C (in press) Perception of Music and Dimensional Complexity of Brain Activity. International Journal of Bifurcation and Chaos. [133]

Birchmeier-Nussbaumer AK (1974) Die Penfieldschen Hirnreizexperimente im Lichte einer Sprachanalyse von zugehörigen Patientenaussagen. Schweizer Archiv fur Neurochirurgie und Psychiatrie 114: 37-56. [138, 170]

Bizzi E, Hogan N, Mussa-Ivaldi FA, Giszter S (1992) Does the nervous system use equilibrium-point control to guide single and multiple joint movements? Behavioral and Brain Sciences 15: 603-613. [63, 85]

Bloom FE & Lazerson A (1988) Brain, Mind, and Behavior (2nd ed.). New York: Freeman. [78]

Blum L, Shub M & Smale S (1989) On a theory of computation and complexity over the real numbers. Bulletin of the American Mathematical Society 21: 1-46. [103]

Bower JM & Beeman D (1994) The Book of GENESIS: Exploring Realistic Neural Models with the GEneral NEural SImulation System. New York: TELOS/Springer. [45, 172]

Braitenberg V & Schüz A (1991) Anatomy of the Cortex: Statistics and Geometry. Berlin: Springer. [48]

Breasted JH (1933) The Dawn of Conscience. New York, Scribner's. [7, 10]

Bressler SL (1988) Changes in electrical activity of rabbit olfactory bulb and cortex to conditioned odor stimulation. Journal of Neurophysiology 102: 740-747. [60]

Bressler SL, Coppola R, Nakamura R (1993) Episodic multiregional cortical coherence at multiple frequencies during visual task performance. Nature 366: 153-156. [99, 167]

Bressler SL, Freeman WJ (1980) Frequency analysis of olfactory system EEG in cat, rabbit and rat. EEG and clinical Neurophysiology 50: 19-24. [57, 97]

Brillinger DR (1981) Time series: Data analysis and theory. San Francisco: Holden-Day. [159]

Brothers L (1990) The Social Brain: A project for integrating primate behavior and neurophysiology in a new domain. Concepts in Neuroscience 1: 27-51. [1, 147]

Brown J (1977) Mind, Brain and Consciousness: The Neuropsychology of Cognition. New York: Academic Press. [42, 147]

Bullock TH & Horridge GA (1965) Structure and Function in the Nervous Systems of Invertebrates. San Francisco: Freeman WH. [7, 63, 69]

Brown SL (1994) Animals at play. National Geographic 186: 2-34. [175]

Bulsara A & Maren AJ (1993) Coupled neural-dendritic processes. In KH Pribram (Ed.), Rethinking Neural Networks. (pp. 95-118). Hillsdale NJ: Lawrence Erlbaum Associates. [160]

Burns BD (1958) Mammalian Cerebral Cortex. Baltimore: Williams & Wilkins. [165]

Buzsaki G, Bragin A, Nadasdy Z & Jando G (1994) The hippocampal dentate gyrus is primarily an inhibitory structure. Society for Neuroscience Abstracts 1: 148.17. [170]

Caldwell JD (1992) Central oxytocin and female sexual behavior. In CA Pedersen, JD Caldwell, GF Jirikowski & TR Insel (Eds.),

Oxytocin in Maternal, Sexual, and Social Behaviors. Annals of the New York Academy of Sciences, Vol. 652: 166-179. [121]

Calvin WH & Ojemann GA (1994) Conversations with Neil's Brain. Reading MA: Addison-Wesley. [25]

Calvin WH (1994) The emergence of intelligence. Scientific American 271: 79-85. [182]

Carmichael MS, Warburton VL, Dixen J & Davidson JM (1994) Relationships among cardiovascular, muscular, and oxytocin responses during human sexual activity. Archives of Sexual Behavior 23: 59-79. [122]

Chomsky N (1975) Reflections of Language. New York: Pantheon. [18, 103, 172]

Churchland PS (1986) Neurophilosophy: Toward a Unified Science of the Mind-Brain. Cambridge MA: MIT Press. [107, 159]

Churchland PS & Sejnowski TJ (1992) The Computational Brain. Cambridge MA: MIT/Bradford. [172]

Clarke E & O'Malley CD (1968) The Human Brain and Spinal Cord: A Historical Study Illustrated by Writings From Antiquity to the 20th Century. Los Angeles: University of California. [15]

Cleckley HM (1955) The Mask of Sanity. St. Louis MO: Mosby [128]

Clynes M (Ed.) (1982) Music, Mind and Brain: The Neuropsychology of Music. New York: Plenum. [130, 133]

Collins JJ & Stewart IN (1993) Coupled nonlinear oscillators and the symmetries of animals gaits. Journal of Nonlinear Science 3: 349-392. [63]

Craik K (1943) The Nature of Explanation. Cambridge UK: Cambridge University Press. [172]

Crick F (1984) Function of the thalamic reticular complex: The searchlight hypothesis. Proceedings of the National Academy of Sciences (USA) 81: 4586-4590. [88]

Crick F (1994) The Astonishing Hypothesis: The Scientific Search for the Soul. New York: Scribner's. [18]

Critchley M (1979) The Divine Banquet of the Brain. New York: Raven. [91-92, 154]

Cytowic RE (1989) Synesthesia. New York: Springer. [171]

Damasio AR (1994) Descartes' Error: Emotion, Reason, and the Human Brain. New York: Grosset/Putnam. [25]

Darwin C (1872) The Expression of Emotion in Man and Animals. London: Murray. [13, 91]

Dempsey EW & Morison RS (1942) The electrical activity of thalamocortical relay systems. American Journal of Physiology 138: 283-289. [88]

Dennett DH (1991) Consciousness Explained. Boston: Little, Brown. [13, 18, 93]
Derrida J (1972/1988) Limited Inc. Evanston IL: Northwestern University Press. [109]
Descartes R (1641/1946) Discours de la Methode. Montreal: Variete. [3, 28, 38, 140, 157]
Dewey J (1896) The reflex arc concept in psychology. Psychological Review 3: 357-370. [23, 30, 41]
Dewey J (1914) Psychological doctrine in philosophical teaching. Journal of Philosophy 11: 505-512. [23]
Dreyfus HL (1979) What Computers Can't Do: The Limits of Artificial Intelligence. New York: Harper Colophon. [12]
Dreyfus HL (1991) Being-in-the-World: A Commentary on Heidegger's Being and Time. Cambridge MA: MIT Press. [12]
Dreyfus HL & Dreyfus SE (1986) Mind Over Machine. New York: The Free Press. [12]
Durkheim E (1915/1926) The Elementary Forms of the Religious Life: A Study in Religious Sociology (JW Swain, Trans.). New York: Macmillan. [129]

Eccles JC (1994) How the Self Controls Its Brain. Berlin: Springer. [42, 82, 162]
Eckhorn R (1991) Principles of global visual processing of local features can be investigated with parallel single-cell- and group-recordings from the visual cortex. In A Aertsen & V Braitenberg (Eds.), Information Processing in the Cortex (pp. 385-420). Berlin: Springer. [61, 165, 167]
Eco U (1992) Interpretation and Overinterpretation. Cambridge UK: Cambridge University Press. [108]
Edelman GM (1987) Neural Darwinism: The Theory of Neuronal Group Selection. New York: Basic Books. [20, 36, 172]
Eisenberg J, Freeman WJ & Burke B (1989) Hardware architecture of a neural network model simulating pattern recognition by the olfactory bulb. Neural Networks 2: 315-325. [172]
Eliot TS (1922/1964) The Waste Land. V. What the Thunder Said. In Selected Poems. New York: Harcourt Brace. [155]
Érdi P, Grobler T, Barna G & Kaski K (1993) Dynamics of the olfactory bulb: Bifurcations, learning, and memory. Biological Cybernetics 69: 57-66. [165]

Fischer R (1971) A cartography of the ecstatic and meditative states. Science 174: 897-904. [11, 81, 151, 153]

Fischer R (1990) Why the mind is not in the head but in society's connectionist network. Diogenes 151: 1-28. [1, 147, 169]
Fischer R (1994) Reply to Charles D. Kaplan. Social Neuroscience Bulletin 7: 20. [194]
Fisher HE (1992) Anatomy of Love: The Natural History of Monogamy, Adultery, and Divorce. New York, Norton. [123]
Fodor JA (1990) A Theory of Content. Cambridge MA: MIT Press. [103, 172]
Fort J (1969) The Pleasure Seekers: The Drug Crisis, Youth and Society. New York: Grove Press. [132]
Foster M & Sherrington CS (1897) A Textbook of Physiology: The Central Nervous System (7th ed.). London: Macmillan. [33]
Foucault M (1976/1980) The History of Sexuality: Vol. 1. An Intro-duction (R Hurley, Trans.). New York: Random House. [51]
Frazer JG (1890/1949) The Golden Bough: A Study in Magic and Religion. New York: Macmillan. [132]
Freeman WJ (1967) Analysis of function of cerebral cortex by use of control systems theory. Logistics Review 3: 5-40. [163]
Freeman WJ (1975) Mass Action in the Nervous System. New York: Academic Press. [43, 44, 55-57, 61, 161-166, 170-173]
Freeman WJ (1979) Nonlinear gain mediating cortical stimulus-response relations. Biological Cybernetics 33: 237-247. [163]
Freeman WJ (1984) La fisiologia de las imagenes mentales. Salud Mentale 7: 3-8. [76]
Freeman WJ (1987a) Simulation of chaotic EEG patterns with a dynamic model of the olfactory system. Biological Cybernetics 56: 139-150. [61, 164]
Freeman WJ (1987b) Techniques used in the search for the physiological basis of the EEG. In A Gevins & A Remond (Eds.), Handbook of Electroencephalography and clinical Neurophysiology (pp. 583-664). Amsterdam: Elsevier. [58-60]
Freeman WJ (1988) Analysis of strange attractors in EEGs with kinesthetics and computer graphics in 4-D. In E Basar & H Stowell (Eds.), Dynamics of Sensory and Cognitive Processing in the Brain (pp. 512-520). Berlin: Springer. [176]
Freeman WJ (1990a) On the fallacy of assigning an origin to consciousness. In ER John (Ed.), Machinery of the Mind (pp. 14-26). Boston MA: Birkhauser. [76, 81, 86, 140]
Freeman WJ (1990b) On the problem of anomalous dispersion in chaoto-chaotic phase transitions of neural masses, and its significance for the management of perceptual information in brains. In Haken H, Stadler M (eds.) Synergetics of Cognition. Berlin, Springer-Verlag, Vol. 45: 126-143. [167]

Freeman WJ (1991a) The physiology of perception. Scientific American 264: 78-85. [59, 166]
Freeman WJ (1991b) Nonlinear dynamics in olfactory information processing. In JL Davis & H Eichenbaum (Eds.), Olfaction (pp. 225-249). Cambridge MA: MIT/Bradford. [60]
Freeman WJ (1992a) Tutorial in Neurobiology. International Journal of Bifurcation and Chaos 2: 451-482. [42, 56, 65, 163, 166, 173]
Freeman WJ (1992b) Predictions in neocortical dynamics that are posed by studies in paleocortex. In Basar E, Bullock TH (Eds.) Induced Rhythms of the Brain. Cambridge MA, Birkhaeuser. pp 183-199. [61, 165]
Freeman WJ (1993) Valium, histamine, and neural networks. Biological Psychiatry 34: 1-2. [71, 151]
Freeman WJ & Baird B (1987) Relation of olfactory EEG to behavior: Spatial analysis. Behavioral Neuroscience 101: 393-408. [62, 167]
Freeman WJ & Barrie JM (1994) Chaotic oscillations and the genesis of meaning in cerebral cortex. In G Buzsaki, R Llinàs, W Singer, A Berthoz & Y Christen (Eds.), Temporal Coding in the Brain (pp. 13-37). Berlin: Springer. [2, 61, 94, 98]
Freeman WJ & Grajski KA (1987) Relation of olfactory EEG to behavior: Factor analysis. Behavioral Neuroscience 101:766-777. [97]
Freeman WJ & Schneider W (1982) Changes in spatial patterns of rabbit olfactory EEG with conditioning to odors. Psychophysiology 19: 44-56. [1, 57]
Freeman WJ & van Dijk B (1987) Spatial patterns of visual cortical fast EEG during conditioned reflex in a rhesus monkey. Brain Research 422: 267-276. [61]
Freeman WJ & Viana Di Prisco G (1986) Relation of olfactory EEG to behavior: Time series analysis. Behavioral Neuroscience 100: 753-763. [94]
Freeman W & Watts JW (1950) Psychosurgery, in the treatment of mental disorders and intractable pain, 2d ed. Springfield, Ill., Charles C. Thomas [80].
Freud S (1895/1954) The project of a scientific psychology. In M Bonaparte, A Freud & E Kris (Eds.), The Origins of Psycho-Analysis (E Mosbacher & J Strachey, Trans.). New York: Basic Books. [11, 32, 112]
Freud S (1908/1963) "Civilized" sexual morality and modern nervousness. In EB Herford & EC Mayne (Trans.) Sexuality and the Psychology of Love (pp. 1-40). New York: Collier. [111]

Fulton JF (1966) Selected Readings in the History of Physiology. Wilson (Ed.). Springfield IL: Thomas. [29]
Fuster JM (1994) Memory in the Cerebral Cortex. Cambridge MA: MIT/Bradford. [80]

Gastaut H (1964/1967) Les activités éléctriques cérébrales spontanées et évoquées chez l'homme. Colloque de Marseille (13th). Paris, Gauthier-Villars. [88]
Georgeopolis AP, Schwartz AB & Kettner RE (1986) Neural population coding of movement direction. Science 233: 1416-1419. [163, 165]
Gevins A, Bressler SL, Morgan N, Cutillo B, White R, Greer D & Illes J (1989) Event-related covariances during a bimanual visuomotor task. Electroencephalography and clinical Neurophysiology 74: 58-75, 147-160. [22, 80, 138]
Gibson JJ (1979) The Ecological Approach to Visual Perception. Boston: Houghton Mifflin. [35, 159]
Glass L & Mackey MC (1988) From Clocks to Chaos: The Rhythms of Life. Princeton NJ: Princeton University Press. [25]
Globus GG (1992) Toward a noncomputational cognitive neuro-science. Journal of Cognitive Neuroscience 4: 299-310. [36]
Goldbart S & Wallin D (1994) Mapping the Terrain of the Heart: The Six Capacities That Guide the Journey of Love. New York: Addison-Wesley. [123]
Goldstein K & Gelb A (1939) The Organism: A Holistic Approach to Biology Derived From Pathological Data in Man. New York: American Book. [15, 30]
Gorman J (1989) The Man With No Endorphins, and Other Reflections on Science. New York: Penguin. [119]
Gould SJ (1987) Time's Arrow, Time's Cycle: Myth and Metaphor in the Discovery of Geological Time. Cambridge MA: Harvard University Press. [52, 100]
Granger R, Staubli U, Ambros-Ingerson J & Lynch G (1991) Specific behavioral predictions from simulations of the olfactory system. In JL Davis & H Eichenbaum (Eds.), Olfaction (pp. 251-264). Cambridge MA: MIT/Bradford. [166]
Grassberger P & Procaccia I (1983) Measuring the strangeness of strange attractors. Physica D 9: 189-205. [65, 162]
Graves R (1948) White Goddess. N. Y.: Vintage Books. [125, 132]
Gray CM, Freeman WJ & Skinner JE (1986) Chemical dependencies of learning in the rabbit olfactory bulb. Behavioral Neuroscience 100: 585-596. [119, 165]

Gray CM & Singer W (1989) Stimulus-specific neuronal oscillations in orientation columns of cat visual cortex. Proceedings of the National Academy of Sciences (USA) 86: 1698-1702. [55, 61]

Gray CM & Skinner JE (1988) Centrifugal regulation of neuronal activity in the olfactory bulb of the waking rabbit as revealed by reversible cryogenic blockade. Experimental Brain Research 69: 378-386. [164]

Grene M (1948) Dreadful Freedom: A Critique of Existentialism. Chicago IL: University of Chicago Press. [140]

Griffin D (1992) Animal Minds. Chicago IL: University of Chicago Press. [7, 90]

Grillner S, Wallén P & Viana Di Prisco G (1990) Cellular network underlying locomotion in a lower vertebrate model. Cold Spring Harbor Symposia on Quantitative Biology 55: 779-789. [63]

Grossberg S (1987) The Adaptive Brain. Amsterdam: Elsevier. [165, 170]

Haberly LB & Bower JM (1989) Olfactory cortex: Model circuit for study of associative memory. Trends in Neuroscience 12: 258-264. [165]

Haken H (1983) Synergetics: An Introduction. Berlin: Springer. [42, 49, 85, 138]

Hamel SM, Yorke JA & Grebogi C (1987) Do numerical orbits of chaotic dynamical processes represent true orbits? Journal of Complexity 3: 136-145. [105, 167]

Hamer D & Copeland P (1994) The Science of Desire: The Search for the Gay Gene and the Biology of Behavior. New York: Simon & Schuster. [22, 143]

Hameroff SR (1987) Ultimate Computing: Biomolecular Consciousness and Nanotechnology. Amsterdam: North-Holland. [38]

Hardcastle VG (1994) Psychology's binding problem and possible neurobiological solutions. Journal of Consciousness Studies 1: 66-90. [163]

Hayflick L (1994) How and Why We Age. New York: Ballantine. [109]

Hebb DO (1949) The Organization of Behavior. New York: Wiley. [34, 116]

Heidegger M (1968) What is Called Thinking? (JG Gray, Trans.). New York: Harper & Row. [173]

Heidegger M (1982) Basic Problems of Phenomenology (A Hofstadter, Trans.). Bloomington: Indiana University Press. [17]

Heimer L (1969) The secondary olfactory connections in mammals, reptiles and sharks. Annals of the New York Academy of Sciences 67: 129-146. [61]

Helmholtz H von (1879/1925) Treatise on Physiological Optics: Vol. 3. The Perceptions of Vision (JPC Southall, Trans.). Rochester NY: Optical Society of America. [31, 84-85]

Herbert N (1993) Elemental Minds: Human Consciousness and the New Physics. New York: Dutton. [13, 36, 41, 138, 156]

Herrick CJ (1926) Brains of Rats and Men. Chicago IL: University of Chicago Press. [11, 69]

Herrick CJ (1948) The Brain of the Tiger Salamander. Chicago IL: University of Chicago Press. [73, 77-79, 167]

Herrnstein RJ & Murray C (1994) The Bell Curve. New York: The Free Press. [142]

Hess WR (1957) The Functional Organization of the Diencephalon. JR Hughes (Ed.). New York: Grune & Stratton. [88]

Hobson JA (1994) The Chemistry of Conscious States: How the Brain Changes Its Mind. New York: Little, Brown. [78, 127]

Hopfield JJ (1982) Neuronal networks and physical systems with emergent collective computational abilities. Proceedings of the National Academy of Sciences 81: 3058-3092. [116]

Hoyle F (1957) The Black Cloud. New York: Harper & Row. [12]

Hubel DH & Wiesel TN (1962) Receptive fields, binocular interaction and functional architectures of the cat's visual cortex. Journal of Physiology 160: 106-154. [13, 54]

Hume D (1739) Treatise on Human Nature. London: J Noon. [144]

Huxley A (1954) The Doors of Perception. Middlesex UK: Penguin. [152]

Hyman R (1994) Anomaly or artefact? Comments on Bem and Honorton. Psychological Bulletin 115: 19-24. [156]

Inhelder B & Piaget J (1955/1958) The Growth of Logical Thinking From Childhood to Adolescence (A Parsons & S Milgram, Trans.). New York: Basic Books. [147, 172-174]

Insel TR (1992) Oxytocin: A neuropeptide for affiliation. Evidence from behavioral, receptor autoradiographic, and comparative studies. Psychoneuroendocrinology 17: 3-35. [122-123, 129]

Jackson JH (1884/1958) Evolution and dissolution of the nervous system: Lecture III. (J Taylor, Ed.), Selected Writings. New York: Basic Books. [13, 20, 32, 168]

James W (1890) The Principles of Psychology. New York: Holt. [10, 136, 156]

Jaynes J (1976) The Origin of Consciousness in the Breakdown of the Bicameral Mind. Boston MA: Houghton Mifflin. [7]

Kalivas PW & Barnes CD (1993) Limbic Motor Circuits and Neuropsychiatry. Boca Raton FL: CRC Press. [76]
Kandel ER, Schwartz JH & Jessel TM (1993) Principles of Neural Science (3rd ed.). New York: Elsevier. [84, 119, 162]
Kaneko K (1990) Globally coupled chaos violates the law of large numbers but not the central-limit theorem. Physical Review Letters 65: 1391-1394. [167]
Kant I (1781/1974) Kritik der reinen Vernunft (W von Weischedel, Ed.). Frankfurt am Main: Suhrkamp Verlag. [8, 11, 17, 107]
Kauer JS (1987) Coding in the olfactory system. In TE Finger & WL Silver (Eds.), Neurobiology of Taste and Smell (pp. 205-232). New York: Wiley. [57]
Kay L (1994) Distribution of gamma and beta oscillations in olfactory and limbic structures during olfactory perception in rats: Evidence for reafference. Proceedings of the World Conference on Neural Networks WCNN'94 2: 675-680. [86]
Kay LM &Freeman WJ (1994) Coherence of gamma oscillations throughout olfactory and limbic brain structures in rats. Society of Neuroscience Abstracts 144.3. [86]
Kelso JAS, Mandell AJ & Shlesinger MF (1988) Dynamic Patterns in Complex Systems. Singapore: World Scientific. [63]
Kendrick KM, Levy F & Keverne EB (1992) Changes in the sensory processing of olfactory signals induced by birth in sheep. Science 256: 833-836. [121]
Kirkpatrick B (1994) Psychiatric disease and the neurobiology of behavior. Biological Psychiatry 36: 501-502. [76]
Klinger E (1978) Dimensions of thought and imagery in normal waking states. Journal of Altered States of Consciousness 4: 97-113. [138]
Klopf H (1982) The Hedonistic Neuron: A Theory of Memory, Learning, and Intelligence. Washington DC: Hemisphere. [41]
Koestler A (1950) The God That Failed: Six Studies in Communism. London: Hamish Hamilton. [124]
Koffka K (1935) Principles of Gestalt Psychology. New York: Harcourt Brace. [33]
Köhler W (1940) Dynamics in Psychology. New York: Grove Press. [23, 33]
Kosko B (1993) Fuzzy Thinking. New York: Hyperion. [116]

Krüger J. (1990) Multi-microelectrode investigation of monkey striate cortex: Link between correlational and neuronal properties in the infragranular layers. Visual Neuroscience 5: 135-142. [165]

Lacan J (1966/1977) Ecrits: A Selection (A Sheridan, Trans.). New York: Norton. [109]

Lancet D, Greer CA, Kauer JS & Shepherd, GM (1982) Mapping of odor-related neuronal activity in the olfactory bulb by high-resolution 2-deoxyglucose autoradiography. Proceedings of the National Academy of Sciences (USA) 79: 670-674. [58]

Lange CG & James W (1922) The Emotions. Baltimore: Williams & Wilkins. [40]

Lashley KS (1942) The problem of cerebral organization in vision. In J Cattell (Ed.), Biological Symposia VII: 301-322. [34, 65]

Laurent G & Davidowitz D (1994) Encoding olfactory information with oscillating neural assemblies. Science 265: 1872-1875. [166]

Lehmann D & Michel CM (1990) Intracerebral dipole source localization for FFT power maps. Electroencephalography and clinical Neurophysiology 76: 271-276. [99]

Leibniz GW (1670/1947) Discourse on Metaphysics Monadology (GR Montgomery, Trans.). La Salle IL: Open Court. [2, 140]

Lettvin JY, Maturana HR, McCulloch WS & Pitts WH (1959) What the frog's eye tells the frog's brain. Proceedings of the Institute of Radio Engineers 47: 1940-1951. [54]

Lewin R (1992) Complexity: Life at the Edge of Chaos. New York: Macmillan. [65]

Li Z & Hopfield JJ (1989) Modeling the olfactory bulb and its neural oscillatory processings. Biological Cybernetics 61: 379-392. [165]

Libet B (1994) Neurophysiology of Consciousness: Selected Papers and New Essays. Boston MA: Birkhauser. [82, 99]

Liljenstrom H (1991) Modeling the dynamics of olfactory cortex using simplified network units and realistic architecture. International Journal of Neural Systems 2: 1-15. [165]

Lindley D (1993) The End of Physics: The Myth of a Unified Theory. Washington DC: Basic Books. [23, 158]

Llinàs R (1988) The intrinsic electrophysiological properties of mammalian neurons: Insights into central nervous system function. Science 242: 1654-1664. [56, 173]

Lorente de Nó R (1934) Studies in the structure of the cerebral cortex: I. The area entorhinalis. Journal von Psychologie und Neurologie 45: 381-438. [34, 81]
Lucky RW (1989) Silicon Dreams: Information, Man, and Machine. New York: St. Martin's. [13, 35, 172]
Luria AR (1966) Higher Cortical Functions in Man (B Haigh, Trans.). New York: Basic Books. [15]

Maclean PD (1969) The Triune Brain. New York: Plenum. [77, 168]
Maclean PD (1973) A Triune Concept of the Brain and Behavior. Toronto: University of Toronto Press. [168]
Magoun HW (1958) Waking Brain. Springfield IL: Thomas. [13, 88]
Malinow R (1994) LTP: Desperately seeking resolution. Science 126: 1195. [113]
Martinez DM & Freeman WJ (1984) Periglomerular cell action on mitral cell in olfactory bulb shown by current source density analysis. Brain Research 223-233. [170]
Maslow A (1968) Toward a Psychology of Being. New York: Van Nostrand. [43]
Maturana HR & Varela FJ (1992) The Tree of Knowledge: The Biological Roots of Human Understanding (R Paolucci, Trans.). New York: Random House. [2]
May R (1969) Love and Will. New York, Dell. [7, 16, 150]
Mayer-Kress G, Yates FE, Benton L, Keidel M, Tirsch W, Poppl SJ, Geist K (1988) Dimensional analysis of nonlinear oscillations in brain, heart and muscle. Mathematical Biosciences 90: 155-182. [65]
McCulloch WS (1969) Embodiments of Mind. Cambridge MA: MIT Press. [34, 115, 159]
McLaughlin WI 1994) Resolving Zeno's paradoxes. Scientific American 271: 84-89. [27, 103]
McNaughton BL (1993) The mechanism of expression of long-term enhancement of hippocampal synapses: Current issues and theoretical implications. Annual Review of Physiology 55: 375-96. [75, 165]
Mealey L (in press) The sociobiology of sociopathy: An integrated evolutionary model. Behavioral and Brain Sciences. [128]
Melzack R & Wall PD (1983) The Challenge of Pain. New York: Basic Books. [82]
Mencken HL (1956) Minority Report: H. L. Mencken's Notebooks. New York, A. A. Knopf. [155]
Menninger KA (1938) Man Against Himself. New York: Harcourt Brace. [127, 128, 135]

Merleau-Ponty M (1942/1963) The Structure of Behavior (AL Fischer, Trans.). Boston: Beacon Press. [30, 42]
Merleau-Ponty M (1945/1962) Phenomenology of Perception (C Smith, Trans.). New York: Humanities Press. [23, 35]
Merleau-Ponty M (1947/1963) The Primacy of Perception (JM Edie, Trans.) (pp. 12-42). Evanston IL, Northwestern. [42, 93]
Milner B (1972) Disorders of learning and memory after temporal lobe lesions in man. Clinical Neurosurgery 19: 421-446. [78]
Milner PM (1974) A model for visual shape recognition. Psychological Review 81: 521-535. [54]
Minsky ML (1986) The Society of Mind. New York: Simon & Schuster. [4]
Mitchell SW, Morehouse GR & Keen WW (1864) Gunshot Wounds and Other Injuries of Nerves. Philadelphia PA: Lippincott. [15]
Mitzdorf U (1987) Properties of the evoked potential generators: Current source-density analysis of evoked potentials in cat cortex. International Journal of Neuroscience 33: 33-59. [105]
Miyashita Y (1993) Inferior temporal cortex: Where visual perception meets memory. Annual Review of Neuroscience 16: 245-263. [164]
Moore FL (1992) Evolutionary precedents for behavioral actions of oxytocin and vasopressin. In CA Pedersen, JD Caldwell, GF Jirikowski & TR Insel (Eds.), Oxytocin in Maternal, Sexual, and Social Behaviors. Annals of the New York Academy of Sciences, Vol. 652: 156-165. [122]
Mountcastle VB (1978) An organizing principle for cerebral function: The unit module and the distributed system. In G Edelman & VB Mountcastle (Eds.), The Mindful Brain (pp. 7-50). Cambridge MA: MIT Press. [48, 81]
Mpitsos GJ & Burton RM (1992) Convergence and divergence in neural networks: Processing of chaos and biological analogy. Neural Networks 5: 605-625. [113]

Nagel T (1974) What is it like to be a bat? Philosophical Review 83: 435-450. [137]
Nietzsche F (1872/1993) The Birth of Tragedy (S Whiteside, Trans.; M Tanner, Ed.). New York: Penguin Books. [133]
Nietzsche F (1885/1961) Thus Spake Zarathustra (RJ Hollingdale, Trans.). Baltimore MD: Penguin. [154, 155]
Nietzsche F (1887/1974) The Gay Science (W Kaufmann, Trans.). New York: Vintage, Random House. [5]
Nunez PL (1981) Electric Fields of the Brain: The Neurophysics of EEG. New York: Oxford University Press. [44]

Ojemann G (1986) Brain mechanisms for consciousness and
conscious experience. Canadian Psychology 27: 158-168. [170]
O'Keefe J & Nadel L (1978) The Hippocampus as a Cognitive Map.
Oxford UK: Clarendon. [73, 75]
Orwell G (1949) Nineteen Eighty-Four. New York: Harcourt Brace.
[124]

Pavlov IP (1955) Selected Works. (J Gibbons, Ed.; S Belsky,
Trans.). Moscow: Foreign Languages Publishing House. [124]
Pedersen CA, Caldwell JD, Jirikowski GF & Insel TR (Eds.) (1992)
Oxytocin in Maternal, Sexual, and Social Behaviors. Annals of
the New York Academy of Sciences, Vol. 652. [121, 127]
Pellionisz A & Llinàs R (1985) Tensor network theory of the
metaorganization of functional geometries in the central
nervous system. Neuroscience 16: 245-273. [159, 173]
Penfield W (1975) The Mystery of the Mind: A Critical Study of
Consciousness and the Human Brain. Princeton NJ: Princeton
University Press. [78, 88, 169]
Penrose R (1994) Shadows of the Mind. Oxford UK: Oxford
University Press. [13, 37, 39, 41, 160-161]
Peterson I (1993) Newton's Clock: Chaos in the Solar System.
San Francisco: Freeman. [27]
Pirsig RM (1974) Zen and the Art of Motorcycle Maintenance: An
Inquiry Into Values. New York: Morrow. [13]
Plato (~400 BC/1961) Phaedrus (R Hackforth, Trans.). New York:
Bollinger Foundation, Pantheon Books. [7, 168, 175-176]
Poincare H (1913/1963) Mathematics and Science: Last Essays
(JW Bolduc, Trans.). New York: Dover [158]
Popper KR & Eccles JC (1977) The Self and Its Brain. Berlin:
Springer. [82, 162]
Pribram K (1982) Brain mechanisms in music: Prolegomena for a
theory of the meaning of meaning. In M Clynes (Ed.), Music, Mind
and Brain: The Neuropsychology of Music (pp. 21-36). New York:
Plenum. [133]
Pribram K (1991) Brain and Perception: Holonomy and Structure
in Figural Processing. Hillsdale NJ: Lawrence Erlbaum
Associates. [29]
Price R (Ed.) (1982) Shamans and Endorphins. Washington DC:
Society for Psychological Anthropology. [129]
Prigogine I (1980) From Being to Becoming: Time and Complexity
in the Physical Sciences. San Francisco: Freeman. [42, 49, 173]

Prochaska G (1784/1851) Principles of Physiology. (T Laycock, Trans.) London, Sydenham Society. From Adnotationum academicarum. Prague: Wolfgang Gerle. [29, 31, 34, 71]

Putnam H (1988) Representation and Reality. Cambridge MA: MIT Press. [18]

Putnam H (1990) Realism With a Human Face. Cambridge MA: Harvard University Press. [8, 17, 144-145]

Rabin MD & Cain WS (1984) Odor recognition: Familiarity, identifiability, and encoding consistency. Journal of Experimental Psychology 10: 316-325. [61]

Ramachandran VS (1992) Blind spots. Scientific American 255: 86-91. [11]

Ramón y Cajal S (1911) Histologie du Systeme Nerveux de l'Homme et des Vertèbres (Vols. I & II). Paris: Maloine [54, 160]

Rank O (1932/1968) Art and Artist (CF Atkinson, Trans.). New York: Knopf. [10]

Rapp P (1993) Chaos in the neurosciences: Cautionary tales from the frontier. Biologist 40: 89-94. [25, 65]

Rilke RM (1982) Liebes-Lied. In Deutsche Liebeslyrik. H Wagener (Ed.). Stuttgart: Philipp Reclam. [4]

Rilke RM (1984) Letters to a Young Poet (S Mitchell, Trans.). New York: Random House. [4, 68, 124]

Roederer JG (1984) The search for a survival value of music. Music Perception 1: 350-356. [131]

Rollins CD (1967) Encyclopedia of Philosophy (P Evans, Ed.). New York: Macmillan. [2, 3]

Rolls ET, Miyashita Y, Cahusac PBM, Kesner RP, Niki H, Feigenbaum JD & Bach L (1989) Hippocampal neurons in the monkey with activity related to the place in which the stimulus is shown. Journal of Neuroscience 9: 1835-1845. [75, 165]

Rose SP (1992) The Making of Memory. New York: Anchor. [113]

Russell B (1948) Human Knowledge: Its Scope and Limits. New York: Simon & Schuster. [11, 37, 93]

Ryle G (1949) The Concept of Mind. New York: Barnes & Noble. [28]

Sacks O (1985) The Man Who Mistook His Wife for a Hat. New York: Summit. [25, 81, 90, 173]

Santayana G (1905/1922) The Life of Reason. Volume 1. Reason in Common Sense. New York: Scribner's. [1, 3]

Santayana G (1923) Scepticism and Animal Faith; Introduction to a System of Philosophy. New York, Scribner's. [27]

Sargant WW (1957) Battle for the Mind. Westport CT: Greenwood. [125, 126, 130]

Sargant WW (1974) The Mind Possessed: A Physiology of Possession, Mysticism and Faith Healing. Philadelphia PA: Lippincott. [126]

Schiff SJ, Jerger K, Duong DH, Chang T, Spano ML & Ditto WL (1994) Controlling chaos in the brain. Nature 230: 615-620. [25, 101]

Schild D (1988) Principles of odor coding and a neural network for odor discrimination. Biophys. Journal 54: 1001-1011. [165]

Schlitz MJ & Honorton C (1992) Ganzfeld psi performances within an artistically gifted population. Journal of the American Society for Psychical Research 86: 83-98. [156]

Schneider LH (1989) Orosensory self-stimulation by sucrose involves brain dopaminergic mechanisms. In LH Schneider, SJ Cooper & KA Halmi (Eds.) The Psychology of Human Eating Disorders. New York Academy of Sciences 575: 307-320. [149]

Schwartz E (Ed.) (1990) Computational Neuroscience. Cambridge MA: MIT/Bradford. [172]

Searle JR (1990) Consciousness, explanatory inversions, and cognitive sciences. Behavioral & Brain Sciences 13: 588-638. [41, 145]

Searle JR (1992) The Rediscovery of Mind. Cambridge MA: MIT Press. [12]

Seligman AW & Hilkevich JS (1992) Don't Think About Monkeys: Extraordinary Stories by People With Tourette Syndrome. (Available: Hope Press, P.O. Box 188, Duarte CA 91009) [143]

Shaw RE, Kugler PN & Kinsella-Shaw JM (1990) Reciprocities of intentional systems. In R Warren & A Wertheim (Eds.), Control of Self-Motion (pp. 579-619). Hillsdale NJ: Lawrence Erlbaum Associates. [36, 159-160]

Shepherd GM (1991) Computational structure of the olfactory system. In JL Davis & H Eichenbaum (Eds.), Olfaction (pp. 3-41). Cambridge MA: MIT/Bradford. [165]

Sherrington CS (1906) The Integrative Action of the Nervous System. New Haven CT: Yale University Press. [54, 84, 160]

Sherrington CS (1940) Man on His Nature. Cambridge UK: Cambridge University Press. [35]

Sholl DA (1956) The organization of the cerebral cortex. New York: Wiley. [48]

Sillito AM, Jones HE, Gerstein GL & West DC (1994) Feature-linked synchronization of thalamic relay cell firing induced by feedback from the visual cortex. Nature 369: 479-482. [88]

Singer M & Yakovlev P (1954) Human Brain in Sagittal Section.
Springfield IL: Thomas. [109]
Singer W (1994) A new job for thalamus. Nature 369: 444-445.
[88]
Skarda CA & Freeman WJ (1987) How brains make chaos in order
to make sense of the world. Behavioral and Brain Sciences 10:
161-195. [42]
Slezak P (1994) Situated cognition: Empirical issue, "paradigm
shift" or conceptual confusion? Proceedings of the Sixteenth
Annual Conference of the Cognitive Science Society (pp. 806-
811). Hillsdale NJ: Lawrence Erlbaum Associates. [103]
Slotnik BM & Kaneko N (1986) Role of mediodorsal thalamic
nucleus in olfactory discrimination learning in rats. Science
214: 91-93. [61]
Smythies JR (1994) The Walls of Plato's Cave: The Science and
Philosophy of Brain, Consciousness and Perception. Aldeshot
UK: Avebury. [2, 11, 138, 158]
Spatz H (1967) Gehirnentwicklung (Introversion-Promination)
und Endocranialausguss [Brain development (introversion-
promination) from endocranial casts]. In R Hassler & H Stephan
(Eds.), Evolution of the Forebrain (pp. 136-152). New York:
Plenum. [80, 135]
Spencer H (1863) Essays: Moral, Political, and Aesthetic. New
York: Appleton-Century-Crofts. [31]
Sperry RW (1950) Neural basis of the spontaneous optokinetic
response. Journal of Comparative Physiology 43: 482-489. [85]
Sperry RW (1958) Physiological plasticity and brain circuit
theory. In HF Harlow & CN Woolsey (Eds.), Biological and
Biochemical Bases of Behavior (pp. 401-424). Madison WI:
University of Wisconsin Press. [33]
Sperry RW (1969) A modified concept of consciousness.
Psychological Review 76: 532-536. [13]
Sperry RW (1982) Some effects of disconnecting the cerebral
hemispheres [Nobel Lecture]. Science 217: 1223-1226. [147]
Spinoza B (1674/1955) Ethics (WH White, Trans.; J Gutman, Ed.).
New York: Hafner, Macmillan. [8, 140]
Squire LR (1987) Memory and Brain. New York: Oxford University
Press. [80]
Stearns MW (1958) The Story of Jazz. New York: Oxford
University Press. [174]
Sutton JP, Rittenhouse CD, Pace-Schott E, Stickgold R & Hobson
JA (1994) A new approach to dream bizarreness: Graphing

continuity and discontinuity of visual attention in narrative reports. Consciousness and Cognition 3: 61-88. [138]

Tank DW, Gelperin A & Kleinfeld D (1994) Odors, oscillations, and waves: Does it all compute? Science 265: 1819-1820 [166]
Targ R, Putoff H (1977) Mind Reach. Scientists Look at Psychic Ability. New York: Dell. [38]
Taylor J (1994) When the Clock Struck Zero: Science's Ultimate Limits. New York: St. Martin's. [23, 88]
Tolman EC (1948) Cognitive maps in rats and men. Psychological Review 55: 189-208. [73]
Tolman EC (1951/1967) Purposive Behavior in Animals and Men. New York: Appleton-Century-Crofts. [73, 159]
Tovee MJ & Rolls EJ (1992) The functional nature of neuronal oscillations. Trends in Neuroscience 15: 187. [56, 163]
Tsuda I (1991) Chaotic itinerancy as a dynamical basis of hermeneutics in brain and mind. World Futures 32: 167-184. [100]
Turing AM (1950) Computing machines and intelligence. Mind 59: 459-476. [115, 137, 172, 175]

Verger P (1954) Dieux d'Afrique. Paris: P Hartmann [130, 174].
Viana Di Prisco G & Freeman WJ (1985) Odor-related bulbar EEG spatial pattern analysis during appetitive conditioning in rabbits. Behavioral Neuroscience 99: 962-978. [57, 96]
von der Malsburg C (1983) How are nervous structures organized? In E Basar, H Flohr, H Haken & AJ Mandell (Eds.), Synergetics of the Brain (pp. 238-249). Berlin: Springer. [55]
von Holst E & Mittelstadt H (1950) Das Reafferenzprinzip (Wechselwirkung zwischen Zentralnervensystem und Peripherie). Naturwissenschaften 37: 464-476. [85]
von Neumann J (1958) The Computer and the Brain. New Haven CT: Yale University Press. [35, 115]

Wallin NL (1991) Biomusicology: Neurophysiological, Neuro-psychological, and Evolutionary Perspectives on the Origins and Purposes of Music. Stuyvesant NY: Pendragon. [133]
Walter WG (1963) The Living Brain. New York: Norton. [12, 82, 116, 172]
Watson JB (1924) Behaviorism. Chicago IL: University of Chicago Press. [13]
Webster's New International Dictionary (1949) WA Nielson, TA Knott & PW Carhart (Eds.). Springfield MA: Merriam. [136]

Whipple B, Ogden G & Komisaruk BR (1992) Physiological correlates of imagery-induced orgasm in women. Archives of Sexual Behavior 21: 121-133. [122]

Whitehead AN (1938) Modes of Thought. New York: Macmillan. [11, 37, 38, 40, 41, 93, 140]

Williams L (1967) The dancing chimpanzee: A study of primitive music in relation to the vocalizing and rhythmic action of apes. New York: Norton. [131]

Wilson MA & Bower JM (1992) Cortical oscillations and temporal interactions in a computer simulation of piriform cortex. Journal of Neurophysiology 67: 981-995. [165]

Wilson MA & McNaughton BL (1993) Dynamics of the hippocampal ensemble code for space. Science 261: 1055-1058. [75]

Wilson SG (1992) The Drummer's Path: Moving the Spirit With Ritual and Traditional Drumming. New York: Destiny Books. [131, 174]

Wimsatt WC (1976) Reductionism, levels of organization, and the mind-body problem. In GG Globus, G Maxwell & I Savodnik (Eds.), Consciousness and the Brain: A Scientific and Philosophical Inquiry (pp. 205-267). New York: Plenum. [52]

Winslow JT, Hastings N, Carter CS, Harbaugh CR & Insel TR (1993) A role for central vasopressin in pair bonding in monogamous prairie voles. Nature 365: 545-548. [123]

Wolfe T (1979) The Right Stuff. New York: Farrar, Straus & Giroux. [132]

Worringer W (1953) Abstraction and Empathy (M Bullock, Trans.). New York: International Universities Press. [10]

Wright JJ, Kydd RR & Sergejew AA (1990) Autoregression models of EEG. Biological Cybernetics 62: 201-210. [161]

Xerri C, Stern JM & Merzenich MM (1994) Alterations of the cortical representation of the rat ventrum induced by nursing behavior. Journal of Neuroscience 14: 1710-1721. [121-122]

Yao Y & Freeman WJ (1990) Model of biological pattern recognition with spatially chaotic dynamics. Neural Networks 3: 153-170. [61]

Yeats WB (1921/1947) The Collected Poems. New York: Macmillan. [1, 149]

Young JZ (1966) The Memory System of the Brain. Berkeley: University of California Press. [90]

Young JZ (1971) The Anatomy of the Nervous System of Octopus vulgaris. Oxford UK: Clarendon. [70, 107]

Index

Glossary of Terms used with Special Meanings [page]

activity density function - a spatiotemporal pattern of numbers that models an evolving spatial pattern of Neuroactivity [43]

awareness - update of intentional structure, back-dated about a half second after a self makes a decision to act [155]

bifurcation - an abrupt change in the function of a brain part with a chemical or structural change in its connections [63]

causality - quale of the process of observation in cyclic action-reafference-perception; a basis of intentional action [142]

consciousness - the social attribution of awareness by humans to other humans, animals, objects, and imagined spirits [138]

conversion - dissolution of intentional structure by endogenous neurochemicals, followed by learning new patterns of actions and beliefs; also pejoratively called *brainwashing* [124]

Eureka reaction - the feeling of insight; based in neuromodulator action having no relation to truth; antidote: skepticism [149]

forcing function - cortical input preceding state transitions [63]

intentionality - the process of a brain in action having the properties of unity, wholeness, and "stretching forth"; a combination of action, perception, and learning [15]

intentional structure - synaptic web of neuropil in a forebrain, modified by learning and unlearning; actualizing behavior [19]

intent - stretching forth; reduced by metonymy to "purpose" [17]

itinerancy - a form of change in which a sequence of brain states returns sufficiently close to earlier states that they are classed together, though they differ in detail [100]

meaning - the location of a focus of intentional relations; a part of a trajectory traced by chaotic dynamics in a brain [134]

mind - the structure of behavior, unfolding as experience [40]

neural activity - chemical events comprising Neuroactivity [39]

Neuroactivity - what neurons do; in models, state variable Q [39]

neuromodulator - an endogenous brain chemical that changes the strength of synaptic action of neurons onto other neurons [47]

neurotransmitter - an endogenous brain chemical that carries the synaptic action of neurons onto other neurons [47]

neuropil - tissue formed by branched threads of neurons, densely intertwined, allowing each cell to contact many others [48]

reafference - process of relaying messages from limbic system via entorhinal cortex to sensory cortices, in parallel with limbic commands to motor systems, serving (1) to compensate in advance for changes in sensory input accompanying actions, and (2) to sustain states of expectancy and attention [86]

representations - intentional gestures, words, numbers, and constructed objects that elicit meaning in the process of communication, but which themselves have no meaning [106]

solipsism - theory that a self knows only its own constructs [2]

state transition - abrupt change in activity pattern in a brain that follows sensory stimuli or neuromodulator inputs [50]

state variable - a representation by a symbol, Q, in a dynamical equation for Neuroactivity in a brain part during behavior [29]

thought - a process by which Neuroactivity constructs meaning, modifies intentional structure, and makes representations for purposes of communication among humans and animals [107]

transmarginal inhibition - a state of behavioral collapse induced by physical and emotional stress prior to conversion [125]

unlearning - meltdown of intentional structure by stress [120]

unity - state of integration by which a self distinguishes itself from nonself; found in bacteria, immune systems, neurons, brains, bonded pairs, tribes, and nations [19]

wholeness - a process in which a self actualizes by stages its mature form, and dies; found in brains and healing bodies [19]

wisdom - the apogee of wholeness in intentionality [110]